Fighting Chance

Fighting Chance

GLOBAL TRENDS AND SHOCKS IN THE NATIONAL SECURITY ENVIRONMENT

Edited by **NEYLA ARNAS**

CENTER FOR TECHNOLOGY AND NATIONAL SECURITY POLICY

NATIONAL DEFENSE UNIVERSITY PRESS

POTOMAC BOOKS, INC.

WASHINGTON, D.C.

Library of Congress Cataloging-in-Publication Data
Fighting chance : global trends and shocks in the national security environment / edited by Neyla Arnas.
   p. cm.
 Includes bibliographical references and index.
 ISBN 978-1-59797-495-0 (pbk. : alk. paper)
 1. Security, International. 2. United States—Strategic aspects. 3. National security—United States. 4. World politics—21st century. I. Arnas, Neyla.
 JZ5588.F544 2009
 355'.033073—dc22

                                 2009016949

Printed in the United States of America on acid-free paper that meets the American National Standards Institute Z39-48 Standard.

Potomac Books, Inc.
22841 Quicksilver Drive
Dulles, Virginia 20166

First Edition

10 9 8 7 6 5 4 3 2 1

Contents

Part III: Conclusions

Illustrations

Acknowledgments

THIS VOLUME is the product of the many scholars who brought their collective intellect, creativity, and sustained commitment to the "Trends and Shocks" project. They have my deep gratitude. In addition to the scholars and authors, many hands helped shape the finished volume, and I would like to acknowledge a few of them.

Much appreciation goes to Dr. Hans Binnendijk, Director of the Center for Technology and National Security Policy (CTNSP) at the National Defense University, for giving me the freedom to oversee this project. Dr. Binnendijk's thoughtful imprint can be seen in a myriad of subtle ways throughout our work.

Special thanks are due to Mr. Terry Pudas, then-Deputy Assistant Secretary of Defense, Forces Transformation and Resources, who brought the "Trends and Shocks" project to CTNSP. Without his fulsome encouragement and financial support, this volume would not have been possible.

I am especially grateful to Dr. Tom Mahnken, Deputy Assistant Secretary of Defense for Policy Planning, and his dedicated staff for their intellectual contributions to the concepts presented here and their overall support for this project.

Thanks also are due to Kathleen Toomey Jabs for her unsparing editorial corrections and many constructive suggestions. I also would like to thank Dr. Ozer Arnas for proofreading the final manuscript and offering his improvements.

Finally, I would like to acknowledge with sadness and deep respect the unparalleled intellectual devotion of my CTNSP colleague and friend, Dr. Bob Armstrong, who succumbed to cancer before he could see his good work finished. From his hospital bed and throughout his final days, Bob continued to offer substantive contributions to this volume along with his trademark wit and wisdom. Bob's daughter, Katie Armstrong, was instrumental in revising the summary portions of the chapters and deserves special thanks.

1

Introduction

Neyla Arnas

THE OFFICE of the Deputy Assistant Secretary of Defense for Forces Transformation and Resources asked the Center for Technology and National Security Policy at the National Defense University to build on ongoing Department of Defense (DOD) work identifying long-range trends. We invited a select group of experts from academia, private industry, government, and nongovernmental organizations to a 2-day workshop in September 2007, at which they presented the papers that became the chapters of this book.

DOD has been examining strategic trends, their defense relevance, and how they may overlap to produce strategic "shocks"—like the launch of Sputnik or the fall of the Berlin Wall—and how we might prepare for such events to mitigate risks and capitalize on opportunities. Through a preliminary survey of the extensive futures and trends literature, DOD identified six major trend categories (see table 1–1).

Definitions

For the purposes of this project, a *trend* is defined as a predictable path along which events are expected to evolve. A *shock* is defined as an event that punctuates the evolution of a trend (a discontinuity that either rapidly accelerates its pace or significantly changes its trajectory) and, in so doing, undermines the assumptions on which current policies are based. For our purposes, a shock would be a major disruptive event that changes the way we think about defense and national security.

There have been numerous shocks in the course of the last century, events for which we were not fully prepared and that ultimately changed the way in which we behaved within the international system—the guns of August of 1914, the financial crash of 1929, Hitler's rise to power, Pearl Harbor, the descent of the

1

Table 1–1. Shaping the Future: Key Trends

CATEGORIES	TREND EXAMPLES
Conflict	• Increasing lethality and scope of irregular challenges and agile nonstate threats • Military operations in new domains: outer space, cyberspace • Rise of new military competitors: Asia, petrodollar states • Increasing nuclear proliferation
Demographics	• Youth bulge: 87 percent of people ages 10–19 live in developing states • Global aging: The ranks of those over age 60 are growing about 2 percent each year—60 percent faster than the overall population. Primarily affects Europe and Japan. • Urbanization: By 2025, nearly 60 percent of global population will live in cities • Migration between and within states to economic opportunity and away from conflict
Economy	• Continued economic growth and trade facilitated by globalization and rise of Asia • Growing gap between rich and poor within and between countries • Increasing regional and global integration of economies • Increasing Asian influence in international markets
Environment	• Growing overall resource consumption (food, water, energy, minerals, timber) • Resource scarcity and disruptions to distribution (water, energy) • Disruptive climate change leading to rise in sea level, changing climatic zones, and environmental stress
Culture, Identity, and Governance	• State remains dominant unit in international system • Strong but challenged U.S. leadership in international arenas (global commons) • Increasing influence of the individual, group, private sector, and nongovernmental organizations on the international system • Strong national and subnational bonds sustained and reinforced through Internet communication and remittances • Increasing tension between individual rights and group rights
Science and Technology	• Technology: information, miniaturization/nano, bio, power, robotics • Increased proliferation of technologies and knowledge

Source: Department of Defense.

Iron Curtain over Europe, the Soviet development of nuclear capability, Sputnik, the Cuban missile incident, the energy shock of 1973, the Soviet invasion of Afghanistan, the fall of the Berlin Wall, and 9/11.[1] In hindsight, it appears we could have identified the onset of most of these events if not for the "noise" that got in the way.

In writing about the lead-up to Pearl Harbor, Roberta Wohlstetter notes how the signals that seemed to announce the attack were always accompanied by competing and contradictory signals—"noise." She further states that to understand the surprise, it is equally important to examine the characteristics of the noise as well as the signals that after the event clearly are seen to have heralded the attack.[2] She concludes that Pearl Harbor might have been a foreseeable event but for the clutter of noise.

Thomas Schelling writes about a government that was fully expectant regarding Pearl Harbor, but that it "expected wrong." He goes on to warn against the "poverty of expectations" that manifests itself in "a routine obsession with a few dangers that may be familiar rather than likely."

This book attempts to look at broad trends, go beyond the obvious dangers they might pose, and see through the clutter of noise.

The 2008 National Defense Strategy recognizes that "increasingly, the Department of Defense will have to plan for a future security environment shaped by the interaction of powerful strategic trends. These trends suggest a range of plausible futures, some presenting major challenges and security risks."[3] The strategy goes on to note that over the next 20 years, the confluence of trends with rapid social, cultural, technological, and geopolitical change will present greater uncertainty. "The uncertainty is exacerbated by both the unprecedented speed and scale of change, as well as by the unpredictable and complex interaction among the trends themselves."[4] Defense policy must account for this uncertainty by acting to reduce risk and by developing the capacity to hedge against it. This will require "institutional agility and flexibility," as well as cooperation with "interdepartmental, non-governmental, and international partners." The aim of this book is captured in the strategy's observation that "how these trends interact and the nature of the shocks they might generate is uncertain; the fact that they will influence the future security environment is not."[5]

The Experts

We asked our experts to work from the premise of the six trend categories identified by the Department of Defense: conflict; demographics; economy;

environment; culture, identity, and governance; and science and technology. We identified functional experts to address the trends: Michael Moodie covered conflict; Carl Haub, demographics; David Gates, economics; Geoffrey Dabelko, environment; Dale Eickelman, culture and identity; and Peter Katona, health. For science and technology, Neil Jacobstein addressed nanotechnology; Greg Rattray, cyberspace; and Mark Drapeau and Bob Armstrong, life sciences.

Because we were interested in trend intersections, or shocks, we asked a group of regional experts to consider the six trend categories in the context of their respective regions. Mark Bellamy looked at Africa; Robert Ross, China; Ian Lesser, Europe and the North Atlantic Treaty Organization; Steven Pifer, Russia and Eurasia; Michael Krepon, South Asia; and Edward Schumacher-Matos, Latin America.

In preparing their presentations and papers, we instructed our experts to consider issues not already captured through the Office of the Secretary of Defense's extensive review of future trends literature and to focus instead on the potential shocks or unexpected events that may radically alter the trend projections. A list of possible shocks by chapter is included as an appendix.

Key Questions

For each region and major trend area, we asked the experts to apply out-of-the-box thinking to the following questions, focusing on adding new data, ideas, and alternatives to the existing body of knowledge and only briefly summarizing or referring to previous work:

- How do various trends intersect and interact to create strategic shocks?
- How should the shocks be ranked in terms of impact and likelihood of occurrence in 5 years, 10 years, 15 years, 20 years, and beyond?
- What are the implications for U.S. national security?
- How might DOD influence the trends and/or mitigate the shocks?
- Where might DOD have the highest impact?

Chapter 18 summarizes the trends and shocks presented in each previous chapter by functional and regional area.

Role of the National Security Community

In a concluding chapter, the Transformation Chairs Network[6] considers how we might prepare ourselves as a government within a trends and shocks context where some issues are outside the bounds of what we normally think of as national security. The network suggests a whole-of-government approach, including an early warning mechanism, enlightened leadership, organizational capacity to respond, broad spectrum of capabilities and people, and an educational base.

Expecting the Unexpected

Finally, as a postscript, Bob Armstrong reminds us of the limitations of trend analyses in a discussion of the unpredictable events that Nassim Nicholas Taleb calls "black swans."[7] A black swan event has three attributes:

- it lies outside the realm of regular expectation; nothing in the past can convincingly point to its possibility
- it carries an extreme impact
- in spite of its outlier status, human nature makes us concoct explanations for its occurrence after the fact, making it explainable and predictable.

As this volume was going to press, the economies of the United States and many other countries were hit by the economic shock of 2008. Chapter 4, which was updated in October 2008 to reflect these developments, concludes that while this current economic crisis is a shock, it does not qualify as a "black swan." The shock is an example of the confluence of several economic trends, "none of which on their own would have resulted in anything extraordinary but which together have led to an unprecedented disruption of the world financial system." The trends that contributed to the crisis include an extended period of low interest rates; an unprecedented runup in commodity prices; errors by institutions in creating and exploiting new financial instruments; errors in government policy and execution, including regulation of financial practices; and finally, the decisions of households and consumers to spend beyond what historically would have been considered their means. What this means for the U.S. economy remains to be seen. Without doubt, debate will continue on the steps necessary to restore confidence and vitality to the global markets.

Given the limits of our knowledge and foresight, how do we build a resilient system that can best cope with unexpected crises? How do we build a whole-of-government approach to national security that will enable a comprehensive and coordinated response? This book aims to stimulate a productive debate as a step toward answering these questions. As the 2008 National Defense Strategy underscores, the Department of Defense "must continue to improve [its] understanding of trends, their interaction, and the range of risks [it] may be called upon to respond to or manage."[8] Our goal with this book was to contribute to that understanding.

Part I: Functional Trends

2
Conflict

Michael Moodie

As the Cold War was coming to a close, most of the world had never heard of the small Yugoslavian provinces of Bosnia-Herzegovina or Kosovo, let alone considered them regions that would demand global attention. Nor would the world have believed that a state such as North Korea, deemed a "basket case" with respect to many fundamental functions of government, would acquire nuclear weapons and maintain chemical and biological capabilities. A global network of extremists based on the perversion of one of the world's great religions that was willing to resort to sustained acts of violence resulting in the deaths of thousands of civilians was a scenario worthy only of a movie script. The identification of U.S. national security priorities as waging a "global war on terror" and the deployment of tens of thousands of U.S. troops to preempt a "gathering" threat to the Nation's security, who would then become engaged in a protracted attempt to create a democratic nation-state in the midst of a civil war, were on no one's radar.

Far from promoting peace and stability, the end of the Cold War invited disorder and conflict. It took the lid off confrontations thought too dangerous at a time of superpower confrontation, unleashed rivalries and competitions whose fires had been banked by the chill of the East-West standoff, and fostered a succession of violent eruptions that the world could not ignore, even though they occurred in parts of the globe long considered peripheral to the central security dynamic.

Trends

It has become a cliché to argue that the major challenges today are instability and conflict fostered by regional and local tensions stemming from such diverse sources as historical animosity; ethnic, religious, or other forms of communal hostility; control over resources; or attempted regional hegemony. These conflicts frequently have little or no politically ideological character and can erupt in unexpected places and ways. Their inherent dangers are made more ominous by the proliferation of chemical, biological, radiological, and nuclear (CBRN) weapons and their means of delivery.

As with most clichés, these views contain a central element of truth. It is generally agreed that war between great powers is unlikely, although not impossible. In 2005, for example, the Stockholm International Peace Research Institute's conflict database reported no interstate conflicts for the first time. Some analysts even argue that major war has become "obsolete," not in the sense that it is not possible, but that it is improbable because war no longer serves political purposes. While many other analysts think this view overstates the case, considerable agreement seems to exist that the "total war" of the World War II variety is not and should not be a major concern for today's or tomorrow's policymakers.

Caution, however, should be the watchword in evaluating trends related to conflict. In 1838, Lieutenant General Antoine-Henri Baron de Jomini wrote in his *Summary of the Art of War* that "the means of destruction are approaching perfection with frightful rapidity."[1] Jomini was wrong. It took more than 100 years for nuclear weapons to make their appearance. Even good analysts can be wrong about trends. In less than 20 years, prevailing paradigms that ordered both thinking and policy with respect to conflict have been shattered and replaced with paradigms entailing profound differences. When the prospects of "shocks" are added, confidence in prediction should give way to reflection.

An examination of trends in conflict can be conducted by addressing three dimensions: the nature of conflict, why it occurs, and how it is waged.

WHAT KINDS OF CONFLICT?

It is useful to remember Donald Kagan's admonition that the one great truth of history is that "there is always one other possibility besides all the ones that you can imagine."[2] Even if World War II–style conflicts are no longer serious prospects, a wide array of state actors could interact in diverse ways to create multiple potential scenarios that are anything but benign. Major power competition, for example, has a military dimension, even if it is not prominent at the moment. The continuing centrality of U.S., Chinese, and Russian nuclear weapons in national security policies provides an important reminder of this reality, as does the Chinese modernization of its conventional forces. A second tier of aspiring major powers or regional powers is in a position to capitalize on the global diffusion of technology that will become even more prevalent in the years ahead, and they appear to believe they are not getting their due from an international system they see as designed by and for the major powers. As a result, they sometimes nurture animosity toward those major powers and often toward one another. The environment is further complicated by states that do not play by the rules. North Korea, for example, may not be particularly powerful in absolute terms, but it is unwilling to abide by international norms, and its national priorities elevate power in all forms, especially military, both for internal consumption and external profit. These traits create major uncertainty and potentially profound international instability.

The potential for conflict arising from these dynamics is not particularly unique to the current and emerging security environment. What is new is the complicating presence of proliferation, not just of CBRN weapons, but of a variety of militarily relevant technologies.

Proliferation has become an important feature of the current security landscape because of the changing dynamics between supply and demand. On the demand side, CBRN proliferation might be attractive for a number of well-identified reasons: leverage against regional rivals or major powers, the United States in particular; prevention of the exercise of leverage by others; prestige; diplomatic influence; a "ticket to the top table"; and others.

With respect to the supply side, the combination of rapidly advancing science and globalization have brought the knowledge and technology of CBRN weapons within reach of a much wider range of actors than previously could exploit them. Technological advances, particularly in the life sciences, also are creating capabilities that never before existed.

This supply-side trend is fostering a changing relationship between intent and capability. Conventional wisdom holds that "intent drives capability," in which the proliferation process is marked by a systematic move down a path toward the deployment of specific capabilities following a government's decision to acquire them. This assumption may no longer represent the exclusive dynamic in play. Rather, a second dynamic has also emerged in which advancing science and technology (S&T) combines with globalization to generate an environment in which "capability shapes intention." Indeed, a 2006 study by the National Research Council argues that future decisions to seek chemical and biological weapons (CBW) are not likely to be driven as much by the perceived efforts of an adversary as by ongoing scientific and technological advances.[3]

In a security context, the combination of what is interesting and what is doable—of curiosity and capability—could yield worrisome results. Although the Biological Weapons Convention bans any work on offensive biological weapons, particularly in a deteriorating security environment, states might be willing to explore the CBW potential of the life sciences, for example, not because they are committed to an institutionalized program or deploying a complete weapons system, but because they are curious. They might begin such an exploration merely because knowledge and capabilities exist somewhere in their scientific or economic establishments, and they are interested in what possibilities these capabilities might offer. Work might go forward with no sense of an ultimate objective, certainly without the highest levels of government intent on fielding a CBW capability. "Dabbling" could become the order of the day. Why would government officials, scientists, or others push for the creation of a dangerous capability? Often the only answer is because they can.

The challenge posed by the combination of curiosity and capability has been identified by the Lawrence Livermore National Laboratory's Center for Global Security Research as proliferation "latency, which could"—possibly the greatest conundrum confronting those responsible for addressing proliferation.[4] How does one counter proliferation in a world in which key actors—primarily states but increasingly nonstate actors as well—enjoy through the diffusion of technology developed for legitimate purposes a "breakout capability" that need be activated only when it is decided to do so?

In terms of conflict dynamics, if North Korea and Iran become recognized nuclear powers, no one could be certain of the chain of consequences. More countries might feel compelled to seek a countervailing capability. Current assessments seem to assume that the other countries would opt for nuclear weapons. Is such an assumption warranted? A nuclear weapons program is very expensive, technically challenging, lengthy in development, and politically risky. A case could be made, therefore, that rather than expending the massive resources required for developing a nuclear capability that takes years to come to fruition, countries would instead seek a more immediate response by exploiting what they already have on hand, which increasingly will be life sciences–based capabilities.[5]

The impact of proliferation on future conflict has been hotly debated. Some analysts argue that proliferation, especially of nuclear weapons, will increase the prospects of at least a limited nuclear war for actors that are not major powers, such as those in South Asia. Others argue the opposite, contending that the presence of nuclear weapons in second-tier countries will spur a reversion to more prolonged, lower level conflicts by other means—intimidation, subversion, terrorism, proxies, and insurgency operations—that are less likely to provoke escalation. Which side is right is impossible to know. What can be said, however, is that proliferation will give potentially global and unlimited dimensions to conflicts that would otherwise be localized and perhaps limited.

While conflict between states, including with CBRN weapons, cannot be dismissed, today's primary conflict contingencies are those complex conflicts in what Phil Williams has described as the "growing number of increasingly disorderly spaces" across the globe, spaces that are geographic, functional, social, economic, legal, and regulatory.[6] These conflicts are often among communities, defined either by some concrete factor such as ethnicity, religion, or language, or increasingly by self-defined and self-selected criteria. They usually are not motivated by political ideology as were the major conflicts of the 20th century, but rather by the age-old goal of control—of territory, resources, or political, economic, and social power. One should resist describing such conflicts as "internal" or "civil," however, in that they do not always remain contained within the boundaries of a single state, and the fighting can occur not only between nongovernment entities and government, but also among a variety of nongovernment players, and even among multiple governments. The conflict in the Democratic Republic of the Congo, for example, has been "transnational" in that it has been in part a civil war involving several insurgent groups and warlords, and in part an international war for regional power and influence, with Angola, Chad, Namibia, Sudan, and Zimbabwe providing forces to one side, and Rwandan and Ugandan troops fighting for the other.

These contemporary community conflicts often share a number of characteristics. First, they involve failed/failing states or "anocracies," regimes between democracy and autocracy that have an incoherent mix of the characteristics of each. The concept of a failed or failing state is well established. Recent analysis suggests an alarming likelihood that such states will become participants in crises either at the regional or global level. According to data analyzed by the University of Maryland's Center for International Development and Conflict Management, 77 percent of all international crises in the post–Cold War era have involved at least one state classified as unstable, fragile, or failed.[7] This leads analysts to conclude that the "extension of the dangers of instability from the domestic to the international realm is . . . a defining characteristic of the current international system."

Anocracies also appear to be closely associated with contemporary violence. Again, according to University of Maryland data, countries with these forms of government are as much as two and a half times more likely than either democracies or autocracies to experience instability and be associated with violent conflict.

Second, contemporary community conflicts do not usually involve classic military confrontations in at least two respects. Most importantly, they involve a wider range of participants. Although formal military forces might be engaged, they are not always—in fact, not usually—the dominant participants. Rather, community-based conflicts are usually waged by competing militias, warring ethnic groups, warlords, and informal paramilitary organizations.

Moreover, these kinds of conflicts tend to be crude, with brutal and often indiscriminate violence. Few if any of the participants take notice of the "laws of war" as defined by the Geneva Conventions or other international legal agreements. The conditions that Lawrence Freedman has identified as necessary to leave civil society relatively unscathed in conflict—refined and discriminatory military means, operations in relatively unpopulated areas, and restraint that allows belligerents to restrict their options—are all unlikely to exist.[8]

A third quality community conflicts share is that they are hard to end. Data suggest that in any given year over the last decade, most active conflicts have been going on for some time. According to Dan Smith, in 1999, for example, 66 percent of existing conflicts were more than 5 years old, and 30 percent were more than 20 years old.[9] No participant usually is in a position to claim victory. Several of the conflicts that now disfigure the global landscape have lasted for many years at a low level. Others have gone into abeyance following conclusion of a ceasefire or peace agreement, but they have resumed (as happened recently in Sri Lanka and Azerbaijan). The reasons for the difficulty in truly ending contemporary conflicts are many: one or more parties are insincere and use the hiatus to rebuild combat capability; one or more are disappointed with political or other developments following the agreement; one side or the other may fragment, with more radical elements continuing to resort to violence; or the underlying causes of the conflict are not addressed.

The impact of the conflict on the psychology of the participants also plays a part. Attempts to destroy an adversary's community and infrastructure—homes, schools, places of worship, and other social fixtures—seem to have become a permanent part of current conflicts. These efforts leave lasting scars that blend into existing community mythology to promote a "never forget" mentality, which fosters a willingness to return to violence.

Lastly, community conflicts are localized. One reason some conflicts can endure for decades is that they remain contained geographically (even if they cross national borders). Most of the decade-long violence in the Democratic Republic of the Congo, for example, has occurred in the eastern portions of the country. Darfur remains an ongoing challenge, but the conflict is not defined in terms of Sudan as a whole. In such cases, neither side has the capability—or sometimes the desire—to precipitate a decisive confrontation, allowing a level of violence to continue that neither side necessarily wants, but with which both can live.

A variant of community warfare, one in which the "communities" are globally defined, is transnational terrorism of the kind promoted by al Qaeda and its affiliates. Osama bin Laden is the leader of a self-defined community—those committed to a particular brand of Islamic fundamentalism—that is neither bounded by territory nor, in their minds, accountable to any authority other than God. In part, its members achieve their sense of community by posing themselves in opposition to another community, the West, in particular the United States and those "apostate" regimes associated with it.

Although more global in scope than many contemporary conflicts, transnational terrorism shares several characteristics with other forms of community conflict. While it is not necessarily state-sponsored, al Qaeda has benefited from the existence of failed states and anocracies, which provide it important room for maneuver. It also has a proclivity for brutality, with high casualties rather than a particular political objective as the primary goal of an attack. And most certainly, transnational terrorism is a kind of conflict that will be difficult to bring to an end.

WHY SUCH CONFLICTS?
The nature of conflicts and the manner in which they are conducted are closely related to the reasons for which they are waged. The causes of today's conflicts are a mix of political, economic, social, psychological, and environmental elements.

One concept that describes this combination is what has been called "new medievalism" or "neomedievalism." Philip Cerny captured the elements of this phenomenon by identifying the interaction of the following factors as the source of an ongoing "durable disorder":

- competing institutional and overlapping jurisdictions of state, nongovernment, and private interest groups
- more fluid territorial boundaries both within and across states
- growing alienation between entities in the global system responsible for innovation, communications on one hand and disfavored, fragmented hinterlands on the other
- increased inequalities within and isolation of permanent underclass and marginalized groups

- growing importance of identity politics, ethnicity, and multiple, fragmented loyalties
- contested property rights, legal status, and conventions
- the spread of geographic and social "no go" areas where the rule of law does not run.[10]

Whether these factors truly represent sources of conflict similar to those in the Middle Ages is, of course, not really the point. Rather, what must be understood is the combination into a complex pattern of state, group, and individual elements interacting to yield today's unique conflicts. Moreover, to this neomedieval mix must be added forces of contemporary modernity that have the effect of turbo-charging conflicts that otherwise would have little international impact. The forces of globalization, particularly the interconnectivity provided by modern information technology, as well as S&T advancing at unprecedented speed, are perhaps the two key elements in this regard.

Another school of thought emphasizes the psychological factors that generate today's small wars. It argues that the search for basic human needs such as identity, belonging, dignity, and self-respect can only be expressed through specific channels in today's international system and combine with massive, accelerating, and disorienting processes of modernization to produce enormous social discord and, ultimately, conflict and violence. Michael Mazarr summarized the argument in contending that "the nature of conflict has shifted from a largely rational enterprise waged by elite-dominated states in pursuit of power objectives to the product of mass psychological trauma attendant to modernization."[11] In this view, future conflict will increasingly have more to do with psychology and identity than military forces.

Yet another school of contemporary analysis regarding the sources of conflict focuses on competition for and the need to protect vital resources. Not surprisingly, this discussion is most often cast in terms of oil and natural gas, not only in connection with the geographic sources of these key resources, but also the security of the systems by which they are transported (pipelines, tanker routes, and ports) and processed and used (refineries and power stations). This orientation has also revived attention to other important resources, which have been a key objective in recent conflicts. Perhaps most notable in this regard are diamonds in Africa. Valuable timber stands have similarly been the object of conflict in Southeast Asia, particularly in Borneo. Also reappearing has been concern over the prospects of "water wars," given a new impetus by attention to climate change and the implications it might have in altering the availability of water resources in some vital regions, not least the Middle East. It should be noted that water-related disputes have tended to be resolved without resort to violence. Under the pressures of climate change, however, this might not be the case in the future.

A final trend related to the purposes for which conflicts are fought may not have as much to do with the causes of conflict as the reason for their continuation. That is, in the current environment, those involved may have either little choice or desire to end the conflict. The issue of choice is in part related to the participation in contemporary conflict of child soldiers. Many of the conflicts discussed here are conducted by participants not out of, and in some cases not even into, their teens. For them, conflict is a way of life; they have virtually no other experience, opportunities, or prospects. Thus, they provide a pool of people who can do nothing but fight for at least a generation. They contribute to what has been called "supply-side war"—conflict driven by the availability of men who have no other skills but those of a fighter.

Even if they know nothing else, whether all these individuals want to fight is questionable. But for another category of individuals the perpetuation of conflict is important, and they want it to continue because their power, status, and economic privilege result directly from it. This line of thought begins with the view that traditional interpretations do not fully take into account the rational economic calculations that drive many current conflicts. Rather, to understand contemporary violence one must also understand the economic dimensions underpinning it. David Keen, for example, identifies seven economic activities arising from war: pillage; extortion of protection money; control or monopolization of trade; exploitation of labor; access to land, water, and mineral resources; theft of aid supplies; and advantages for the military. This is the "greed rather than grievance" school. For example, Paul Collier of the World Bank argues that greed is a principal cause of contemporary conflict, and that warring factions have an economic interest in initiating and sustaining war. While Collier provides macroeconomic evidence in support of his position, the more widely accepted view is that economic agendas account less for the origins than for the longevity of violent conflict.

HOW ARE SUCH CONFLICTS WAGED?

The final set of trends related to contemporary conflict relates to how conflict is conducted. At this level, the issues are less about the conflict and more about the war and the battle. The characteristics of the conduct of conflict will depend in large measure on the respective capabilities of the adversaries, particularly whether they are relatively balanced or whether the fighting is between adversaries in which one, such as the United States, has markedly greater military wherewithal than another. Despite these differences, however, one can suggest some commonalities that will manifest themselves somewhat differently depending on the combatants.

Future conflicts will not usually be fought with advanced conventional weapons. According to some figures, 80 to 90 percent of all casualties in recent wars have been caused by small arms and light weapons. One estimate puts gun deaths in conflicts between 60,000 and 90,000 people per year. This is no surprise when one considers who is doing most of the fighting today and why. Those engaged in many community conflicts, especially in Africa, not only do not have access to more sophisticated technologies, but also, given their opponents, they do not need them. In some cases, machetes do just fine.

Where the adversary is a more advanced military, such as the U.S. Armed Forces, the opponent has little ability to match its conventional capabilities. The use of less advanced weaponry reflects the goals of the weaker combatant, which are not to impose a decisive military defeat on an opponent such as the United States, but rather to undermine the legitimacy, authority, and determination of its government, as well as diminish its popular support, whether among noncombatants within the area of conflict or domestically.

The use of unsophisticated arms also reflects those who use them. Most combatants in contemporary conflicts are not professional soldiers. Rather, they are individuals, often unskilled and unemployed, recruited on the basis of their enthusiasm for a cause, or attracted by the camaraderie and sense of purpose provided by such enterprises. Over time they may become hardened veterans with honed skills who know nothing but conflict. But this still does not make them military professionals, although they can be formidable fighters.

In such cases, small arms, light weapons, and armaments with some degree of precision and other advanced characteristics predominate. They are enhanced by the use of common explosives, albeit in increasingly sophisticated and innovative ways. In this regard, the appearance of improvised explosive devices using chlorine in Iraq might be a harbinger of things to come. A variant in the use of explosives is suicide bombing.

The point is that those involved in such conflicts have learned what limited capabilities can do. As Major General Robert Scales, USA (Ret.), points out, they have recognized that unsophisticated weapons with increased killing power made possible by the use of technologies that exploit "simple craft improvements" can reduce the margin in effectiveness that would otherwise favor the few but very effective (and expensive) weapons of their adversary.[12]

The technology of conflict will not remain static. Some technologies, several of which are still concepts more than finished products, have the theoretical potential to influence the conflict environment significantly over the next 15–20 years. Among those considered to have the greatest potential to alter the relative capabilities of combatants are biotechnology, nanotechnology, directed energy weapons, advanced information systems, and cheaper and more reliable space-lift systems. Importantly, the development of the underlying technologies will be driven more by the private sector than the military, which will have to find ways to translate those commercially driven developments into military capabilities.

Since technological innovation does not automatically translate to new military capabilities, technical hurdles will need to be overcome, not least of which is the research and development cost of new or improved systems. Organizational, bureaucratic, social, and other factors also may retard the process. In reality, then, few actors—state or nonstate—will have the resources, expertise, and motivation to integrate these new technologies fully.

But perhaps they do not need to. An important example in this regard is the potential terrorist use of chemical and biological weapons. Some experts contend that terrorists are both unwilling and unable to exploit the life sciences. With respect to biological weapons, for example, they may not be able to handle advanced genetic engineering capabilities, despite the prevalence of genetic engineering competence, because it does not necessarily translate into terrorist capabilities. Other commentators disagree, contending, for example, that increasingly sophisticated practical knowledge related to the life sciences is available, that the full potential of past programs was never unleashed, and that biological weapon use by small groups historically was relatively unsophisticated and far from representative of what moderately well-informed groups might do today.

Even if terrorists cannot exploit the most cutting-edge science and technology, it does not mean they can do nothing. Terrorists do not need the most advanced capabilities. They do not demand the same operational performance as militaries. Their science and technology have to be just "good enough."

Predicting how technological change will affect international conflict, therefore, is difficult. Technology is neutral, and how it is used will depend on human choices. Those choices, in turn, are influenced by the perceived utility of a given technology, the costs of acquiring it and making it usable for operations, the timelines to achieve that, and the negative consequences that may be attached.

While many technologies have the *potential* for providing those who harness them with new capabilities, the *actual* impact is not guaranteed.

The target set is more expansive. Because of the disparity in capability, major direct assaults on the forces of a well-equipped adversary are often avoided. This does not mean those forces are not attacked, but such operations are usually far removed from the force-on-force battles generally thought to characterize conventional warfare. Rather, superior forces are targets of more classic guerrilla or insurgent operations of a kind that go back far into history.

The military, however, represents only one set of targets in today's violent conflicts. Another set is economic assets, whether they relate to the source of a government's income (such as attacks against tourists in Egypt) or its infrastructure. In this regard, especially in the context of conflicts over resources, pipelines emerge as attractive targets—as they have been, for example, in Colombia. Another key infrastructure causing growing concern is the communications sector, which is vulnerable through cyberwar. Attacks against computer networks in the financial sector and against such security entities as the Pentagon have been widely publicized. Yet little or no publicly available evidence exists that terrorist groups or other adversaries engaged in conflict have perpetrated such attacks. Nevertheless, that sort of contingency is now considered one of the risks for which significant planning is necessary.

A third category of targets is symbols, again useful in undermining the legitimacy and authority of the adversary. The 9/11 attacks represented an assault against both economic and symbolic targets.

Finally, an important set of targets in many contemporary conflicts reflects a new phenomenon and illustrates the brutality of modern clashes. In today's conflicts, civilian populations have become fair game. It is not a question of "collateral damage," which is a tragic dimension of any conflict, but of the conscious targeting of noncombatants as part of a strategy to destroy the adversary psychologically as well as physically. This strategy accounts for such measures as the deliberate use of rape against women, assaults against medical personnel (even those from international organizations) whom the laws of war consider neutral, and the use of violence to control food supplies and manipulate dynamics in refugee camps.

The world is watching. Although media coverage has been a feature of conflict for more than a century, the globalization of information and related technology has fundamentally altered the relationship between the media and conflict and significantly changed how conflicts are waged. The foundation for these changes is the openness and availability of information made possible by new technology. As the journalist Michael Ignatieff has commented, "When war becomes a spectator sport, the media becomes the decisive theater of operations."[13] Ayman al Zawahiri, al Qaeda's second in command, made the same point another way: "I tell you that we are in a battle and that more than half this battle is taking place in the battlefield of the media."[14] The chief theater of modern war has, in some ways, become a television or computer screen. Not every conflict receives major media attention, and some continue to be ignored. Even combatants in those situations, however, give priority to getting their stories before the global community.

Modern conflict is less and less about defeating the enemy in the physical arena, and more about prevailing in the cognitive domain. That is what the "battle for hearts and minds" is all about. Achieving victory in that domain requires a compelling narrative about the conflict— its causes, course, and consequences—that will be supported by those where the conflict is being waged, by allies, friends, and supporters, and at home. The media is the means for relating that narrative. All sides in a conflict, then, use the tools the media provides— especially images, but also stories, "scoops," commentaries, and new forms such as blogs, discussion threads, and others—to make their narrative the most convincing of those to which critical audiences are exposed. The claims of all sides are carried to the world by someone, somewhere. Military operations are often presented from the viewpoint of both those who launch them and their targets. A cynic would suggest that conflict, like much else in modern life, has become primarily an exercise in media "spin."

Giving insufficient attention to the potential impact of the media, however, and not incorporating media planning as part of one's strategy could produce disaster. The stakes are high. Small mistakes can become more costly, perhaps even strategic in their consequences, because they are more transparent. Not only have the formal media been facilitated in their coverage of conflict by direct satellite transmissions, global positioning systems, and more, but also the easy and uncontrollable forms of global, instantaneous communications have, as Lawrence Freedman has pointed out, exponentially increased the number of actors who are able to shape that narrative. Even the actions of a single person can achieve strategic dimensions, whether the individual is an actor whose behavior is transmitted around the world (a guard at the Abu Ghraib prison, for example) or a person doing the transmitting, using technology as simple as a cell phone.

Many contemporary conflicts are made possible by the exploitation of illicit activities that involve what some analysts call "dark networks." Those networks facilitate conflicts in two ways. First, they provide a source of income that funds both acquisitions and operations. Commentary has been widespread on the involvement of terrorist groups in the drug trade and other forms of illicit trafficking. Reports also indicate al Qaeda's efforts to raise money through the sale of diamonds from Africa. For most terrorist groups, these activities are largely instrumental in the sense that they allow the groups to continue doing those things they most want to do. Some conflicts, however, have become inseparable and indistinguishable from such activities, especially when it comes to control over key resources. In these cases, the violence is intended to ensure control, reflecting again the greed rather than grievance phenomenon.

Second, dark networks provide operational support. Most important here is the exploitation of a globalized financial system to manage the money required to continue the violence. But such networks clearly provide other forms of support as well, including logistical, transportation, and special services, such as documentation.

Combatants operate out of remote or inaccessible locations. The mountains of Afghanistan and the inhospitable territory on the Afghanistan-Pakistan border are examples. In the future, however, inaccessibility is equally likely to be found in the sprawling urban areas that have become a feature of the early 21st-century landscape. These slums and shantytowns are often already "no go areas," where authority is asserted by actors other than representatives of the government, including those responsible for public security. As such, they are likely to contribute significantly to the dispersed, distributed, protected, and non-nodal kinds of operations that contemporary combatants are perfecting.

Legal restraints are likely to be asymmetrical. Contemporary conflicts can be remarkably brutal, and combatants appear increasingly disinterested in observing the Geneva Conventions and other instruments defining the laws of armed conflict. The most striking example of this trend is the growing practice of willfully targeting civilian noncombatants in attacks that aim to destroy the adversary's social and communal cohesion, if not causing his physical destruction altogether. A particularly heinous method is the growing use of rape as a weapon, especially if it also entails spreading HIV/AIDS.

Today's conflicts are of a form in which any restraint is being abandoned, not just in terms of targeting noncombatants, but also in other ways that seek to deny an adversary any advantage. Deliberate attacks against medical and health care workers, whom the laws of armed conflict define as neutrals and therefore not to be targeted, are increasing, for example, because those personnel are seen as strengthening the enemy by ministering to troops and community health needs.

This growing disregard for the international laws of armed conflict is not limited to community conflicts, however. It has also been seen in confrontations involving professional armed forces. During the Kosovo conflict, for example, Serbs located sensitive missile sites adjacent to hospitals to avoid being hit by North Atlantic Treaty Organization airstrikes. They also deployed their forces next to convoys of civilians. Another trend in current conflicts that further exacerbates this problem is the growing use of mercenaries, who often write their own rules.

These attitudes create an operational asymmetry, especially for Western forces, including those of the United States. Such forces will remain constrained by the laws of armed conflict, and properly so. They will continue to observe such principles as seeking to use the least amount of force necessary to achieve a given objective, not attacking civilian noncombatants, and minimizing collateral damage. But such restraint creates a dilemma: the more observant of the rules a military is, the more likely an adversary is to exploit that observance. Such exploitation of legal restraint is a central component of terrorism, and it is becoming increasingly common in other forms of armed conflict as well. The challenge to regular forces, then, is how to play by the rules when the other side does not.

This dilemma is made even starker in the transparent media world. In such an environment, any rule violation is likely to be documented in some form and could prove costly.

A further legal dilemma also should be highlighted. Many current conflicts—while the combatants might be fighting to enhance their economic, social, or political power—also entail military intervention intended to enforce a set of universal values often cast in terms of human rights or the principles of the United Nations (UN) Charter. Such thinking, for example, is at the core of the principle now being promoted in some quarters of the "responsibility to protect." Jean-Marc Rickli makes the point that, to the extent that some conflicts are about "enforcing the world vision enshrined in the UN charter," a state's decision to engage in conflict, as well as the conduct of its forces in that conflict, must strictly follow international law.[15]

As the debate prior to the invasion of Iraq in 2003 so strikingly demonstrated, however, a major problem exists because of the absence of a universally recognized and accepted authoritative interpretation of international law regarding armed conflict. In particular, that debate found many arguing that the UN is the only international institution that can provide legitimacy for undertaking military operations. This view has two problems. One, those who initiate conflict never seem to care about the view of the UN, again playing by a different set of rules. Two, internal transgressions, structural deficiencies, and inadequate performance have all called the "legitimizing" role of the UN into question, at least for some major members of the international community. Continuing debate over the legitimacy of an ongoing military operation represents a potentially significant obstacle to effective performance, particularly for coalition operations or those that would benefit from involvement of allies or even their political support. As such, it represents yet another asymmetry in contemporary conflict.

Trends giving shape to international conflict in the years ahead portray a turbulent, volatile, and multidimensional dynamic. They suggest a wide set of diverse participants at the state and nonstate levels motivated by a complex combination of political, economic, social, and other reasons related to the international system, national governmental performance, group dynamics, and individual alienation and psychological trauma. The spectrum of instruments used will be both brutal and savage, and sophisticated and discriminate. Military and civilian personnel and areas will be targets, facilitated by disorderly spaces and dark networks, most likely for the long term. This is not a pretty picture, nor is it a familiar one. As a result, it places enormous demands on thinking and operating creatively at both the policy and operational levels.

Shocks

A number of shocks could make this situation even more disturbing. Shocks could occur across any of the dimensions mentioned above, and, given the complex nature of the processes fostered by current conflict trends, the number of shocks is almost limitless. The following list of shocks is offered, therefore, to highlight some of the different challenges such shocks might pose. It attempts not to repeat examples provided elsewhere, such as a successful cyber attack, although such developments are obviously important from the perspective of future conflicts. Nor does the list include shocks characterized by the emergence of new technologies, although any number of possibilities exists in this realm.

USE OF A CBRN WEAPON

Beyond the physical and psychological impact such weapons could achieve, the "next use" of CBRN, especially if successful, would have a profound impact on the perceived utility of such capabilities. Successful use could change actors' calculations regarding the costs and benefits of pursuing these options, and propel a more serious exploration of their potential utility. Moreover, concepts of use bear directly on the technical and operational requirements needed to conduct a successful attack, and, therefore, on proliferation cost-benefit calculations. For a considerable time, some measure of relief has been taken from the view that an attack producing catastrophic casualties is beyond the technical or operational capacity of most nonstate actors and even many states. In the future, this is likely to be less and less the case. Moreover, the requirements for contingencies producing fewer victims are less stringent. It is important to understand the implications of these less demanding requirements so as to guard against underestimating the likelihood of such an event, which, even if not catastrophic, could nevertheless generate disastrous implications.

A REVOLUTIONARY COLLAPSE SUFFERED BY A MAJOR REGIONAL ALLY

Depending on the specifics, the impacts of such a contingency could be felt not only in the country itself, but also regionally and perhaps globally. First, it could represent the loss of important resources, particularly if that ally was an oil-rich nation in the Middle East. Second, it could also create a new "disorderly space" that becomes the site of conflict or facilitates the activities of others engaged in conflict in the region or with the United States. Third, even if it does not become adversarial in this way, its loss could undercut or impede the ability of the United States to perform important security-related operations, such as through the loss of access to facilities. Fourth, the armed forces of the country may be operating in coalition with the United States somewhere, or be involved in peacekeeping or other operations that Washington supports, creating a gap as they are withdrawn by the new leadership.

An important variant of this contingency is the coming to power by extremists in a nuclear-armed country. This scenario, which is playing out in Pakistan, has received considerable attention. While such an eventuality might not come as a surprise, it would nevertheless still represent a shock, profoundly changing the country's bilateral relationships with its neighbors, altering regional dynamics in a major way, and creating intense international concern.

A "WATER WAR"

Most scenarios of resource conflicts center on oil—shocking, perhaps, but not surprising. A scenario that would be both surprising and shocking would be a major conflict over water. It would be surprising because, as mentioned, such a development has been rare historically; it would be shocking for the impact it would have on regional security dynamics, but also in terms of the broad psychological impact it would spark across the international community regarding how the prospect of climate-related security issues will have to be handled.

The most likely region for such a scenario is the Middle East, especially between Israel and one of its neighbors. It is in this context that the term "transnational conflict" should be used deliberately because such an event would almost certainly involve not only the national militaries of the adversaries, but also nonstate actors with a high stake in the outcome, such as Hamas, that increasingly are acquiring at least some of the characteristics of national governments.

COMMUNITY CONFLICT IN THE EUROPEAN CORE

Demographic and social pressures created by immigration and population trends and national policies have created increasingly high levels of anxiety in Europe. The French experience in the summer of 2005, problems in Germany, and alienated youth engaging in terrorism in the United Kingdom can all be cited as possible symptoms of domestic situations that, while not combustible today, might erupt under certain circumstances. An explosion on the periphery of the "new Europe" might be more easily accommodated in terms of national and international reactions; it might be deemed a problem but not a major shock to the system. That view would change entirely if the eruption occurred in what might be considered Europe's core, particularly in Western Europe. Such a development would set off alarm bells in all Western countries, each of which has its own particular challenge with respect to minority populations. It might also attract foreign "combatants" who identify with the violent minority and are interested in striking a blow against a despised adversary, fostering the kind of imported violence that some say is a major part of the problem in Iraq. It might also provide an example of an important issue to consider in understanding the battle between governments and insurgents. That issue has been described by Phil Williams in the following terms: "During the day, the forces associated with the formal authority structure are often dominant; during the night, the constellation of forces is very different. Indeed, the issue of who controls the night is perhaps one of the best single indicators of the progress of the struggle."[16]

A DOMESTIC CBRN TERRORISM CAMPAIGN

No one would underestimate the impact of the Oklahoma City bombings. One of the most important shocks from that attack was the realization that the United States could confront home-grown terrorism unrelated to the international conflicts waged by Islamic extremists. Since 9/11, U.S. Government officials have demonstrated an increased awareness of the threat of terrorist CBRN use, resulting in substantial efforts to improve the Nation's ability to respond to and mitigate the effects of these attacks. Enormous amounts of time and money have been expended on prevention, response planning, and bolstering response capacity. Yet these efforts have too often revolved around a terrorism incident—the single use of a CBRN weapon by a terrorist. Planning and capacity-building efforts have failed to account for the possibility of a series of interconnected incidents in the form of a terrorism campaign. Moreover, planning has assumed that both the incident and the response will progress in a linear fashion. This concept of a neatly phased progression is likely to prove untenable in the face of a CBRN terrorism campaign involving a series of attacks, separated temporally and spatially. Under campaign circumstances, prevention, crisis and consequence management, and recovery likely will need to take place concurrently. Finally, attention to home-grown terrorism has receded in the face of continued pressure from al Qaeda and the diminished activities of militias and other groups that spawned Timothy McVeigh and were the object of considerable concern a decade ago. There is no guarantee, however, that something—either at home or abroad—will not spark their resurgence.

The prospect of confronting a terrorist CBRN campaign raises questions about prevention and preparedness and response requirements, making difficult tradeoffs regarding the allocation of limited resources, reconciling competing political and economic interests, promoting international cooperation, and reassuring publics. Answers to these questions that might be suitable for dealing with a single incident are unlikely to address CBRN campaigns.

U.S. WITHDRAWAL FROM THE WORLD STAGE

If the American leadership and public were to decide the country should no longer play the security role it has played since World War II, the impact might represent the biggest shock of all. Competition to fill the vacuum would become intense, leading to widespread instability and conflict. U.S. allies would not only feel the effects, but could also become endangered. U.S. adversaries—state and nonstate alike—would become emboldened. International governance regimes would struggle to remain relevant, if they did not break down altogether.

Conclusion

This chapter has provided some thoughts on trends and shocks related not to war but to conflict, albeit conflict involving often intensive and extensive violence.

For U.S. policymakers, keeping this distinction in mind is important because clarity of view with respect to the real challenges will help to ensure appropriate policy responses. War in its traditional sense of the engagement of adversaries' armies is complicated enough and is getting more so as the potential battlefield expands into more dimensions. But the conflicts discussed here have a complexity and multifaceted dynamic that pose perhaps even more vexing challenges for the future.

Some of these challenges will involve decisions about when to engage in a conflict. At times, no choice will exist—for example, if the United States or its interests are the direct target of violence. In most cases, however, the choice will not be so clear-cut, and the criteria for determining when the United States should engage or intervene will remain the subject of intense debate. Other questions will relate to how we engage. In this regard, two issues come immediately to mind. First, with whom will we engage, and under whose auspices? The occasions in which the United States will act alone will be rare if they arise at all. So with whom will Washington act, and by whose authority? Again, answers to these questions are not self-evident, and they could be hotly contested. The second issue pertains to whether U.S. involvement will necessarily entail the military. This issue is controversial and will plague future debates over engagement. Traditionally, the view of the U.S. military has been that its role is to "fight and win America's wars." But most future conflicts will not be America's wars or even America's conflicts. What the U.S. military response should be in such circumstances, therefore, needs careful calibration.

This chapter tries to convey the close interaction between why conflict will occur, the many diverse participants who will be involved, and the characteristics of those conflicts, not least being the difficulties of bringing them to a close. Such a complex relationship suggests the need for an understanding of conflict across the spectrum—from its origins to its amelioration—and the importance of being able to act across that complete spectrum. Doing so effectively will require capabilities that extend far beyond those of the military. The need for such a broad set of nonmilitary capabilities is a lesson being driven home by the experiences of the United States and other polities from Iraq to Georgia to Darfur. It is a lesson that must be taken to heart as we confront conflict-related trends and shocks in the future.

3

Global Demographics

Carl Haub

FOR THE MOST PART, changes in demographic rates, as well as expectations for the future, move at near-glacial speed. For many decades, the outlook for future world population has not varied greatly from the overall pattern shown in figure 3–1. Simply put, practically all future world population growth will be in the developing countries of Africa, Asia, Latin America, and Oceania. In 2007, 18 percent of the global population lived in the developed regions of Europe, North America, plus Australia, Japan, and New Zealand. By 2020, that percentage should decline to about 16 percent and, by 2050, to 13 percent. Trend or shock? In the long term, such a development is *quite* a shock when we consider that the developed regions accounted for 33 percent of the global total in 1900 and for many years had the military and economic power to colonize and even exploit the developing regions. While the horizon for the project that produced this book is 2020, some reference should also be made to a more distant date, such as 2050. Demographic trends are important not simply for what they show now, but also for where they are heading. Population trends, barring any sharp and large reversals, have certain predictability. Many future trends are a direct consequence of what is happening now.

A key consideration is that the trend shown in figure 3–1 is, for all practical purposes, irreversible. While labeling a demographic trend irreversible may seem risky, consider the following: the projection of developing country populations makes the universal assumption that fertility rates in developing countries will soon begin to decline or will continue to do so where they have already begun to. In addition, it is assumed that declines will be continuous once they begin. These are large assumptions that, even today, are not necessarily borne out by actual developments. A second reason why the trend can be labeled irreversible is that

Figure 3–1. World Population, 1950–2050

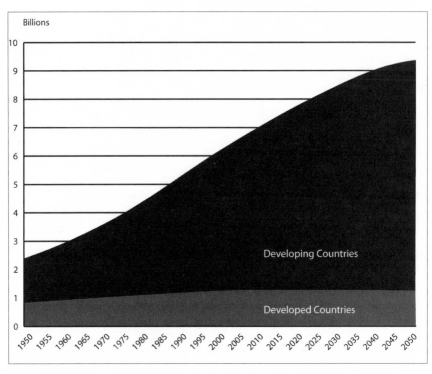

Source: United Nations, *World Population Prospects as Assessed in 2006, Medium Variant.*

even an unexpectedly large rise in European fertility will not alter the situation to any great extent. Thus, any future planning must take into account the fact that the past 100 years have produced a world that, demographically speaking, has been turned upside down. Finally, if that were not enough, the dramatic difference in *age structure* between developed and developing regions assures the vast gulf in population growth. Often, one-third or more of a developing country's population is below the age of 15 and about 5 percent above the age of 65, so considerable population growth is a certainty. In Europe, only 16 percent is below age 15 and 16 percent is above age 65. As a result, deaths now equal or exceed births, a situation unprecedented in history.

Yet a simple division of the world into only two discrete groups, developed and developing countries, masks a large variation within regions. For that reason, a region-by-region overview will be far more useful.

Africa

Contemporary Africa is the one world region where present and future population growth still fits the old "population explosion" model. There are three reasons for this: fertility rates are still quite high, at a total fertility rate (TFR)[1] of 5.0 continent-wide and 5.5 in largely impoverished sub-Saharan Africa; fertility decline has either not begun in some countries or has stalled; and current low life expectancy results in considerable room even today for improvements in health conditions to lower death rates, further increasing an already rapid rate of population growth. Current projections call for Africa to add 1 *billion* people to its current 944 million by 2050, and that projection may well prove to be conservative.

Almost every country in Africa has an officially stated policy to slow population growth, although the gap is usually wide between official policies and effective action. In terms of fertility, there are really two Africas. In the North African countries, efforts to reduce the birthrate have been quite successful. The TFR in Algeria is now 2.4, in Egypt 3.1, and in Tunisia 2.0. The situation in sub-Saharan Africa is quite different.

Sub-Saharan Africa has produced one of the demographic shocks of recent years. Fertility rates, which had been in gradual decline, now appear to be slowing their decrease in many countries. As shown in figure 3–2, the TFR has shown practically no or extremely slow decline in Chad and Uganda, while declines from previously high levels have slowed in Ethiopia, Kenya, and Zimbabwe. The significance of this trend grows when we realize that, as mentioned above, standard population projections assume that the TFR will decline continuously until reaching a point near the two-child level. That level is also referred to as *replacement level* fertility, since couples simply replace themselves without increasing the size of successive generations. As a result, population growth eventually reaches zero, although that can take some time. Current trends in sub-Saharan Africa raise the question of the likelihood that African countries will reach such a low level of fertility.

The implication for population projections is enormous. Sub-Saharan Africa is the world's most youthful region, with 40–50 percent of the population below the age of 15 in most countries. The possibility of sub-Saharan Africa growing from the present 800 million to 2 billion by 2050 is quite realistic.

A second shock has been provided by new, lower estimates of HIV prevalence in the region. This information has been provided by Demographic and Health Surveys (DHS), a series of nationally representative surveys that have been

Figure 3–2. African Fertility Decline Slowdown

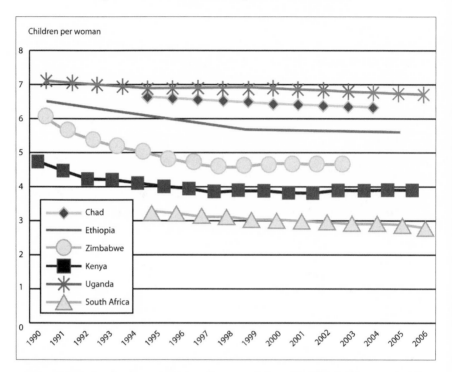

conducted in developing countries for several decades. The DHS program was initiated by the U.S. Agency for International Development and often receives additional funding from organizations such as the World Bank, the Department for International Development of the United Kingdom, the United Nations Children's Fund, and the United Nations Population Fund.[2] Recently, DHS surveys began testing interviewed men and women for HIV infection. Before such surveys, estimates of national levels of HIV prevalence could only be based on HIV testing performed at selected locations, such as antenatal clinics at government hospitals or among military recruits. Such measurement points were not representative of the general population by definition. As a result, estimates were subject to a considerable margin of error. The lower figures are good news, although levels remain quite high in many countries of eastern and southern Africa. Among the consequences of lower HIV prevalence levels will be lower mortality and less disruption of the economy, and also higher population projections, once the lower mortality from HIV can be taken into account (see figure 3–3).

Figure 3–3. HIV Prevalence in Selected Sub-Saharan African Countries Before and After Demographic and Health Surveys, 2003–2006

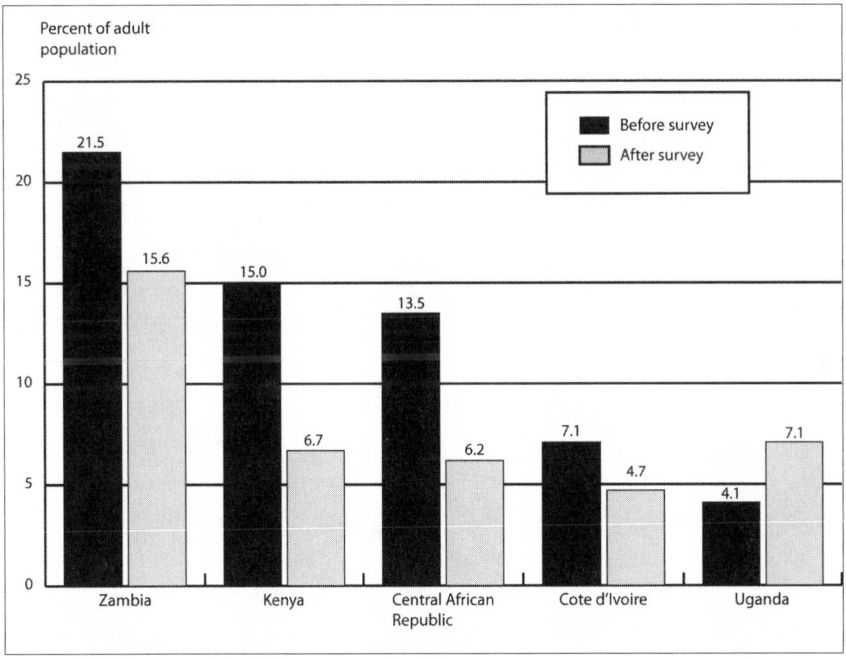

Source: UNAIDS and Demographic and Health Surveys.

Sub-Saharan Africa combines many ingredients that could be of concern to the Department of Defense (DOD), not the least of which is the most rapid population growth in the world's most poverty-stricken region. The World Bank estimates sub-Saharan Africa's gross national income adjusted for purchasing power parity (GNI PPP) at $2,000 per capita, the world's lowest. This increase in population is combined with ethnic conflict, unstable and ineffective government, and economic growth that have been hampered by many factors.

Asia and Oceania

Trends are as diverse in Asia and Oceania as they are homogeneous in Africa. In Western Asia/Middle East,[3] the TFR exhibits quite a wide range. TFRs in some of the larger countries are: Iran, 2.0; Iraq, 4.9; Israel, 2.8; Jordan, 3.5; Palestinian Territory, 4.6; Saudi Arabia, 4.1; Syria, 3.5; Turkey, 2.2; and Yemen, 6.2. Of the larger countries, only Iran and Turkey have achieved a low, "secular" TFR and are at, or even below, the replacement level. Those countries have fertility more in line with France and the United States.

Overall, the region is projected to increase from 294 million in 2007 to 358 million by 2020 and to 467 million by 2050, a modest level overall compared to Africa, although the projected growth is naturally larger in the countries with both the higher TFRs and the potential for political instability. Along with North Africa, low fertility in countries such as Iran and Turkey can be described as a "shock," an unexpected decline in countries that in the past had traditionally high fertility. This is particularly true in the case of Iran.

At the same time, a low TFR is often associated with an improving economy and rising national income. GNI PPP per capita in Iran and Turkey were $8,480 and $9,060 respectively in 2006. Such improvements in economies can be a favorable sign but can also lead to internal conflict should rising expectations not be met in terms of adequate employment for youth entering the labor force years.

In South Asia, the three major players in terms of population are Bangladesh, India, and Pakistan. Of the three, India receives by far the greatest attention in its emergence as a new economic force. Along with Pakistan, it is also a member of the nuclear club and is in negotiations with the United States on a new nuclear agreement. It is the contention here, however, that the rapidity of India's development has been greatly overstated in the Western media. While there is no doubt that a small segment of the population, primarily in a few major metropolitan areas, has benefited from less stringent economic policies and direct foreign investment in new businesses, little else has changed from decades ago for the vast majority of the population.

India would appear to be one of the developing countries well on the way to completing the demographic transition from high fertility and mortality rates to low ones, but national rates can be deceiving. In 2005, India's TFR stood at 2.9, down from about 6.0 in the 1960s. This national rate, however, hides wide variation at the state level (see figure 3–4).

Much of the decrease in India's TFR has been in its southern states, such as Kerala and Tamil Nadu, where TFRs are now below 2.0. These states can make no further contribution to fertility decline in the country. It is the large northern states that hold the key to India's demographic future. Just two of these states, Bihar and Uttar Pradesh, today contain one-fourth of the country's population and have the highest fertility, with TFRs above 4.0. But these are also the country's poorest states and those with the greatest illiteracy (see table 3–1).

Figure 3–4. Total Fertility Rate in Selected Indian States, 2005

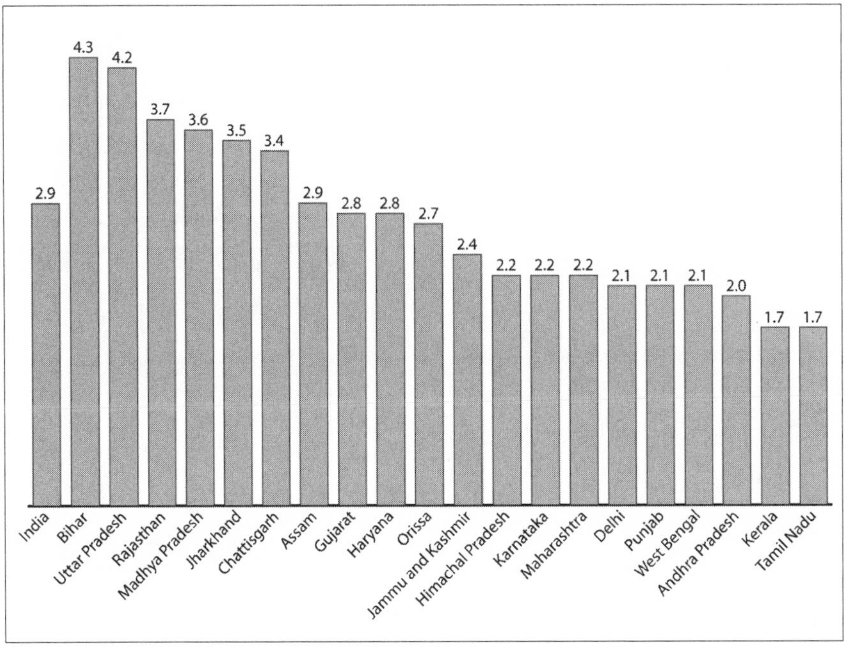

India remains a nation of villages, in that the average Indian lives in a village of a little more than 4,000 people. The country's population is officially 28 percent urban, but, in India, an urban center is considered a settlement where the population is 5,000 or more and at least three-fourths of the adult male population is not engaged directly in agriculture. Thus, we must change the way we look at India—not as a nation of computer experts, but of farmers and laborers, with a few areas showing signs of economic success (Delhi, Mumbai [formerly Bombay], Bangalore, Hyderabad, and a few others). But even Mumbai is 54 percent slum. Currently, India's gross national product is 6 percent of that of the United States, and while no good figures on income distribution are available, much of the wealth resides in the hands of a few.

Much of India's future population growth will happen among its poorest segment over the next few decades. In many states, particularly in the north, corruption in state capitals has left much of the rest of these states with little or no infrastructure development. This is not the case everywhere, to be sure, but when considering India, the reality of its massive and widespread poverty must be kept in mind. To date, the country has functioned well as a democracy

Table 3–1. India's Demographic Divide: The Example of Three States

	UTTAR PRADESH	BIHAR	KERALA
2001 population (millions)	166	83	32
Male/female literacy (percent)	69/42	60/33	94/88
Total fertility rate	4.2	4.3	1.7
Urban population (percent)	21	11	26
Population below age 15 (percent)	41	42	46
Households with electricity (percent)	32	10	70
Households in permanent-type house (percent)	53	41	68
Households with television (percent)	25	9	39
Households with 4-wheeled vehicle (percent)	2.2	0.9	4
Households with 2-wheeled vehicle (percent)	3.6	10.4	10.0
One-room households (percent)	30	43	11
Underweight children under age 3 (percent)	47	58	29

Source: 2001 Census of India, National Family Health Survey-3.

within the limitations of its political reality. A major drawback has been the proliferation of political parties since India achieved independence in 1947, in part due to the many linguistic, ethnic, and caste groups. Illiteracy and lack of understanding on the part of much of the electorate have contributed to this political diversity. One result of a large number of parties has been the difficulty of forming effective governments at the state and national levels. Even without political fragmentation, widespread corruption acts as a major impediment to development. While there is no reason to fear a collapse of India's democratic system, we should be aware that an India with a population of 1.7 to 2 billion, with most of that growth among the impoverished, will be a very different place from what it is today (see figure 3–5).

Bangladesh did provide a shock in the early 1990s, when its TFR began a fairly rapid decline. Today, the TFR stands at 3.0, essentially the same as India's. However, the country's small size and large population must be kept in mind. With a low-lying land area of about 50,000 square miles, Bangladesh is about the size of Louisiana. Its population of 150 million gives it a density of 3,000 persons

Figure 3–5. Projected Population in Selected Indian States, 2001–2051

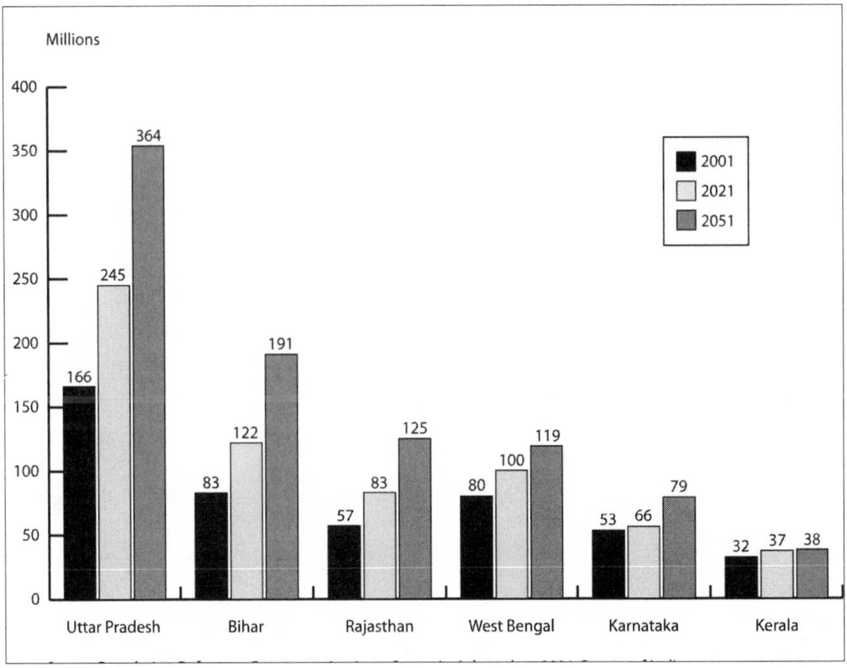

Source: Population Reference Bureau projections, Scenario A, based on 2001 Census of India.

per square mile, the world's highest among noninsular countries/city-states. Overcrowding has led to illegal emigration to India, an issue that has raised tensions between the countries. A recent DHS survey (2006–2007) in Pakistan measured a TFR of 4.1. While the TFR has reached a medium level, decline has been quite slow. Further, fertility is higher in the rural areas, a common observance in most countries. Pakistan is 66 percent rural, and the TFR was 4.5 in rural areas in 2006–2007, compared to 3.0 in large cities.

In East Asia, China is well known for its stringent "one child" population policy. That policy was certainly a shock when it was imposed in the 1970s. Today, China's TFR is about 1.6, an astoundingly low rate for a developing country. In fact, China's effective population policy is really for 1.5 children, not 1.0, since exceptions are made for couples whose first birth is a girl, and different rules apply to minorities (see figure 3–6).

A TFR as low as China's will have a pronounced effect on the country's age structure. Figure 3–6 shows that the proportion of younger children who will

Figure 3–6. Population Pyramid, China, 2007

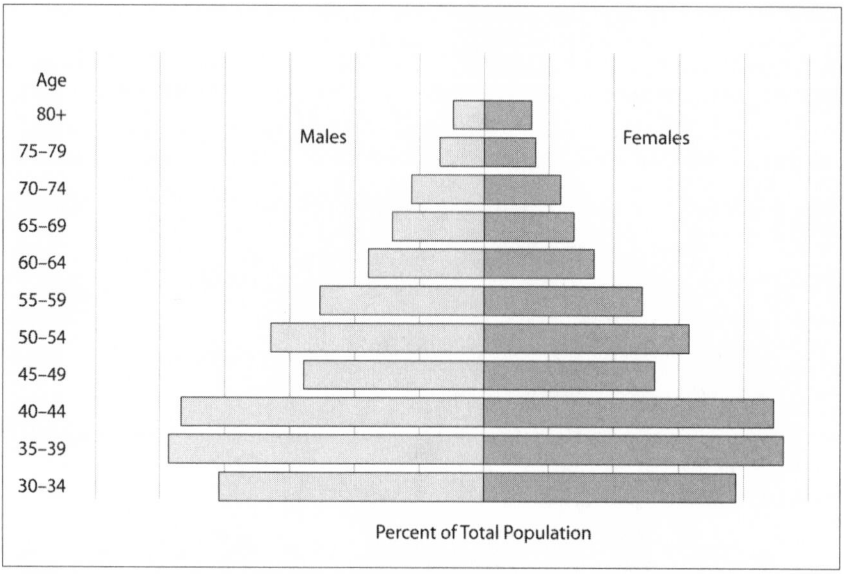

Source: U.S. Census Bureau, International Database.

be tomorrow's parents has been greatly diminished. It is clear that when these smaller age cohorts enter the childbearing years, they will be unable to produce sufficient births to offset deaths occurring among the much larger older groups.

The rapidly diminishing size of the youngest age cohorts is, of course, a direct result of China's national policy. There are additional disturbances in China's age pyramid due to temporary declines in the birthrate, particularly during the Cultural Revolution of the late 1960s and early 1970s. But the country's very low birthrate has now given the country's pyramid a European appearance. This can be compared to India's age structure (figure 3–7), which, as would be expected, retains the classic youthful appearance of a developing country with a more normal demographic history—one of a relatively smooth decline in the birthrate. It is clear from figures 3–8 and 3–9 that India will remain a much more youthful country for quite some time. However, between now and 2020, the measure of China's youthfulness, the percent of population below age 15, is projected to change only from 20 percent in 2007 to 19 percent in 2020. The so-called age burden, the percent above age 65, will rise from 7 to 11 percent. The longer term consequences of China's low birthrate will not be felt until later. By 2050, the percent below age 15 should decline to 15, while that above age 65 should rise to a very high 24 percent. These figures are as projected by the U.S. Census Bureau on the assumption that fertility will remain at the current level. While there have been rumors over the years that China would relax its population policy in response to the specter of severe societal aging, the government has denied any such change on many occasions.

India's population, on the other hand, will maintain much of its youthful character well beyond 2020. The percent below age 15, about 32 percent in 2006, should still be about 28 percent in 2021, declining to 22 percent in 2051. The percent above age 65, 5 percent in 2006, is likely to increase to only 6 percent in 2021, and then to 13 percent by 2051.

In both countries, lower fertility has led to reduced proportions of the population below age 15 and a reduction of the proportion of the population in the dependent ages. This development is often referred to as the demographic

Figure 3–7. Population Pyramid, India, 2006

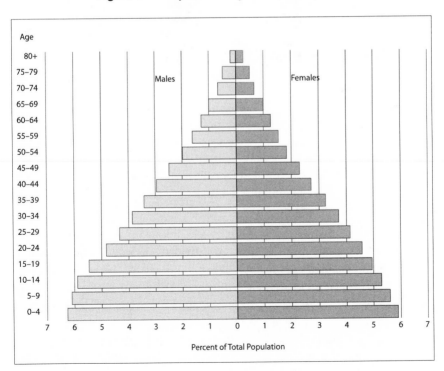

Source: Population Reference Bureau projections, based on 2001 Census of India.

Figure 3–8. Population Below Age 15 and Above Age 65, China and India, 2006 and 2021

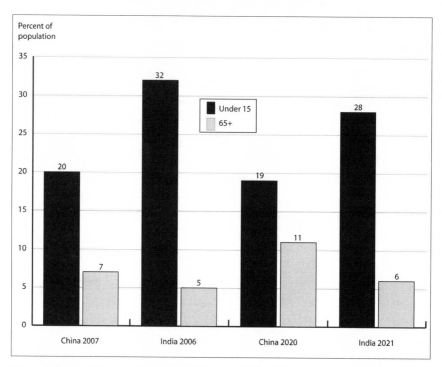

Source: U.S. Census Bureau, International Database and Population Reference Bureau projections, based on 2001 Census of India.

dividend, in that a large portion of the population is in the working age group and less national expense is required for education. While there is some truth to the notion of a dividend, numbers of people in the working ages do not constitute any sort of dividend absent productive employment.

With a labor force that is heavily agricultural and untrained, India has done little to take advantage of its demographic dividend. (Vietnam finds itself in a similar condition.) There are highly publicized pockets of "high-tech" employment in several major cities, along with significant industrial development in states such as Gujarat, Jharkhand, Maharashtra, Uttarakhand, and Uttar Pradesh, but such development has made only a small economic contribution in such a large and growing population. At present, it would seem that China is in a better position to utilize its labor pool because of its much more developed economy and industrial base, at least until 2020. But China will subsequently face

**Figure 3–9. Population Below Age 15 and Above Age 65,
China and India, 2007 and 2050**

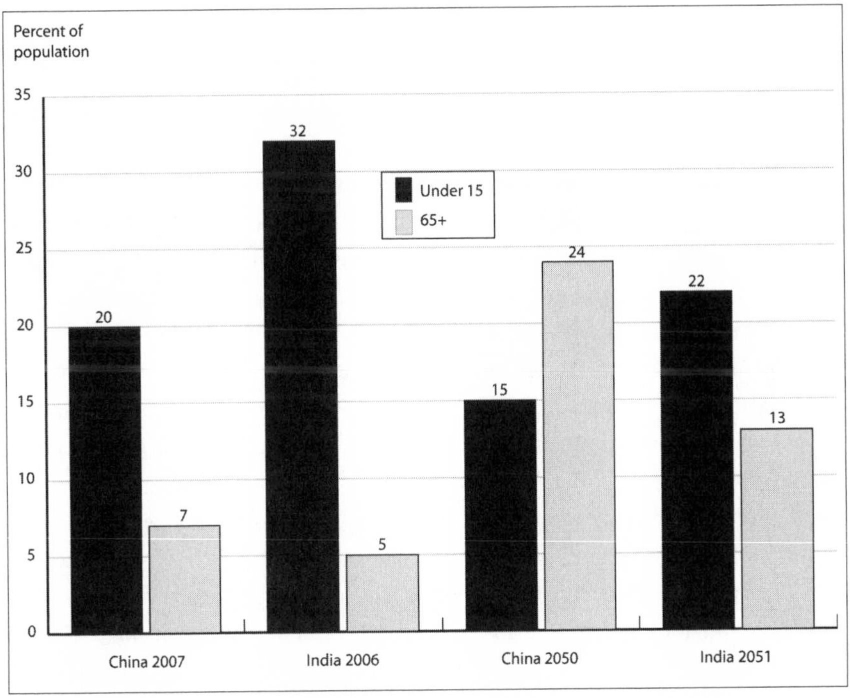

Source: U.S. Census Bureau, International Database and Population Reference Bureau
projections, based on 2001 Census of India.

the significant problem of societal aging beyond 2020. Still, the ratio of workers
to the dependent population will remain favorable in China until that time, perhaps beyond. The recent announcement that China intends to compete with
Airbus and Boeing in the construction of large airliners gives evidence of the
country's continuing emergence as an economic power. Its increased participation in the aerospace field is certainly one area of concern for DOD.

The Low Fertility Countries

One of the great demographic shocks of recent years has been the collapse of
the birthrate in industrialized countries, first in Western Europe, then in the
former Soviet bloc and the newly industrialized countries (NICs) of East Asia. An
aftershock is that the birthrate collapse has not been a temporary phenomenon
but has become chronic.

Since the issue of low fertility is not confined to one geographic region, these countries will be discussed as a group. Certainly, TFRs as low as 1.1 (Taiwan and South Korea) and 1.3 in Germany were never anticipated. Once such low levels were reached, it also was never expected that they would continue. The effect of such catastrophically low birthrates will, of course, be significant natural decrease (more deaths annually than births) and an unprecedented level of societal aging. This will have serious economic and social impacts upon countries that have historically been among the most valued U.S. allies. At least three major impacts can be identified: severe economic consequences, such as declining markets and labor force shortages; increased pension and health care expense, reducing funds available for defense; and greater reliance on foreign labor in competition with xenophobic tendencies.

The low fertility countries have become very concerned over the negative aspects of greatly reduced numbers of young people, and stories on the subject are common. Many countries are moving quickly to encourage births and make raising children less burdensome on families. One factor, however, stands out: the longer the birthrate remains at a low level, the more damage is done to a country's age distribution.

The drastic reduction in the size of South Korean age cohorts from ages 10–14 is quite obvious in figure 3–10; it is also irreversible. Note that the 0–4 male age group represents about 2.5 percent of the population, while the age group 35–39 is 4.5 percent. This is nearly a *50 percent* reduction. The situation is similar in the very low fertility countries of Europe.

What are the prospects for "recovery" of birthrates in Europe? The concern expressed by countries for many years has recently become action. Countries have begun to increase or introduce incentives for childbearing, such as larger payments to families and improved daycare. To date, there have been increases in TFRs in some countries, particularly in Northern Europe. Several countries with the lowest rates, such as Italy and Spain, have also evidenced a slowly rising birthrate, although this has not been the case among the Germanic countries of Western Europe, Austria, Germany, and Switzerland. Figure 3–11 provides the TFR trend for countries with low TFRs and those with completely reported data on births and deaths beginning in 1995 up to the most recent year for which figures are available.

In addition to the possible effects of national policies on the TFR, it is also possible that some childbearing in Europe has simply been "delayed." In Spain, the TFR did rise from 1.17 in 1995 to 1.37 in 2006. Looking at age-specific rates

Figure 3–10. Population Pyramid, South Korea, 2007

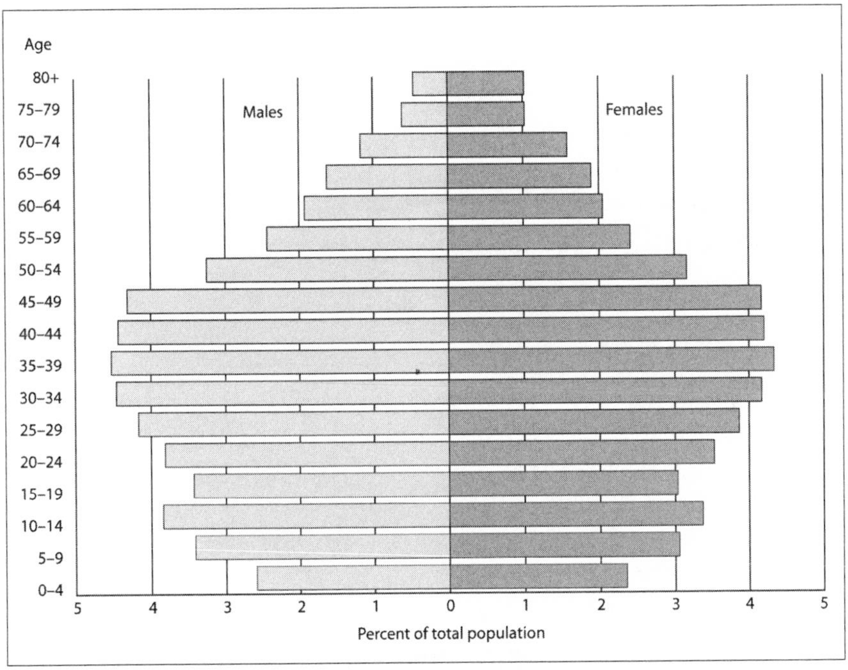

Source: National Statistical Office, Republic of Korea.

(figure 3–12), it is evident that childbearing shifted to ages above 30 from 1995–2005 rather dramatically, giving credence to the delayed childbearing hypothesis. However, the TFR in Spain is still very low, and it is doubtful that shifts in the age of childbearing alone could raise the TFR to anywhere near 2 children per woman. While there is evidence that most low TFRs have "bottomed out" in the lowest fertility countries, and that some increases are possible and even likely, the small age cohorts produced during the period of low fertility cannot be undone.

The Americas
While there have not been any demographic developments in Latin America that could be described as shocks, it is worth noting that the poorest countries, primarily in Central America (notably Guatemala and Honduras), have the highest fertility and population growth rates. However, recent migration trends northward could be considered something of a shock.

Figure 3–11. Total Fertility Rate, Selected European Countries, 1995–2006

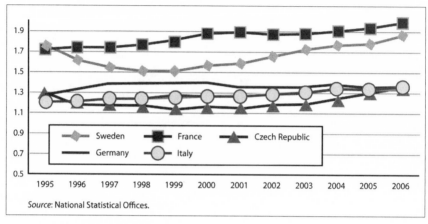

Source: National Statistical Offices.

Source: National Statistical Offices.

Figure 3–12. Age-specific Birthrates, Spain, 1995 and 2005

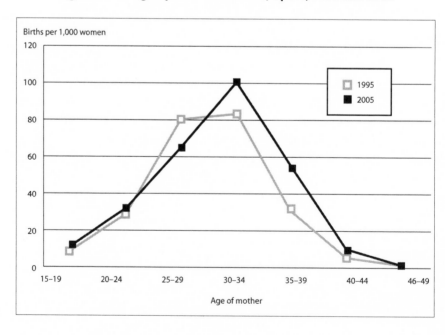

The 2000 U.S. Census produced a count that was 7 million higher than anticipated, the largest gap ever between the pre-censal population estimate and the census count itself. As a result, the U.S. Census Bureau has raised its estimate of annual net immigration to the United States to 1.2 million, up from 0.8 million prior to the 2000 census. The effect of the change is striking when we look at the ethnic composition of the country's youngest age group, ages 0–4. In 2006, 45 percent of that age group was "minority," which is counted as all groups excepting white non-Hispanic; and 23 percent of the 0–4 group was Hispanic. The increase in immigration will have two main effects: U.S. population growth will be more rapid than expected, and the country will be more youthful.

Conclusion

This discussion suggests that, while demographic trends do move slowly, there are several broad issues that can be considered shocks and could be of concern to DOD. First, the overall shift of population numbers from the developed to the developing countries is changing the balance of global power and economic influence. Second, population growth in the developing world has become a phenomenon of both the poorest countries and the poorest states and regions within countries. And third, population decline and extreme societal aging among traditional U.S. allies have become chronic and are unlikely to be offset by increases in birthrates.

4

Economics and Energy

David F. Gates

THE "TRENDS AND SHOCKS" construct works well as an approach to economic activity and the implications of that activity. Trends in aggregate economic activity tend to be reasonably long-lived. In addition, it is not unusual for trends to set up shocks and for shocks to result in changes in trends that otherwise might have been expected to continue for years. Obviously, not all economic shocks are endogenous, but many, if not most, have their roots in preexisting trends and often give rise to security concerns.

Much of this discussion will focus on real gross domestic product (GDP), which is the most commonly used, broad-based measure of economic activity. But economic trends and shocks involve more than GDP, as we are seeing in the current turmoil in world financial markets. Thus, the discussion will touch on other economic indicators, including measures such as international reserves that traditionally do not generate much attention—except when countries run short of them—but have raised concerns and now, in some cases, hope for relief, as we have observed with the accumulation of reserves in Asia and the Middle East. The chapter will also touch on the role of the international financial architecture, including the way the International Monetary Fund (IMF) has traditionally dealt with countries in crisis. This architecture came into being some 60 years ago and is now in the process of being changed, if not replaced completely, by developments in international financial markets, the rise of new economic powers, and changes in countries' willingness to play by traditional rules.

The chapter concludes with an assessment of some of the consequences of current and projected long-term economic trends as they relate to energy demand and supply. The world energy picture—and the energy architecture we have known since the end of World War II—is changing dramatically. Here again, the implications for security are potentially important.

Long-term Economic Trends

The long-term economic assumptions that are the basis for the U.S. Department of Energy's long-term energy outlook will be used as a starting point for the discussion of future economic trends.[1] This outlook, as summarized in an annual report of the Energy Information Administration (EIA), consists of two historical data points (1990 and 2004) and three sets of projections (reference, high, and low) for three forecast years (2010, 2020, and 2030).[2]

The United States and its continental neighbors, Canada and Mexico, were the largest country and region respectively in total real GDP in 1990, and they are expected to retain those positions in 2010 and in 2030, according to the EIA reference case projections (see figure 4–1). The Organisation for Economic Cooperation and Development (OECD) Europe, which now comprises some 23 countries, including Turkey, was second among regions in 1990 and is expected to retain that ranking in 2010 and 2030. Japan was second among all countries, and OECD Asia (Japan, Korea, Australia, and New Zealand) was third among regions in 1990. Each of these will retain its position in 2010, although probably not in 2030. China, India, and the rest of Asia were still in the back of the pack in 1990, but that has changed dramatically over the past 17 years, and this region likely will rank third, if not second, in total real GDP by 2030. GDPs in the other regions are fairly modest in total, both historically and in the forecast through 2030.

While overall these trends are more or less reasonable, some specifics warrant comment, both because the outlooks for different parts of the world differ in degree of certainty, and because the performance of some countries and regions could turn out substantially different from what is projected here.

Before going further, it may be useful to think about how these projections might have looked had they been prepared in, say, 1970, 1980, or 1990. It is sobering but instructive to recall how reasonable numbers of economists saw the outlooks for the various countries and regions and how things worked out 10 or 15 years later. In 1970, for example, most forecasters expected great things from Brazil and little or nothing from China, India, or what came to be known as the Asian tigers (Korea, Hong Kong, Taiwan, and Singapore). In 1980, many economists were projecting slower growth across most of the world in the aftermath of the second oil shock. Few were assuming a major realignment of the prospects of the various countries and regions, including the Soviet Union and China, which at that point was just starting to stir. By 1990, the world had seen nearly 10 years of strong growth in China (interrupted by the turmoil in Tiananmen Square),

Figure 4–1. Projections for Real Gross Domestic Product by Region, 1990, 2010, and 2030

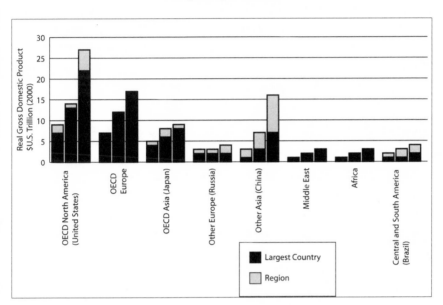

several years of strong growth in Korea and Southeast Asia, and the beginnings of the collapse of the Soviet Union—all of which looked reasonable in retrospect but none of which had been reflected in most forecasts 10 years earlier.

So, which countries and regions are most likely to grow substantially faster or slower than assumed in the projections summarized above?

OECD Countries

It is hard to imagine vastly different outcomes than the trends projected for most of the OECD countries. Perhaps the most questionable forecast is that for the United States, where the reference case assumption that growth in real GDP will average 2.9 percent per year from 2004 through 2030 could be 0.5 percent—50 basis points—too high. With a higher rate of population growth, it is not unreasonable to assume that the United States will continue to grow faster than OECD Europe or Japan. But to assume that the United States grows 0.9 percent—90 basis points—higher than these other regions over the next 20 to 25 years would seem to give too little weight to some U.S. problems—physical and social infrastructure, to name two—and too much weight to those confronting OECD Europe and Japan.

Non-OECD Countries

Within the non-OECD group, the countries and regions with the greatest potential for surprises appear to be China, India, Russia, and the Middle East. Longer term relative positions may prove to match the projections shown in figure 4–1, but surprises are clearly possible. And even if things turn out much as expected, it is worth hitting some of the key points on what is driving these strategically important countries and regions.

CHINA

Over the past 15 or 20 years, the key question on China's economy has shifted from the durability of the reform program to the durability of rapid growth.[3] Questions on the durability of reform were largely settled by the mid-1990s, when it became clear that there was no turning back and restoring all or major parts of the system of comprehensive controls that had been the hallmark of the Chinese economy until the start of reform in 1978 to 1980. Indeed, by the mid-1990s, some analysts were making the case that a decision to lift all controls, as had recently been done in Russia, would pose a bigger threat to the future performance of the Chinese economy than a decision to freeze or roll back the controls then in place. In these analysts' view, removing controls would have led to chaos, whereas freezing or rolling them back almost certainly would have been temporary, as imbalances between the various sectors—caused in most cases by differences in the degree to which controls remained in place—would have required further reform to proceed.[4]

The durability of China's current extraordinarily high rate of growth is another matter. The rate of growth in real GDP has averaged nearly 10 percent per year since reform began, and over the past 3 years has been even faster—an average of nearly 11 percent per year.[5] It had been expected to slow for several reasons, including the growth in the size of the economy that has already occurred; the growing complexity of the economy, which continues to pose challenges for China's economic institutions; and the emergence of resource constraints ranging from water and energy to air quality. In the current situation, with much slower growth in the United States and the European Union (EU) likely leading to a much lower trade surplus, how well the Chinese economy performs will depend on how fast domestic consumption grows, how much nongovernment investment slows, how much government spending for all purposes increases, and how well the agricultural sector can be managed. As things look today, growth in real GDP will slow but probably not to more than about 7 or 8 percent in the near term

(2009 and 2010). While this is slow by recent Chinese standards, it is still fast enough to allow the government to meet most of its objectives.

Once the current crisis is over, China could again see growth rates approaching 10 percent. But if this happens, the likelihood is that growth would again begin to slow to 7 or even 6 percent per year by the middle of the next decade.

INDIA

Consensus forecasts for long-term economic growth in India had been increasing in recent years as economists have taken better-than-expected performance and changing perceptions of long-term potential into account. In fact, recent performance has been so good that the question is whether India might be on the verge of challenging China for leadership in GDP growth, even at China's extraordinary pace.

A more rational view was a bit more tempered even before the current crisis. India has been growing faster than many expected 10 or even 5 years ago. Without the current crisis, the rate of growth in real GDP would have been expected to continue at about 8 percent for some years to come. Now, near-term growth will be lower, but if it stabilizes at about 6 percent and edges upward, this would be a tremendous accomplishment and—if China begins to slow as projected—could well result in India challenging China for leadership in the rate of economic growth, not immediately, but over time.

For the period under consideration, India's demographics are projected to become more favorable than those of China.[6] This will clearly be helpful if conditions are such that growth in the labor force can be mobilized in productive employment. Whether this happens probably depends on whether all Indian states choose to adopt the pro-growth economic policies of the current economic leaders—Gujarat, Maharashtra, and several of the southern states—or continue to focus on securing what they can in the way of welfare and support from the central government. In China, different provinces—and even parts of provinces—have vastly different economic performance and prospects. The same is true for different states and parts of states in India. A key difference is that all parts of China have seen improvements in living conditions, and all seem to be determined to do what it takes to see these improvements continue. That may still happen in India, but for the moment, the jury is out.

RUSSIA

The question is often asked why Russia has had so much more trouble than China in establishing itself on a path of strong economic growth following its emergence from communism and the introduction of economic reforms in the late 1980s and early 1990s. The simple answer is that, at the start of reform, China was largely an underdeveloped agricultural economy, with pockets of inefficient state industry, whereas Russia was a moderately developed industrial economy that had invested too much capital in too many dead-end industries. China started with more or less a blank sheet, whereas Russia had to dismantle unproductive industries before growth could proceed. Obviously, other reasons came into play, including the much longer period that Russia had operated under communist control and the absence of anything comparable to the support that China has received from Chinese working overseas.

The other reason the two economies have performed so differently is the way they went about reform. China proceeded pragmatically and experimentally, step by step, trying things that, if they worked, were tried elsewhere and, if they did not, were modified or replaced. With the benefit of Western economic advisors, Russia adopted more of a free-market approach, removing controls and then standing back to see what would happen. In the end, both approaches entailed risks. In China's case, those risks proved to be more manageable than they did in Russia.[7]

Looking ahead, a big question, aside from the adverse demographics and the deteriorating state of the society, is whether Russia can be successful in building a competitive industrial base on a foundation of less than world market prices for energy. Most forecasters are clearly skeptical, as evidenced in the forecast referenced above, which assumes that real GDP will grow by just under 4 percent per year through 2030. Looking at how Russia is managing or mismanaging its energy sector—the assumption, for example, that Russian companies will continue to find and develop all the domestic reserves the country needs while selling their production to domestic companies at less than world market prices—many have reservations about future reform. On the other hand, economists who have been working the details, including developments in sectors other than energy, have been decidedly more optimistic. Basically, the thinking is that after 17 years of poor economic performance, Russia now could be in the early stages of what could be an extended period of reasonably good growth in real GDP.

MIDDLE EAST

Events also seemed to be running ahead of perceptions in the Middle East. For obvious reasons, most assessments of the area tend to focus on the problems in Iraq, while dismissing the rest of the region as oil and gas exporters whose economies will fade in importance as oil and gas production stabilizes, prices decline, or the instability in the rest of the region spills over. Until the collapse of oil prices in summer 2008, the perception had been growing that this time would be different and that the combination of continued growth in demand for oil and gas with an expected flattening out in supplies would lead to steadily rising prices.[8] In addition, there was an emerging sense that this time, Saudi Arabia and the smaller Gulf countries—especially the United Arab Emirates—were taking the steps to develop their industrial and commercial bases such that economic growth would continue.

The current crisis has disrupted this vision of continuous and growing prosperity. Oil prices rose too high in late 2007 and early 2008, and the resulting bubble and subsequent collapse in asset prices may mean years of adjustment. In time, if the projections for world oil and gas demand/supply are correct, the prospects for the Middle East should return to the status quo ante. Such a development will be important for a number of reasons, including the volumes of exports of oil and gas that are likely to be available—or not available—to the rest of the world. Export volume is more a future issue that involves both how fast these countries will develop their reserves and how much they will decide to use for themselves. The bottom line is that it looks now as if many of these countries may well produce less and make less available than is generally assumed in the West.[9]

Past Shocks

In looking back over the recent history of the world's economies, it is impossible not to be impressed by the role of shocks in changing the direction of economic activity and/or giving rise to or adding to security concerns. Some of these shocks are mainly endogenous, others are mainly exogenous, and most are a combination. A list is necessarily subjective, but table 4-1 lists reasonable candidates.

The Current Financial Crisis

The current world financial crisis qualifies as a shock but not yet a "black swan." For most of the world, it is still early in the crisis, the picture is changing rapidly, and it is impossible to say how serious the crisis could become before it is over. At this point it is fair to say that the basis of the crisis was the convergence of a large number of factors, none of which on their own would have resulted in anything extraordinary but which together have led to an unprecedented disruption of the world financial system and almost certainly a long and deep worldwide recession.

Table 4–1. Past Shocks

DECADE	SHOCK	ECONOMIC CONSEQUENCES
1970s	First and second oil shocks, including embargoes	Recessions followed by slower growth in Organisation for Economic Co-operation and Development economies
	Emergence of favorable demographics, especially in China and Southeast Asia	Important as a source of manpower (with the labor force growing faster than the total population) and as a stimulus for government policies to encourage job creation
1980s	China's introduction of market mechanisms in agriculture and later in industry	First steps in what has become one of the greatest economic transformations in modern economic history
	Plaza Accord (1985)	Major strengthening of the yen (and the European Union [EU] currencies) leading inter alia to stronger growth in Southeast Asia and easy monetary policy in Japan that in turn led to the emergence of the so-called twin bubble economy with excessive growth in stocks and real estate prices
	Collapse of former Soviet Union	10 years of economic decline
1990s	Collapse of Japan's "twin bubble" economy	10 years of sub-par economic growth
	Kyoto Protocol	Agreement by the Kyoto Protocol signatories (principally the EU and Japan) to limit their carbon dioxide emissions to levels approximating those prevailing in 1990 by 2008–2012
	Asian financial crisis	Slower economic growth in the crisis countries, plus the beginning of a major reassessment of the International Monetary Fund's traditional response to economic crises
2000s	9/11 attacks	Much easier monetary policies on a sustained basis contributing to a strong expansion in the world economy and a run-up in housing, stock, oil, and commodities prices
	Rise of oil and commodity prices	Major shift in international reserves for the oil- and commodity-exporting countries

The lengthy list of factors contributing to the crisis includes an extended period of low interest rates; an unprecedented run-up in commodity prices; errors by institutions in creating and exploiting new financial instruments; errors in government policy and execution, including regulation of financial practices; and finally, the decisions of households and consumers to spend beyond what historically would have been considered their means.

What is surprising in all of this is not that one or more of these factors caused a crisis but that a crisis in mortgages and mortgage-related financial instruments in the United States led to nearly simultaneous crises in so many markets across the OECD and around the world. Other surprises include a sudden and profound loss of confidence in most Western governments for their failure to anticipate and prevent the crisis and the relatively strong leadership of the British and European governments, in comparison to the United States, once it became clear that strong leadership was required.

It is not yet clear whether the steps taken or the initiatives in place will be enough to stabilize financial markets or if more action will be needed to ensure that stability eventually will return. The one clear implication is that world financial markets will never return to the status quo ante. The structure and the players will be different, and the rules under which they operate will be much more restrictive.

In terms of the outlook for the United States and other developed economies, some implications are already clear. The United States, Europe, and Japan are in for a long and deep recession. Declines in real GDP may be moderate but unemployment will be substantially higher, and the effects on particular sectors such as autos and consumer durables will be very severe. To put these sectoral problems in perspective, they are in many respects a function of most consumers in the United States living beyond their means in an environment of rising housing prices and low interest rates. The problem now is that weakness in these sectors will not end soon, especially in an environment in which bank lending is likely to be seriously constrained for years to come.

Regarding the rest of the world, the picture is mixed. Some emerging markets, such as China, will continue to perform well. Others that are more heavily dependent on trade with the United States and Europe—either directly or through China—will struggle. And others, including those that have enjoyed years of strong growth as commodity prices have surged, may face some difficult adjustments, at least until commodity prices stabilize and move upward. On average, much of the rest of the world is likely to continue to grow more rapidly than the OECD and some countries such as China will do quite a bit better. However, all countries likely will grow more slowly than they or the rest of the world would have expected.

Potential Shocks

Looking ahead, other potential shocks are worth noting. One is the continuing, but as yet incomplete, transition to a new financial architecture that will certainly affect the outcome when one or more countries runs into financial problems, as they have repeatedly in the past and are beginning to again. A second is not so much a shock as a shift in one of the fundamentals underpinning the recent growth in the world economy—namely, acceptance of globalization. More and more countries are opting to pursue what they see as their own immediate interest rather than simply agreeing to adopt policies favoring free trade and free flows of capital.

CRACKS IN THE INTERNATIONAL FINANCIAL ARCHITECTURE

In thinking about the future of the international financial architecture, three aspects of the Asian financial crisis in 1997–1998, widely known as "the Asian flu," are extremely important: the role of the IMF in deepening the crisis in Thailand, Korea, and Indonesia; Malaysia's decision to go its own way; and the emergence of China as a regional power, capable of taking on some of the traditional IMF roles of rescuing countries that get into trouble.

The Asian financial crisis began in Thailand in May-June 1997 and over the next 6 months spread to Malaysia, Indonesia, and Korea. The IMF intervened, essentially from the outset, and imposed or attempted to impose its usual prescriptions in return for its financial support. The disruption that followed was not as remarkable as the criticism that resulted from the disruption, both from outside observers and from within the IMF.[10] Adding to the questions regarding the role of the IMF in future crises was Malaysia's decision to refuse the organization's help and to plot its own course, intervening extensively to restrict capital flows, threatening to intervene even more widely, and ultimately emerging from the crisis with substantially less economic damage than the other crisis countries. Needless to say, Malaysia's actions and their effects on the performance of its economy since 1997–1998 have not gone unnoticed, especially by countries such as Thailand and Indonesia, which were affected much more severely and have been much slower to recover.

Adding to the questions on the international architecture are the steps taken by China to minimize the disruption experienced by its smaller regional neighbors in 1997–1998. With other regional currencies collapsing, China was perceived to be under tremendous pressure to lower the price of the yuan.[11] In fact, at that point the only disagreement among the financial commentators was not if, but when, the yuan would be devalued, with some suggesting a few days and others 6 months or so. China did not devalue. It took other steps to solidify its own financial situation—shifting some of the financing for state-owned enterprises from the government to the enterprises themselves—but it held the value of the yuan and, in the end, put itself on track to displace the United States and Japan as regional economic leaders. The United States worked through the IMF, while Japan made noises about regional solutions. Neither response came off as being as aggressively supportive as China's.

China's decision to maintain the value of the yuan, thereby limiting the damage suffered by its Southeast Asian neighbors, was made at a time when its international reserves were $143 billion. Now these reserves are approaching $2 trillion.[12] If the current crisis were to threaten the economic viability of particular emerging markets (as is clearly starting to happen) and if it were in China's interest to help, is it reasonable to expect that the countries in crisis would refuse China's help and turn instead to the IMF? The bottom line here is that, economically at least, China's influence in the region—and probably beyond—is clearly growing stronger, while the influence of the United States and Japan is not.

This shift in economic power will have implications for the future of the World Bank. Given the countries that are likely to be seeking development aid, if the choice is between China—or, at some point, Russia—and the World Bank, access and terms almost certainly would seem to favor reliance on the individual countries. Whether this works out over time remains to be seen, but it is hard to imagine the aid-seeking countries opting for the World Bank over these alternatives.

PUSHBACK ON GLOBALIZATION

Judging by the popular literature, globalization is the present and the future of the world economy.[13] But if this is the world of globalization, how does it square with the world's two most liberal free traders, the United States and the EU, who apparently decided even before the current crisis that free trade is fine, but only up to the point that some of their domestic industries begin to lose ground to their international competitors? Clearly, the case can be made that China has pushed exports too hard and has done so in ways that would not be acceptable in the United States or EU. The question at this point is whether the United

States and Europe will allow the growth in Chinese exports to continue as their economies sink into recession or whether they will respond with tariffs and other non-tariff barriers, a reaction that hardly seems compatible with the continued growth of globalization.

If it were just this particular situation, the argument could be made that China-U.S./EU trade is a special case. But there are other examples—some involving trade, since the pushback on China's exports is not limited to the United States and EU—involving issues like openness to foreign investment, deregulation, and privatization. On openness or the lack thereof to foreign investment, prospects may be better now with the crisis than they were before since countries clearly need the money. But the United States recently took a number of actions that, if taken by other countries, would have been criticized as unreasonable interference in international commerce once things stabilize.[14] In some cases, there were reasonable arguments for the actions. In others, there were not. But the bottom line is that each was inconsistent with what many economists would consider a worldwide rush toward globalization.

Ten years ago, much of the industrial world seemed solidly embarked on a course toward deregulation of public utilities, especially electricity and gas. Following the example of the United States, deregulation and privatization were widely accepted as the way that a modern industrial country should organize these services. As a result, much of the industrial world, including emerging industrial countries such as South Korea, enacted laws to deregulate their utilities over some set period of time. Prospects of deregulation led to the widespread expectation that foreign investors would compete with domestic producers for opportunities to supply power or gas. In many countries the necessary legislation was put in place, but in most, the legislation has been implemented only partially or not at all. Some foreign investment has occurred, but not nearly to the extent expected at the end of the 1990s. In most cases, this seems to be a matter of governments looking at the legislation, talking to their domestic utilities, asking whether implementation is in their country's interest, and deciding it is better to delay.[15]

Clearly, there is more to globalization than trade, foreign direct investment, and deregulation. But indications that countries are starting to ask what is really in their interest would seem to have the potential to go a lot further. The trend toward globalization may well continue, but the path is likely to be less smooth—and the outcome less clear-cut—than is usually assumed. This, in turn, has implications for the future course of the international economy and also for international initiatives, such as the Kyoto Protocol.

OTHER POSSIBLE SHOCKS

Other possible sources of shocks that might be considered are poverty, income misdistribution, and inflation. Poverty and great disparities in income distribution are widespread, and the security implications of either problem are not necessarily remedied simply through growth in GDP. Obviously, poverty and inequality often contribute to tensions and conflict both in and between countries. But it is not entirely clear how often these are primary drivers rather than secondary contributors, where such factors as ethnicity, religion, corruption, or urbanization are the principal causes.

Inflation, particularly very high rates of inflation, has been another important cause of economic disruptions and even conflict. Yet for various reasons, including improved effectiveness of the world's central banks and the emergence of low-cost competitors, such as China, India, and Southeast Asia, there have been far fewer instances of runaway inflation than there were 10 or 15 years ago.

Economic Conclusions and Implications

The United States, Western Europe, and Japan will remain the dominant economic powers, but their advantage will narrow as China, India, and possibly Russia continue to grow rapidly. Continued expansion in the smaller economies, especially in Southeast Asia, in combination with changes in the financial architecture and the distribution of international reserves, will change the nature and outcomes of future shocks and likely reduce U.S. influence in countries that previously might have been open to partnership in efforts to contain China and Russia.

Economic Activity and Energy Demand/Supply

Assuming world economic activity continues to grow, world energy demand will do so as well during the period covered by this assessment, unless we see an unprecedented and massive technological breakthrough that today seems unlikely.[16] This is the first unshakeable truth about energy. The second is that most of the energy that is usable with current technologies is at some point limited in supply.

From an economist's perspective, these two truths will eventually be reconciled as the price of those energies in limited supply gradually rises until either economic trends or the relationships between economic activity and energy demand are tempered or alternative sources of supply begin to become available (see figure 4–2). The problem is that no one knows when or how this will happen, what tensions may emerge as it does, and, perhaps most importantly, what interventions these tensions may provoke.

One persuasive indication of a positive linkage between economic activity and energy demand can be found by examining the ratio of total energy demand and real GDP for a series of countries from 1980 through 2005.[17] In 1980, China and India were arguably among the least efficient users of energy with ratios of energy demand to real GDP some five and three times higher, respectively, than those of the OECD. Over the next 25 years, both were able to effect major reductions and by the end of the period had only about twice the ratio of the OECD countries. The key point, however, is that the ratio of energy demand to real GDP in the OECD countries, while continuing to decline, is still positive and, at this point, largely stable. Comparable ratios in China and India may continue to decline, but even if they do, there is little question that they will not drop below those of the OECD, which remain positive. Indeed, the risk at this point is that the ratio of energy demand to real GDP in both China and India may now begin to stabilize or even increase. The bottom line is that absent a technological breakthrough, energy demand will likely continue to grow as long as world economies continue to expand.

Figure 4–2. Trends in Energy Efficiency

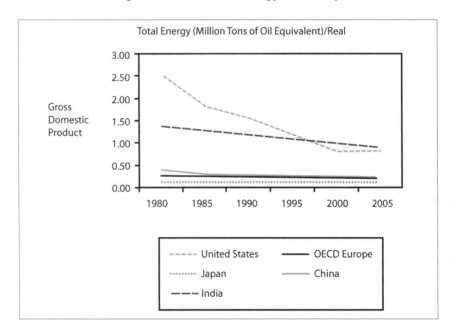

One reason for thinking the ratio of energy to GDP in China and India may stabilize or even move upward for a time is that these countries, like most emerging markets, use relatively little energy in transportation. Reasons for their comparatively high ratios of total energy to real GDP include large volumes of energy in other end uses, especially residential. As development proceeds, this tends to change as incomes rise and more people can afford to switch from bicycles and buses to motorcycles and eventually private cars. Statistically, analysis comparing cars per 1,000 people with purchasing power parity GDP for a range of countries over a number of years (the solid line on figure 4–3) shows a strong S-shaped (logistics curve) relationship with low numbers of cars at low levels of income, sharply rising numbers at intermediate levels of income, then high but relatively stable numbers of cars at high levels of income.[18] China and India are still at the bottom of the curve, but China at least is beginning to approach the average income level at which numbers of cars begin to rise quite sharply. As this happens, China's demand for transportation energy is likely to begin to rise quite rapidly, and the ratio of total energy demand to real GDP, which has been falling as industry becomes more efficient, may begin to stabilize and even move upward. Contributing to this flattening out and possible upturn is the fact that much of the capital stock in China and other emerging markets now embodies the same technology as the industrial countries, such that future improvements in energy efficiency will be a function of research and development rather than simply replacing obsolete equipment as growth proceeds.

Turning to supply, there has been much talk over the years on the subject of peak oil. Given what we know of how oil was formed, it is reasonable to assume that only so much of it is to be found. The question, therefore, is when production will reach its peak and volumes will begin to decline. Some, mainly outside observers, argue that the peak already has been reached. Most of the industry would argue that, while volumes already have peaked in many countries, when and how high the peak will be worldwide is a question of economics and technology. If prices are high enough and/or technology good enough, the peak will be later and higher than if prices are lower or the technology less effective. This debate has gone on for years and generally supports the industry view that oil has not peaked yet. What is new in the debate is an argument that shifts the focus from the physical volume of oil remaining to be discovered to the volume that may be available as a result of the increasing concentration of resources in the hands of countries and national oil companies that may or may not want to produce as much as the rest of the world may want to consume at affordable prices.[19]

Figure 4–3. Cars per 1,000 People through 2003–2004

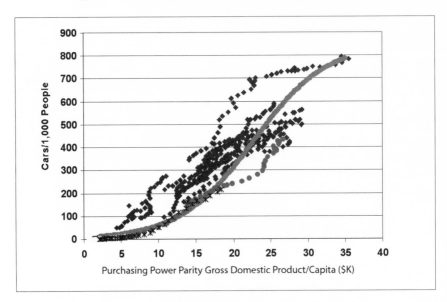

This shifts the focus from physical limits that are not known to a question of politics and economics—namely, what do the countries that increasingly control the world's oil and gas resources want to do with those resources, and what, if anything, does the rest of the world plan to do in response?

When the Organization of the Petroleum Exporting Countries (OPEC) first emerged as a factor in the world oil market roughly 35 years ago, there was a spirited debate among industry economists as to whether OPEC would be successful or would go the way of other cartels in economic history and be done in by external competition or internal dissent. In general, the conclusion was that it would be successful. In retrospect, it has clearly taken a lot longer than expected, as there has been more production from non-OPEC countries, and management of the cartel proved to be more challenging than expected during periods of slack demand. Initially, most of the demand was concentrated in the OECD countries, which never developed a unified response to OPEC. In the interim, much of the production outside OPEC has been developed or is now being produced, and eventually will begin to decline. In some areas, this decline has already begun. This is extremely important, as is the fact that we now have countries like China and India that are emerging as competitors for the available production from OPEC.

On its own, the emergence of these new markets is important, because it means increased demand for an increasingly concentrated volume of resources. But what makes it more important is that these emerging consuming countries view access to resources as at least as important as the traditional consuming countries do and are prepared to cut their own deals to secure access, regardless of whether these deals would be acceptable to their more established competitors.

Examples abound. For years, the Western international oil companies have been trying to gain a foothold in China's oil refining and marketing as one of the last great potential downstream markets. Thus far, progress has been limited mainly to joint venture refineries in which the Western oil companies provide technology—especially facilities integration—and the Chinese National Oil Companies (NOCs) provide access to the market. Now that the Chinese are securing the technology, it is reasonable to speculate that the foreign partner in most future joint ventures will be the third-party NOCs with access to resources.

Realistically, given the distribution of resources, this means more and more bilateral energy and non-energy deals between large, rapidly growing emerging markets and energy-rich regions, such as the Middle East countries, Russia, and countries in Central Asia.[20]

From an economist's standpoint, energy is no different from any other factor of production, and increased international demand should simply result in higher prices, reduced demand, and increased supply. Countries with energy resources should concentrate on producing more of those resources, while countries without energy resources should focus on opportunities to help with exploration and production, conservation, and increasing production of other goods and services that they can sell internationally to pay the higher prices for the energy that they need to import. Unfortunately, the world energy market does not seem to work this way. For countries that have formal energy policies, security of supply is usually the first objective, with economic considerations second or third, and then mainly expressed as minimizing costs.

The result is a seemingly endless series of initiatives and possible initiatives, many of which seem to potentially cause headaches for American security. Examples of such initiatives include investments in upstream oil and gas, especially those being pursued by China in various Middle East countries and investments by many of the same Middle East countries in downstream oil refining and petrochemicals in China.

Energy Conclusions and Implications

Continued growth in demand, slow progress on technology, and constraints on access to resources will mean continued uncertainty in energy markets. Concentration of resources (in a limited number of countries) in combination with concentration of demand growth (in a limited number of countries) will mean a new energy architecture, probably dominated by bilateral deals and alliances, many of which may not involve the Western countries that created the current architecture.

5

Environment and Energy

Geoffrey D. Dabelko[1]

ENVIRONMENTAL AND ENERGY factors are central ingredients in a range of potential challenges for the U.S. Department of Defense within a 20-year time frame. Environmental and energy trends or vulnerabilities will contribute to shocks as they interact with other key political, economic, demographic, and security developments.

At first glance, environmental change appears to occur gradually and incrementally, allowing humans time to adapt and develop coping strategies to counter negative trends. New technology developments in the energy sector, for example, have led to a techno-optimistic faith that new discoveries and technologies will keep expanding energy supplies to meet growing consumption in perpetuity. Despite this faith in human ingenuity and institutional adaptation, history is replete with examples of crossing unknowable environmental thresholds that, in turn, produce rapid environmental change. Furthermore, social, political, and economic institutions have often proven slow to anticipate or respond to sudden ecological shifts that demand rapid institutional change. These environmental thresholds, the product of environmental as well as social developments, could combine to produce a diversity of shocks meriting the attention of the U.S. national security community.

This chapter attempts to anticipate U.S. national security shocks that may result by 2027 due to trends in environmental and energy realms and that are not easily imagined or widely discussed within a national security context. The emphasis is on low-probability, high-negative-impact events. Some or even all of those identified may never come to fruition. The analysis is meant to highlight unlikely but nevertheless worrisome potential trends and shocks.

This chapter builds on key research and analysis already completed by the Office of the Secretary of Defense (OSD) Policy Planning. The office conducted a broad range of trend analysis in the environmental and energy realms. Its wide-ranging efforts highlighted growth in overall resource consumption (for example, food, water, energy, minerals, and timber); resource scarcities and disruptions to resource distribution, such as water or energy; anticipated climate change leading to a rise in sea level; changing climatic zones; water scarcities; and a range of social, economic, and political knock-on effects. It also flagged energy supply locations, distribution, and chokepoints, particularly for fossil fuels in the future. This research foundation was provided to the author, who was explicitly asked to build on it and not restate those trends here. Environmental and energy trends are quite diverse and complex, and a chapter of this length could not begin to do them justice. Significant scientific assessments in the last 2 years have provided easily accessible detail in environmental trends from which this chapter departs.[2] As a result of OSD Policy Planning prioritization of climate change and energy supply, these two specific areas for shocks receive less attention in this chapter in order to avoid duplication and to focus on topics less typical of traditional U.S. national security community analysis. Their omission should not be viewed as suggesting lower priority or probability for those areas of potential shocks.

The OSD Policy Planning analysis captures key trends for critical aspects of environmental and energy topic areas. This analysis becomes even more robust when it is supplemented with trend data on additional environmental variables, such as water, food, and forests, which can amplify into broader geopolitical shocks. On the global scale, trends in water quality and quantity, food availability, or deforestation are worrisome but are less likely to cross thresholds of concern for U.S. security analysts, at least in the short term. But when analyzed in specific country or regional contexts, in combination with potential geopolitical developments, this wider set of environmental variables becomes crucial for security observers to track.

This chapter features shock scenarios related to energy and environment in specific contexts. The examples listed are not comprehensive and do not include a number of potential climate change–related shocks (connected to sea level rise and accompanying population movements, or agricultural production declines due to soil moisture and precipitation pattern change, for example) that could be included if the time period were extended beyond 20 years. Potential shocks are grouped into four categories: water-, forest-, energy-, and climate-related. A subsequent section examines positive opportunities for addressing the negative trajectories of energy and environmental trends, breaking their links to conflict and instability, and utilizing environmental engagement to build partner capacity and foster strategic communication. In many cases, traditional security institutions are not well positioned to influence trends or mitigate shocks in the environmental or energy realms. Yet the U.S. national security community is far from powerless in the face of energy- or environment-related trends and shocks. This chapter ends with opportunities for the U.S. military to engage key actors in some of these shock scenarios—sometimes in the lead and sometimes in supporting roles.

Environmental and energy trends may be shocking in their magnitude on a global scale, but they do not necessarily constitute shocks of direct concern to the U.S. national security community as they are defined by OSD Policy Planning. Approximately 1.1 billion people do not have access to clean water, and 2.6 billion do not have rudimentary sanitation. The yearly casualty rate from diarrheal diseases is 2 million to 4 million deaths and grows much higher if waterborne infectious diseases such as malaria are considered. Rapidly growing populations across much of sub-Saharan Africa will face severe per capita water shortages within 20 years (see figure 5–1).

Water scarcity is only the beginning of a long list of large-scale negative environmental trends. The United Nations (UN) estimates that desertification, exacerbated by climate change, will displace 50 million people (primarily Africans) within 10 years. One-third of the world's fish stocks have collapsed and all stocks are predicted to be in collapse by 2050.[3] Estimates of yearly net tropical forest loss range from 5 million to 7 million hectares.

While of great concern, these global trends are less relevant to shock analysis than specific regional contexts and settings, where human activities can rapidly change access to natural resources in destabilizing ways. In this context, it is relative scarcity, especially when caused suddenly and unexpectedly, rather than absolute scarcity of a given resource, that should be most worrying to security planners trying to anticipate shocks.

This emphasis on more specific levels of analysis is not to suggest that incremental environmental changes are not serious concerns for security planners, but rather that gradual change may not reach the high bar of an unanticipated shock with security implications. Worsening environmental conditions in Darfur,[4] for example, have provided conflict entrepreneurs in Khartoum with the opportunity to exploit the longstanding competition for water and land to pit pastoralists against agriculturalists. These links between natural resources,

Figure 5–1. Water Availability in Africa

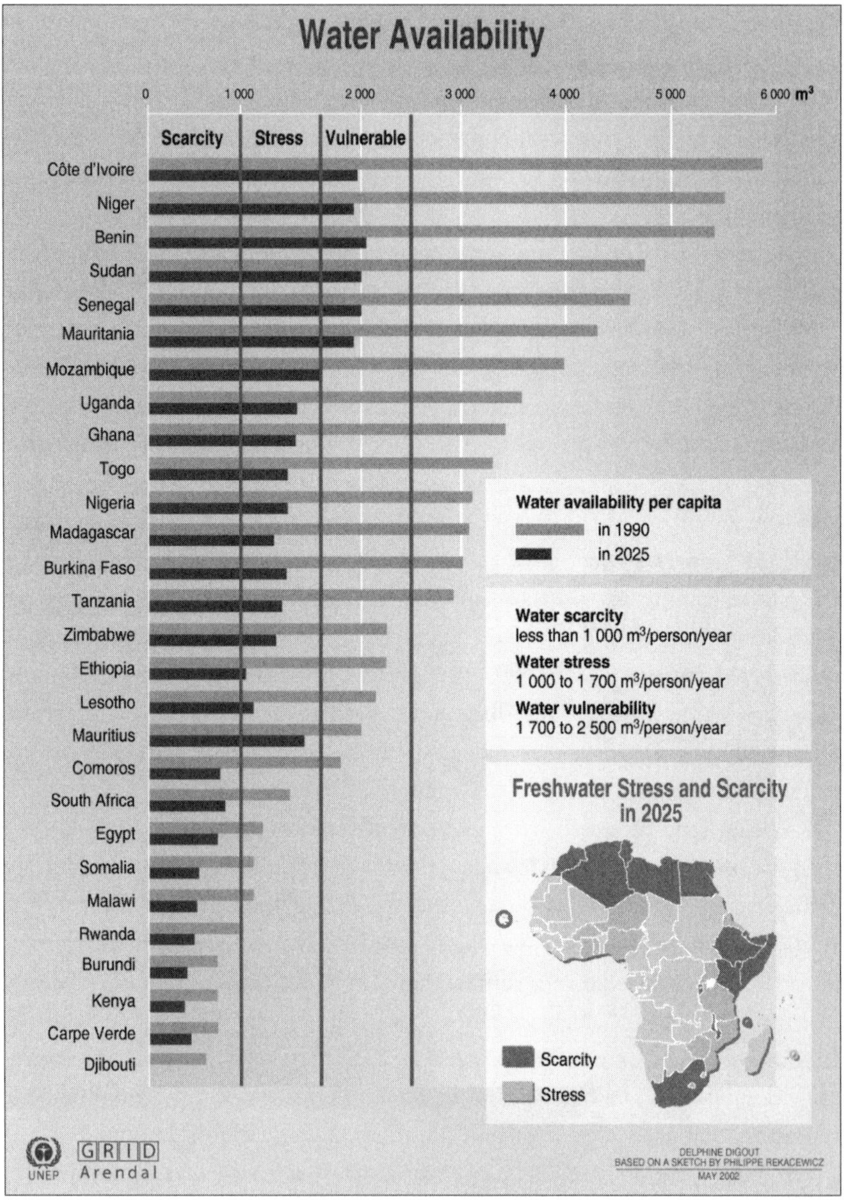

Source: United Nations Environmental Program Web site, available at
<http://maps.grida.no/go/graphic/water_availability_in_africa>.

population dynamics, and conflict are relevant to any security assessment of the Horn of Africa.[5] These types of environment, energy, and conflict connections are largely left out of this particular discussion of shock scenarios, however, unless they combine with larger forces to contribute to a potential shock.

Potential Water-related Shocks

Competition over increasingly scarce water is regularly contributing to conflict within states in a variety of settings, but these water-conflict links do not constitute a potential shock.[6] The greatest threat for conflict or instability around water is not absolute scarcity, although those stresses can have dramatically negative impacts on multiple sectors. Instead, the most likely shocks related to water stem from rapid changes in flow (such as from dams) or rapid declines in quality (as from chemical spills) that put "basins at risk."[7] A sudden decline in flow severely limits the ability of institutions to adapt and mediate conflict disputes. This rate of change differs from situations where gradually worsening water scarcity in already arid environments, even when severe, commonly provides time for institutional coping strategies to avoid the worst conflict outcomes over water resource scarcities.[8]

CHEMICAL SPILL PROTESTS CHALLENGE CHINESE REGIME

Popular environmental protests in politically repressive settings have warranted security community attention; environmental movements in Central and Eastern Europe served as the repositories for broader anticommunist regime expression that contributed directly to the overthrow of those regimes in the late 1980s. Vladimir Putin's Russia has recriminalized the environmental activism that was allowed to flourish in the aftermath of the fall of the Soviet Union.[9]

Today, China is the prime example for environmental/antipollution protests posing threats to regime stability. Because figures vary, it is difficult to precisely categorize the objectives of the demonstrations. The Chinese government figure for 2005 was 51,000 environmental protests.[10] Some have lasted days, attracted thousands of participants, involved significant violence, and required armed police or the military to restore order.

Perhaps the most likely environmental scenario where such protests could fundamentally threaten the reign of the Chinese Communist Party would be a large chemical spill affecting the densely populated lower reaches of the Yangtze River. Many protests to date have involved peasants in rural areas, where authorities could more easily control media access and use force to put down the protests.

Such relatively easy censorship is not possible in more urban settings in China's economically powerful coastal areas, where communications networks are more numerous and sophisticated.

The June 1, 2007, Xiamen protest against a chemical factory had 7,000–20,000 protesters mobilized quickly through text messaging, demonstrating how government authorities can be taken by surprise and fail to stop technology-savvy protesters from organizing protests to be broadcast online in real time. A sustained crisis like the November 2005 benzene spill into the Songhua River that forced the 4-day closure of Harbin's water supply could form the basis for large public protests that could tap into broader frustrations with corruption and the government's inability or unwillingness to protect public health. Such a scenario would become more threatening to the central government if it occurred during the party leadership's annual beach retreat to Beidaihe (as was the case with the mishandled 2003 Severe Acute Respiratory Syndrome outbreak) and/or if party leaders were divided on the appropriate response (as was the case for Tiananmen Square in 1989).[11]

The rapid, and at least initially transparent, Chinese government response to the May 12, 2008, earthquake may reflect a recognition that regime stability can be threatened by less robust responses in times of natural disasters. The relatively high level of information transparency in covering the earthquake also may illustrate the difficulty of controlling information where communications technology is increasingly widespread (and how that transparency can support the mobilization of disaster response resources).

DESTABILIZING DOWNSTREAM: HYDROPOWER IN
THE MEKONG RIVER BASIN

Just as a chemical spill can quickly deprive populations of critical water resources, unilateral dam-building can create destabilizing dynamics through abrupt changes in flow volume and timing. The Chinese desire for economic growth drives an aggressive hydropower strategy. Currently, China has 25,800 dams and plans to double hydropower generation to 250,000 megawatts by 2020.[12] On the Mekong River (the Chinese portion is also known as the Lancang), China has built two dams with a combined total of 2,850 megawatts of power-generating capacity. Three more dams are under construction, and an additional three have been planned (see figure 5–2).[13]

Chinese dam-building already appears to have negative downstream effects on water flow, especially on regional flooding for the recharge of the fertile flood

Figure 5–2. Dams on the Chinese Portion of the Mekong River

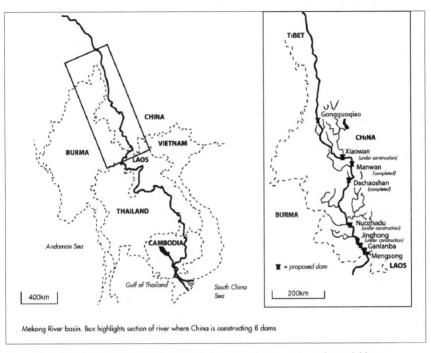

Mekong River basin. Box highlights section of river where China is constructing 8 dams

Source: Reprinted with permission from the International Rivers Network, available at
<http://internationalrivers.org/en/image/tid/216>.

plains.[14] Building dams directly threatens the health of the Mekong ecosystem
because disruption of the seasonal differentiation in water levels can, among
other things, affect migratory fish, aquatic breeding grounds, the amount of silt
deposited downstream for agricultural use, and the flooding cycles that make
this region the rice bowl of Southeastern Asia.

While the Mekong is important to development in China, it is especially
vital for food, water, transportation, and income generation for downstream
neighbors Burma, Vietnam, Laos, Thailand, and Cambodia. Approximately
80 percent of those living along the lower Mekong rely on the river for their
subsistence livelihoods, "either in terms of the fish catch taken from the river or
in terms of agriculture, both through extensive cultivation, principally of rice."[15]
In Cambodia, the population receives 70 percent of its animal protein from fish
caught in the Mekong and its tributaries.

Sustained disruptions to flow and sediment potentially could instigate
countries downstream to act in ways that could lead to a shock rather than

simply widespread regional deprivation, economic dislocation, and political tension. Since 2004, Thailand has been diverting water from Burma, Laos, and Cambodia and has repeatedly raised the possibility of two major diversions (the Kok-Ing-Nan and Khong-Chi-Mun projects) for irrigation that would exacerbate downstream impacts, particularly on Cambodia and Vietnam.[16] Both countries have been publicly critical of such plans.[17]

Chinese dam-building increases pressure for such provocative and unilateral water developments by Thailand. Vietnam could reasonably be expected to consider a military response, given its high dependency on the Mekong.[18] While Vietnam, Laos, Thailand, and Cambodia are members of the Mekong River Commission (MRC), China and Burma are not; they participate as observers. The MRC should be the avenue for quelling these types of unilateral water resource decisions, but it does not have as much influence with national governments as is often assumed.[19] For now, this potential shock remains a low probability; however, it could become more likely in decades hence as more dams come on line.[20] This scenario is meant to illustrate how China's drive to sustain its high level of economic growth can have unintended potential conflict and security implications.

TECHNOLOGICAL BREAKTHROUGH IN DESALINATION

It is commonly assumed that a breakthrough in desalination technology would eliminate a key source of tension in water-scarce regions such as the Middle East. Such a leap forward has been "just over the horizon" for decades, and the processes are highly energy-intensive, allowing only wealthy or energy-rich arid countries to seriously consider it as a viable option for drinking water production. However, long-term analysis of state-to-state interactions involving water finds as much, if not more, evidence for cooperation rather than conflict over water, running against the intuitively appealing but evidence-weak "water wars" hypothesis.[21] In fact, a desalination breakthrough that made this technology more accessible and widely used could lower the countries' interdependence on a common water resource that provides a measure of conflict deterrence—and, at times, a rare avenue for dialogue and cooperation—between adversaries engaged in active or simmering conflicts.

Potential Forest-related Shocks

Trends in rapid deforestation represent a potential ingredient in the destabilization of key strategic states. Indonesia, the world's most populous Muslim country—

with an active Islamic fundamentalist movement—is most likely to experience such a deforestation-related shock. Situated on the narrow Strait of Malacca, through which 70 percent of Asian oil passes, Indonesia is experiencing rapid depletion of its forest resources, which are critical to the livelihoods of millions of its citizens.

REASONS FOR AND EFFECTS OF DEFORESTATION

Under Indonesian President Suharto (1967–1998), natural resources, in particular forests and the timber industry, were tightly controlled by a well-connected cadre with close ties to Suharto and his family. In the wake of Suharto's fall, Indonesia went through a decentralization transition that empowered local and regional governance structures. Decentralization has had a devastating impact on natural resources exploitation by decentralizing corruption and removing official and unofficial barriers to unregulated deforestation for timber sales, farming, and most recently for conversion to palm oil plantations to produce biofuels. The UN estimates that 73 to 88 percent of all timber logged in Indonesia in 2003 was illegal.[22]

Figure 5–3 shows the dramatic change in forest cover on the island of Borneo from 1950 to the present and projects deforestation to 2020 given current rates. These rapid land cover changes present a tremendous hardship to Indonesians living on Borneo who are highly dependent on the shrinking forests for their livelihoods.[23] The tropical soils are nutrient-poor and produce declining yields within a few years once converted to agriculture.

This rapid change in resource access comes on top of a history of violent conflict between ethnic groups over land rights in this part of Indonesia (Borneo contains Brunei and portions of Malaysia and Indonesia). Indonesian Borneo was the recipient of the transmigration of overcrowded populations from Java and Madura in the 1970s and 1980s. A large local ethnic group, the Dayaks, reacted violently to Madurese migrants from 1996–2003 before the Indonesian military suppressed the violence.

The race for biofuels is now further accelerating deforestation and is a new source of conflict over land rights and forests. European, Chinese, Pakistani, and especially Indian policy mandates to dramatically increase the domestic use of biofuels are further accelerating Indonesia deforestation rates. Poorly regulated concessions and takings are instigating angry responses from some small farmers whose land is being converted into palm oil plantations with little or no compensation. "Oil palm cultivation has expanded in Indonesia [Borneo]

Figure 5–3. Extent of Historic and Projected Deforestation in Borneo

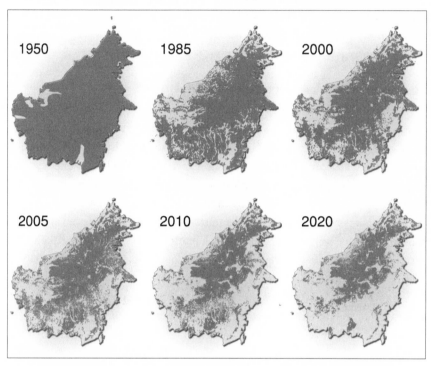

Source: United Nations Environmental Program Web site, available at <http://maps.grida.no/
go/graphic/extent-of-deforestation-in-borneo-1950-2005-and-projection-towards-2020>.

from 600,000 hectares in 1985 to more than 6 million hectares by early 2007, and is expected to reach 10 million hectares by 2010."[24] The price of palm oil doubled between 2006 and 2007.

Deforestation in this shock scenario is a key underlying variable for increased disaffection of unemployed and underemployed Muslim youth who may more easily be recruited to extremist causes, such as Jemaah Islamiyah. With the military historically drawing 50 percent of its budget from for-profit enterprises, including legal and illegal logging, the armed forces have been a deforestation driver rather than protector, further exacerbating the sense of grievance instilled by the loss of forest livelihoods. Borneo's remoteness from Java and the capital, Jakarta, lowers the probability that aggrieved citizens would fundamentally challenge the national government. But the potential for a trend or shock remains.

CONSERVATION-DRIVEN INTERVENTION

The global crisis surrounding the loss of biodiversity may not seem to be the kind of environmental trend requiring significant attention from the U.S. national security community. Yet the pressure for humanitarian deployments that were a factor in instigating Operation *Restore Hope* in Somalia suggests a scenario that cannot be dismissed out of hand. Just as media images of starving children and chaos in the Horn of Africa were integral to the political pressure to intervene in Somalia, so too is it possible to envision a scenario where civil war in eastern Democratic Republic of the Congo (DRC) fundamentally threatens the world's remaining population of 700 mountain gorillas in the DRC-Rwanda-Uganda Virungas border region. The recent killings of five gorillas and one park ranger, probably by irregular forces taking refuge in the area, received widespread international news coverage, mobilized conservation nongovernmental organizations, and increased pressure on the UN peacekeeping mission to protect the gorillas as the eastern DRC fighting escalates in and around the parks.

Setting aside the twisted irony of a scenario in which the loss of gorillas is a stronger motivation for intervention than the loss of many more human beings in the same region, the international community and potentially the U.S. military could be pressured into taking on additional peacemaking and/or peacebuilding missions if there were an acceleration in killings that posed a real threat of extinction. While two UN proposals (in the late 1980s and early 2000s) for a "green helmets" rapid reaction force died on the vine due to developing country sovereignty concerns, the fact that the DRC government is calling for external assistance may increase the likelihood of relief-type missions analogous to flood response in Mozambique.

Such conservation-driven interventions would not rise to the level of a shock, particularly if they remained few in number. The prospect for a truly new type of "humanitarian" mission would come from extending this rationale for intervention to operations designed to keep countries or groups from depleting natural resources deemed vital for the survival of outside countries. Then-Vice President Al Gore's pronouncement that the Brazilian Amazon rainforest is the "lungs of the Earth," implying some limitation on sovereign Brazilian control of its resources, remains an oft-cited basis for Brazilian public and military suspicion of U.S. military intentions.[25]

Energy and the Race for Natural Resources

The drive for access to energy among the rapidly growing economies of India and especially China is increasingly bringing the United States into competition for resources. Valuable minerals, forests, and fisheries are also a focus of these concerted global efforts to gain access to natural resources. Water eventually might be included in this list through trade in "virtual water" in the form of food trade.[26]

These trends in resource availability contribute to civil conflict. The natural resource contributions are commonly incremental and underlying even when they are fundamental to conflicts (such as the pastoralist versus agriculturalist conflict over declining arable land in the Sahel). Even predicted climate change is most likely within a 20-year time frame to add just incremental stress as a "threat multiplier." However, the interactions of these environmental, energy, conflict, and Asian economic trends may create the potential for shocks. The first is a possible return to proxy conflicts between two major powers. The second is illustrated by the fragility of increasingly important African fossil fuel suppliers, particularly when considered in conjunction with other supply-limiting events.

PROXY CONFLICTS IN THE COMPETITION FOR NATURAL RESOURCES

The regular UN Security Council standoffs between the United States and China over Darfur may illustrate the potential for a shock stemming from China's newly assertive strategy to acquire natural resources in Africa, Latin America, and Asia. China's recalcitrance regarding sanctioning the Khartoum regime over the Darfur conflict seems connected to its deepening economic oil links in central Sudan. This dynamic raises the prospect of the United States and China providing financial and security assistance to competing factions in resource-rich countries and expecting favorable or even exclusive trading terms in return. In such a scenario, military assistance to competing claimants to government authority buys favorable natural resource access. Such a dynamic would constitute a financial rather than an ideological motivation for indirect military engagement through proxies reminiscent of Cold War military confrontations between the United States and the Soviet Union.

As a growing number of rebel movements cite the perceived illegitimate sale of natural resources to "foreigners" as a motivation for opposing their governments, this rationale may gain traction as a stated cause of civil war. This grievance and inequity argument pervades the rhetoric of the Niger Delta rebels in Nigeria and the ethnic Somali Ogaden rebels in eastern Ethiopia. Venezuela is another regime China supports and the United States actively opposes, despite the continuing U.S. importation of significant amounts of oil. Such dynamics also could take hold in unanticipated country settings due to technological developments that may rapidly change the value for minerals found in limited geographic locations (for example, columbite-tantalite from DRC is a key input for cell phones).

FRAGILE OIL STATES, THE NIGER DELTA, AND SUSCEPTIBILITY TO TRADE INTERRUPTIONS

The Middle East is rightly perceived as a critical source of imported petroleum. Less appreciated is that the United States imports the same amount of oil products from sub-Saharan Africa as the Middle East (22 percent of its total oil imports). As crude oil imports increase and U.S. oil production steadily decreases, a significant proportion of fossil fuels is imported from these politically unstable regions where petroleum production is susceptible to economic, civil, and political unrest.[27] The widespread fragility of the oil-producing nations in sub-Saharan Africa as well as the Middle East poses a threat to energy supply that could become a critical shock.

One of these resource-rich but volatile areas is the Niger Delta, where armed militias vie for illegal oil revenues and corruption permeates government management of the country's resource wealth.[28] Continued exclusion of Nigeria's poor from oil revenue and development benefits is largely to blame for precipitous increases in violent attacks and kidnappings by militants. As little as 1 percent of the government's oil take trickles down to Nigeria's 144 million people.[29] Yet the United States and the world are highly dependent on Nigeria's oil. Nigeria is the eighth largest oil-exporting country in the world.[30] The country provides about 11 percent of overall U.S. oil imports and ranks as the fifth-largest source for U.S. imported oil (after Canada, Mexico, Saudi Arabia, and Venezuela).[31]

Nigeria is one of a number of fragile states where instability is both the cause and the consequence of oil extraction. Volatile supplies from the Middle East, combined with sabotage or attacks on Nigerian oil facilities, could jeopardize the U.S. oil supply. Taken alone, violence in the Niger Delta, even a civil war, may not rise to the level of a shock in the energy sector. Rebels in the delta have commonly taken 30 percent of Nigerian capacity offline. However, this reduction in production, coupled with other global disruptions (for example, a potential United States-Iran conflict or a dirty bomb in Saudi Arabia's oil fields), could result in disruption of flow that would constitute a shock. If terrorists attacked several chokepoints in the Persian Gulf—the 2-mile-wide shipping bottleneck at the Strait of Hormuz, the two largest oil fields, including Ghawar and Safaniya, or the Abqaiq processing facility—the resulting halt in Saudi oil production could last for at least 6 months.[32]

As global energy demand rapidly rises among developing nations, especially India and China, competition for access to oil will escalate. Adding concerns over climate to a growing energy demand would increase the integrated shock and reverberations from a major violent conflict in the Niger Delta region.

Climate Change and Security

Climate change has the potential to produce enormous shocks.[33] Climate change shocks lie largely outside the 15- to 20-year time frame set for the analysis in this chapter, where the emphasis was to be placed on the immediate 5-year time frame. Most of the predicted impacts that could constitute shocks (for example, massive sea level rise or dramatic declines in food production due to collapsing soil moisture levels) occur during the 20- to 50-year time frame and beyond. To capture climate change shocks, future trends and shocks exercises should extend to the 20- to 50-year time horizon.

Although climate change–related shocks are less likely to appear for at least the next 20 years, minimizing climate change impacts demands action long before the onset of shocks. Mitigation and adaptation measures must be adopted immediately because of the magnitude of the challenges and the momentum built into the Earth's natural systems. Efforts are also widely expected to be more expensive the longer they are postponed.

While shocks due to climate change may not occur for two decades, less catastrophic impacts will occur sooner and are arguably already under way. From a security perspective, they are likely to manifest themselves in the form of human migration, grievances, and loss of livelihoods. The decision to migrate is nearly always a combination of environmental and economic pushes and pulls. Climate impacts will contribute to significant environmental pushes in rural areas due to drought, and in urban and coastal areas due to sea level rise.[34] These migrations will follow many of the existing patterns of movement, including the North Africa-to-Europe trend that lies at the center of scenarios in which poorly integrated immigrant communities change the political landscape in formerly homogenous European countries. Such flows for some constitute a likely spur for the rise of more anti-immigrant and nationalist parties and potentially a test for European-wide institutions such as the free movement of people within the European Union.

Efforts to mitigate the causes of climate change may also contribute to conflict and associated negative secondary effects. The recent surge in subsidies and policy support for biofuels can help create new conflicts as suggested in the Indonesian deforestation/palm oil issue already discussed. This switch to growing fuel rather than food, combined with significantly higher oil prices, also constitutes what some observers view as triggers of riots and social unrest around dramatically higher food prices. While this unrest rarely challenges regime stability fundamentally, the precedent of such protests evolving into receptacles for wider grievances increases their importance and their threat to stability.[35]

The contributions of extended drought and desertification to the conflict in Darfur grab the most media attention, but new research on West Africa indicates that conflict occurrence and intensity correlate significantly with rainfall patterns that are 20 percent below average.[36] The countries and societies likeliest to experience the most severe environmental impacts of climate change are those with the least resources and human capacity to address them. Climate change burdens will fall most heavily on developing countries—both in rural areas and in increasingly urbanized regions concentrated on coastlines, where sea level rise will directly threaten infrastructure. Poor governmental response to "natural" disasters can undercut support for the government or a particular regime. The legitimacy of a regime can suffer an additional blow when grievances are multiplied by the government's siphoning off of humanitarian assistance.

The race to claim newly accessible natural resources as climate change causes Arctic ice to recede presents quite a different set of challenges for security planners. Climate change will raise questions regarding force structure, procurement, doctrine, and training, as the military and diplomats grapple with emerging realities of an assertive natural resource superpower in Russia. These new missions will accompany the expected rise in humanitarian and relief operations responding to increasingly intense extreme weather events, which, in the words of the 2006 National Security Strategy, "may overwhelm the capacity of local authorities to respond, and may even overtax national militaries, requiring a larger international response."[37] These diverse contexts offer a sampling of the many areas in which climate change will add to existing stresses and create entirely new challenges. As the CNA Corporation's Military Advisory Board recently noted, climate change truly is a "threat multiplier."[38] As such, the U.S. military should consider evaluating environmental opportunities for making security gains.

U.S. AFRICA COMMAND AND THE ENVIRONMENT:
BUILDING PARTNER CAPABILITY AND STRATEGIC COMMUNICATION

The U.S. military and security community can make positive contributions on multiple fronts regarding environmental and energy trends and shocks. The Defense Department can help address underlying negative environmental trends that may contribute to shocks. The U.S. military could also reap security benefits from tactically utilizing environmental engagement as a confidence-building strategic communication tool and as a component of military-to-military strategy for building partner capability.

The fall 2007 standup of U.S. Africa Command (USAFRICOM) presents opportunities for the U.S. military to work with military and civilian partners to address negative environmental trends and advance security goals through environmental engagement.[39] Sub-Saharan Africa faces an array of negative environmental trends that become particularly daunting when combined with challenging demographic, economic, governance, and health trends. Arable land and water in the Sahel and the abundance of resources in Central Africa, for example, are critical to African peace and stability. However, the growing scarcity of arable land and water and the potential for looting of natural resources are growing concerns. In Africa's many postconflict settings, environmental and energy priorities are central to restarting agricultural activity, employing former combatants, and restarting economies. Environmental activities in postconflict settings are essential elements of securing peace rather than luxury items that can be left unattended until after elections or even significant economic growth.[40] Fossil fuel–rich states have become a critical source of U.S. oil imports. But these regimes continue to face considerable governance and transparency challenges that prevent large portions of their populations from benefiting from oil rents.

In this setting, USAFRICOM will stand up with an explicit goal of conducting significant nonkinetic missions to build partner capacity and engage in strategic communication. Addressing environmental, health, and poverty challenges is an area ripe for nonkinetic missions for the command and its partners. Models exist, such as the joint exercises in natural disaster preparedness training that were pioneered in U.S. Central Command under General Anthony Zinni, Jr., USMC.[41] Other engagement activities could utilize U.S. military capacities for addressing underlying environmental and health insecurities created by poverty and poor governance.[42]

An environmental confidence-building strategy for USAFRICOM will require an expansion of the definitions of *threat* and *opportunity* within a combatant command. It also will require new models of interaction and collaboration with a range of civilian actors. To be most effective in mitigating negative trends and shocks while gaining stability benefits, the military will have to operate in a supporting role, despite often possessing superior capacities. Traditional military tools are frequently ineffective for addressing environmental problems, and military operations in war and peace often cause environmental damage. Many times, the most constructive approach may be allowing civilians in the international community, or relevant governments or communities, to take the lead in formulating and executing interventions.

NONTRADITIONAL VOICE FOR ENVIRONMENTAL ENGAGEMENT

The spring 2007 experience of the CNA Corporation's Military Advisory Board of 11 retired flag officers illustrates a larger positive strategic role military leaders can play in influencing potential energy and environmental shock trajectories inside and outside the 20-year time frame. In the CNA report "National Security and the Threat of Climate Change," board members identified climate change as a "threat multiplier" with direct implications for threat analysis, mission definition, force structure, procurement, training, and doctrine. In addition to suggesting implications for the security community, the former admirals and generals have proven to be effective nontraditional voices for accelerating the rate of civilian efforts (in the United States and abroad) to address climate change.[43]

LESS CAN BE MORE: CONFLICT PREVENTION IN THE NILE RIVER BASIN

At times, the United States can advance its interests by accepting that it is not an essential part of the solution to every problem. An ongoing successful process of environmental and development conflict prevention in the historically contentious Nile River Basin illustrates this dynamic. Downstream Egypt's heavy dependence on the waters of the Nile River and bellicose statements threatening a military response to upstream water infrastructure development have made the Nile River Basin the most frequently predicted location for a "water war."[44]

Yet for the past decade, all 10 countries in the basin have negotiated at ministerial levels under the Nile Basin Initiative (NBI) to develop a common vision for using water for pressing development needs.[45] The World Bank, United Nations Development Program, and initially the Canadian government provided essential financial assistance and negotiation facilitation. No official documents frame this effort as a conflict prevention effort, yet at its most basic level it is just that, given the repeated Egyptian threats of war in the case of upstream diversions. U.S. efforts to support NBI have remained less direct to avoid the perception that the United States is supporting the Egyptian position. U.S. interests were advanced by playing a more distant and less public role in these natural resource negotiations tied to conflict prevention.

Steps Forward

In focusing on potential energy- and environment-related shocks, this chapter has largely set aside the rich set of environmental and energy trends that contribute directly but more incrementally to instances of conflict and instability of concern to U.S. national security planners. Scarcity of arable land and water availability are ongoing contributors to violence in the Horn of Africa. Rising energy and food prices are sparking social unrest and violence in a wide range of developing country contexts. These continuing linkages do not often cross the high threshold necessary to be deemed shocks, but they remain critical variables in wider analyses of conflict prevention, conflict termination, and postconflict peacebuilding. It is, of course, crucial to examine global environmental and energy trends when identifying shock scenarios in these sectors. However, analyses of global trends can overlook local, national, or regional conditions that cause energy and environment trends to converge with economic, social, and political dynamics in ways that constitute shocks.

This chapter has built upon and expanded the OSD Policy Planning analysis of climate change and energy supply trends to examine a larger set of environmental variables that present salient contributions to potential shocks. Nevertheless, the shock scenarios included here are by no means a comprehensive set of cases. Shock analysis in the area of environment and energy would produce a longer list of potential shocks if the time frame of analysis were extended beyond 20 years. Even "abrupt climate change" scenarios are predicted to take place two decades hence—about the length of time it will take human beings to start seeing the results of their attempts to reduce their contributions to climate change. Dramatic steps must be taken immediately to avoid climate change–related shocks that are likely to fall just outside the 20-year time frame.

If the U.S. national security community wants to prepare for the security implications of these trends and potential shocks, it will have to broaden the range of trends it typically tracks as sources of insecurity. If the security community wants to help mitigate or influence their impacts, it must find direct and indirect means to support greater civilian efforts to address these environmental and energy trends that are bound up with related economic, social, and political challenges. The United States also must adjust its definition of long-term security planning to accommodate the still longer time frames associated with environmental and energy trends.

6
Health Care

Peter Katona

THE INFLUENTIAL 2001 Institute of Medicine's "Chasm" report stated:

> The U.S. health care delivery system does not provide consistent, high quality medical care to all people. Americans should be able to count on receiving care that meets their needs and is based on the best scientific knowledge. Yet, there is strong evidence that this frequently is not the case. Health care harms patients too frequently and routinely fails to deliver its potential benefits. Indeed, between the health care that we now have and the health care that we could have lies not just a gap, but a chasm.[1]

It went on to say that "health care organizations, hospitals, and physician groups typically operate as separate silos, acting without the benefit of complete information about the patient's condition, medical history, services provided in other settings, or medications provided by other clinicians." While our health care system also has great strengths, this criticism will be the starting point for this discussion.

U.S. Domestic Trends
RISING COSTS OF U.S. HEALTH CARE

The cost of medical care is rising rapidly. The United States currently spends 16 percent of gross domestic product (GDP) on health care compared to 7 to 11 percent in the advanced developing countries and less than 2 percent in the least developed states. This equates to more than $2 trillion per year on health care, including $5.4 billion on biodefense. If current trends continue, these amounts are expected to double in the next few decades. Since 2001, premiums for family medical insurance coverage have increased 78 percent, while wages and inflation have gone up 19 and 17 percent, respectively. Meanwhile, health insurance has ranked lower than the postal service in customer satisfaction.

There has been a trend to let the market decide what is covered and how much health care should cost with minimal government interference. Little choice between plans exists for consumers. Businesses provide most coverage, initially because they could write off the expense, and employees have come to expect it. However, economic pressures of global competition are slowly forcing employers to shift health care costs to employees. This trend is giving rise to more consumer-directed health care and health care savings accounts, generating a ripple effect in the health care ecosystem.

The debate revolves around how to get coverage for the uninsured/under-insured; whether it should be primarily government-, insurer-, or consumer-driven; whether the states should take the lead (as Massachusetts, Oregon, and California have done) or the Federal Government; and whether health care is a right or a privilege. The U.S. Government currently pays for almost half of all domestic health care and spends 45 percent of this to cover 27 percent of the population via Medicaid (for the poor), Medicare (for the elderly), and State Children's Health Program (for the young). Appropriations are often wasted on inefficient, top-heavy bureaucracies with little accountability for how much is actually spent on patient care. According to 2005 data from the Center for Medicare and Medicaid Services (which have a low overhead compared to private insurers), over 31 percent of monies spent by Medicaid did nothing to provide any direct medical treatment (or benefit).

The growing uninsured/underinsured population is getting suboptimal care and making inefficient use of current resources. In the United States, 47 million people lack adequate health care coverage (8.5 million more than in 2000). Surprisingly, many of these people are middle class with good incomes who chose not to purchase health insurance; others changed jobs or have preexisting conditions.

MEDICAL INFRASTRUCTURE, REGULATIONS, AND MINDSET

Medical care is a vital component of our country's infrastructure. Much of our medical infrastructure, regulations, and mindset is outdated, inefficient, decaying, and becoming obsolete. Nonetheless, hospital capacity and emergency room (ER) care are declining, while there is greater collaboration between the business world (which holds most of our critical infrastructure) and public health. Ninety percent of ERs are usually overcrowded, and roughly 500 have closed nationally in the past decade. Care has started moving away from hospitals to surgicenters and offices. There will continue to be more 24-hour urgent care centers, often built next to hospitals to relieve ER congestion and reduce cost.

Inefficiencies in medical care are becoming more recognized. With recent reports on medication errors and hospital infections, more initiatives are dictating that providers and hospitals improve their acts. With the help of information technology (IT), we are doing a better job of recognizing inefficiencies in the way medical care is practiced. Nevertheless, there are 1.7 million hospital-acquired (nosocomial) infections per year that cause 99,000 deaths. Based on a recent report on medical mistakes, it is estimated that 44,000–98,000 Americans die each year, not from the medical conditions they checked into the hospital with, but from preventable medical errors. The report estimates that fully half of adverse reactions to medicines are the result of medical errors.

In response to these reports, in October 2008 the Center for Medicare and Medicaid Services stopped reimbursing hospitals for certain complications: blood or air embolisms, bedsores developed in the hospital, injuries caused by falls in the hospital, infections caused by prolonged use of catheters in the bladder or blood vessels, and surgical site infection after coronary artery bypass graft surgery. While this will help in the long run, in the short run it will strap smaller, less efficient hospitals that are losing money.

HEALTH CARE MANPOWER

There is a need for more physicians and dentists, and an even greater need for more nurses and other allied medical personnel. Health care manpower needs are increasingly misappropriated or unmet. Affirmative action initiatives have increased the number of women in medical and dental school classes. But women dentists, for example, practice an average of 7 years, while male dentists practice an average of 30–35 years. Not enough physicians are willing to join the military. Walter Reed Army Medical Center has a shortage of physicians and has to subcontract. Incentives, economics, ethics, and practicality are all part of this picture. Aging baby boomers are beginning to affect the health care system at the very time labor shortages of providers and other health care workers are becoming more acute. Price pressures on the industry will demand more, lower paid workers, causing more reliance on mid- and low-level providers.

For reasons of fear and practicality, one-third of health care workers are expected to be out of commission during an influenza or other major pandemic or bioterrorist attack. Volunteer programs like the Emergency System for the

Advance Registration of Healthcare Professionals, the Medical Reserve Corps, the National Response Plan, and the National Incident Management System will help, especially if more tabletop and practical exercises are done, but we have a long way to go to reverse this expectation.

Because of economics and security, doctors are fleeing from the places they are most needed. Examples include sub-Saharan Africa, India, Russia, and Iraq. Manpower shortages also affect the businessmen who run corporations. Because of the current, rigid, regulated structure of the U.S. health care infrastructure, there is little motivation or incentive for innovative venture capitalists to enter, manage, or improve the decaying health care infrastructure.

CHANGING HEALTH CARE CULTURE AND EDUCATION
Education involves bureaucrats, health care providers, first responders, and consumers. For medical first responders, we need "trimodal" training before, during, and after any disaster involving significant casualties, and we are moving in that direction. If done properly, this will dampen a medical shock. The Center for Domestic Preparedness program at New Mexico Institute of Mining and Technology, Texas A&M University, the Department of Energy's Nevada Test Site, and Louisiana State University's National Center for Biomedical Research and Training bioterrorism program for first responders have all had somewhat effective training programs, but much more needs to be done.

Preventable lifestyle issues are responsible for more than 70 percent of domestic medical care and costs (for example, lack of exercise, smoking, alcohol abuse, and obesity leading to diabetes and coronary heart disease), and psychological issues make up more than half of the visits to many primary care physicians. The sickest 10 percent of patients account for 60 percent of total costs, and even this figure may be low.

What about the physicians of the future? They will want more "evidence-based" data that reflects ethical principles and the latest science. They will have to learn to use IT more efficiently as well as find better ways to cost-effectively treat patients. Doctors often do not know how to evaluate the actual significance of a test result or understand the early bias that enters into their evaluation of a patient and are only now learning how to use IT for other than bookkeeping and billing purposes. Virtual reality will play a larger role in education and, if the bugs and liability are worked out, may even become the dominant mode of medical training. Solo and small practices are shrinking and large group practices are flourishing. Physicians are the gatekeepers of our health and not merely call-center employees entering data into a computer-generated decisionmaking program. Concepts like "risk management" and "disease state management" are being increasingly talked about but require a new mindset to fully incorporate into medical care.

Complementary and alternative medicine are going to decline, while the National Center for Complementary and Alternative Medicine is looking at small niches of effectiveness. Subscribers to "boutique medicine" will increase. IT will enable globalization of the health care economy. Where medical services can be provided remotely and cheaply, they will be. Unless the health care system is restructured, the phenomenon of medical tourism will grow, as people facing higher deductible coverage or no coverage at all seek medical procedures at a lower cost.

CHANGES WITH PUBLIC HEALTH AND CLINICAL MEDICINE

The role of public health is to prevent disease and contain it as efficiently as possible once it has occurred. Yet public health is underfunded, and its interaction with clinical medicine is changing. Although they are usually in agreement, there are inherent conflicts between clinical medicine and public health. The best interests of the individual patient may not converge with the best interests of the public at large, especially in a disaster.

Prevention is a key ingredient of any efficient health care system but is too often neglected. Private medical insurers are reluctant to pay for preventive services because of their 20 percent yearly turnover. The Congressional Budget Office is reluctant to approve prevention initiatives because it looks at the immediate yearly bottom line. And the physician's fee-for-service incentive is to treat, not prevent. Hospitals that provide efficient care may be reimbursed less than hospitals that keep patients longer. The doctor who saves the life of a child dying from tetanus is (appropriately) rewarded, but what about the administered vaccination that prevented another child from getting tetanus in the first place? Is that equally rewarded? The same can be said for treating cholera or preventing it with clean water. Does public health get the same kind of recognition?

Public health gets only about 1 percent of U.S. health care dollars. In our recent efforts to prepare hospitals for pandemic influenza, annual funding is $500 million per year ($100,000 per hospital) versus the estimated need for $5 billion per year ($1 million per hospital) to cover the minimum costs of readiness. Is the need for the Department of Defense (DOD) to support a broad, public health approach to security at home and abroad misguided? I think not. Public health has to be integrated at all levels—local, national, and global—to be effective. The military's resources—manpower, command systems, and protocols—could be invaluable in a crisis.

Public health is making some headway. The cities of Los Angeles and New York have improved collaboration among public health providers, local and national law enforcement, the business community, and various intelligence agencies. This collaboration is a very new post-9/11 trend spurred on by concerns and funding over bioterrorism, and the appreciation by the military and the business community that they need to be part of the infrastructure protection process to survive a major disaster.

KEY HEALTH CARE POLITICAL DECISIONS

Ethics, practicality, and political correctness are sometimes at odds with what is actually needed in terms of health care legislation. Key health care political decisions often are made by the wrong people for the wrong reasons. The Clinton administration plans of competing health maintenance organizations and catastrophic health insurance as well as the Bush administration Medicare prescription drug plan were all failures. Health care is only one of many areas that politicians have to be knowledgeable about, and it is rarely first on the list. Lobbying by drug and insurance companies has been very effective in obstructing needed change. The military's need to provide health care to millions of its personnel can be used to move the system in a positive direction, provided the "military-industrial complex" old boy network does not get in the way.

Very few politicians have technical backgrounds in medicine, so subject matter experts translate the problems and possible solutions into language that consumers and elected officials can better understand. Arbitrary decisions made by government employees—nearly 6,000 in California alone—sometimes overrule recommendations made by doctors and nurses.

Politics and IT are on a collision course in health policy. The explosion of Internet access will drive a new wave of policy debate and government regulation. Medical e-commerce will flourish, and the exchanges of medical and patient data will become virtually universal by 2020. But the medical industry will also face an ethical and social dilemma over the disclosure of patient information, despite regulations like the Health Insurance Portability and Accountability Act.

Online prescribing, security of electronic medical records, and truthfulness of health claims on the Internet are pressing issues in the politics of the information age. Billions of dollars of e-health commerce are at stake over the next 20 years, depending on the political decisions on the regulation of medicine and the Internet. The inefficiencies, inequities, and skyrocketing costs will have to be addressed within the next 5 years by politicians, who are disinclined to attack the lobbying groups (insurers, hospital chains, drug companies, and trial lawyers) who have supported them.

International Trends

It has been said that 90 percent of global medical resources go for conditions affecting about 10 percent of the world's population. Many initiatives are trying to change this trend, which otherwise will eventually cause a major global socio-economic shock. In all disaster management, we must act locally but think globally.

GROWING NUMBERS OF ELDERLY PATIENTS

Due to technological innovations, better diet, vaccinations, and improved sanitation, people are living longer. Growing numbers of elderly patients are straining medical systems and consuming resources. This is true from the United States to China. Elderly patients take more medications and need more medical and social care. By 2040, it is estimated that more than 100 million Americans will suffer from some form of dementia alone. Ethically, is it right to keep a 95-year-old demented patient (who has no quality of life) alive for an additional 2 weeks in the intensive care unit rather than spending those resources to vaccinate 1,000 children for preventable diseases? The increasing number of baby boomers in the United States will not have enough children paying into the system as adults to take care of their parents. These issues will be challenging.

INCREASING TRAVEL AND CROSS-BORDER MOVEMENT

Two million people cross borders every week, and half of these travel between developed and developing countries. International travel and the movement of people across borders are increasing. Travelers on commercial flights can reach most U.S. cities from any part of the world within 36 hours, a span of time that is shorter than the incubation period of many contagious diseases. One million legal and illegal immigrants enter the United States each year. Returning U.S. military forces present infectious diseases, psychological problems, and complex orthopedic problems. The highly contagious and rapidly moving nature of infections like pandemic influenza makes any quarantine initiative virtually useless, although quarantine will be advocated by misinformed politicians and technocrats.

Wars cause refugees, primarily in Africa, where conflicts in Sudan, Congo, and Uganda, for example, have resulted in displacement of millions from their homes. These refugees are fully dependent on the international aid community and still live in horrific conditions with widespread disease and malnutrition. Hope for returning to their homes is only a distant dream. The millions of Darfur refugees in Chad, for example, will be a socioeconomic and medical problem for decades to come.

FLOURISHING TECHNOLOGICAL ADVANCES

Offensive and defensive information and biotechnologies are advancing very rapidly. Beneficial and malevolent technological advances are flourishing internationally and domestically. With the help of genomics and proteomics, diseases will soon be diagnosed by identifying the faulty gene, and therapy will fix or replace the "broken part" or tell us we need to get around it. New rapid diagnostics like the nanotech "lab-on-a-chip" will make cheap, real-time, multidisease diagnosis a reality. Consumer health information accessible via the Internet will surpass pornography as the most in-demand content worldwide. Remote Internet connections will provide services to millions of people who were previously underserved, possibly by linking to cell phones. Advanced genetic technology and bioengineered food will eliminate many diseases, accelerate healing, and increase longevity. Smart drugs, implants, and medical devices will become available. Customized cyberhealth will be designed to monitor, diagnose, educate, and intervene anywhere and at any time. Widely accessible WiFi devices will transform the capability to access information at the point of care and anywhere else it is needed. Consumers will benefit from advanced home-monitoring systems, teleconsultations, personalized care, and individualized treatments.

Physicians in the developed world are slowly becoming more technologically savvy. This started with computers used in billing and accounting and is evolving into clinical information retrieval, such as Epocrates on a personal digital assistant (PDA) and eMedicine on the Internet. The current trend is toward help in decisionmaking using computer-assisted diagnostic programs and artificial intelligence. Within the next 10–15 years, physicians will find wireless, handheld PDAs indispensable in clinical decisionmaking and billing, saving time and expense and improving overall care of patients. These technologies ultimately will be incorporated into some form of a national electronic medical record (EMR) system. EMRs of varying types are becoming the standard among hospitals and large physician organizations and should be universal in health settings by 2020, with most hospitals, clinics, trauma centers, physicians, and patients connected to one large network enabling access to critical medical information. It is estimated that, at a cost of $200 billion, a fully integrated national EMR system would save $1.5 trillion over 10 years.

But technology also has a downside. Weaponization and dissemination technologies, previously only available to the military, are now available from open sources to terrorists. Long, boilerplate medical progress notes are being put into EMRs to facilitate fictitious billings, and medical information will be easier to steal from an electronic source, at least in the short run. Innovations in invasive medical procedures and immunosuppression are curing patients of cancer but also making them more prone to opportunistic infections. By inserting an interleukin-4 gene into a mouse, scientists have created a mousepox virus resistant to vaccine, and we have put together a poliovirus from commercially available products. Should these ideas be published? The "select agent" rule limiting the use of certain dangerous agents has hindered scientific progress, but has it made us more secure? This is where ethics, science, security, and practicality converge.

DRUG RESISTANCE

Microbial drug resistance is increasing, and new antibiotic and vaccine development is floundering. Bacterial and viral drug resistance is rising, caused by widespread drug overuse (a consequence of poor medical treatment and the overuse of antibiotics) and use in cattle feeds. Essential antibiotic development is stymied because it is not economical for drug companies. It now costs over $1 billion to bring a new drug from inception to market, and there is a short window between production and development of resistance. Drugs taken for a lifetime are more lucrative than antibiotics, which are taken for only 1 to 6 weeks.

Microbial adaptation and evolution intersect with bioterrorism, advanced technologies to make better bioweapons, and medical care. As new diseases emerge and old ones reemerge, there is a need for continued "bioprospecting" and an innovative biotech approach to new health care products. Cell-based vaccine production techniques as well as genomic and proteomic advances will be needed to stem this tide.

STRESSES TO THE HEALTH CARE SYSTEM

Societies all over the world are experiencing increased industrialization and urbanization, stressing their health care systems. More and more people are crowding into larger and larger cities with more poverty, pollution, and unsanitary conditions, and fewer medical (and other) resources. Around the world, this tends to break up the family, clan, and village support systems that have traditionally supported health. Lagos, Nigeria, for example, is expected to have a population of more than 30 million people in the next decade, which will have a disastrous effect on medical care. The former Soviet Union, despite staggering oil and natural gas revenues, has deteriorating water treatment and sewage, crowded living conditions (especially in prisons), and surging intravenous drug use and prostitution. These factors are responsible for escalating, and often highly resistant, tuberculosis and HIV rates.

CLEAN WATER

Clean water for drinking and sanitation is becoming scarcer. Lack of clean water is the major cause of disease and hospitalization worldwide. Half of all hospital beds in the world are taken up by patients with waterborne illnesses. Worldwide, 1.2 billion people live without safe, potable water, and more than 2.4 billion do not have access to adequate sanitation. Some 35,000 adults and 10,000 children die every day from waterborne disease. The growing global scarcity of clean water affects health care directly and indirectly. It impacts not only the Middle East and sub-Saharan Africa, but also portions of the United States.

It is ironic that bottled water is sold in the developed world. It is medically unnecessary, very expensive, and not ecologically sound, yet it is a multibillion-dollar industry. It is also ironic that there are untapped deep sources of fresh water in Africa, which are only now being funded by the Hilton and Carter Foundations. Communities have been completely changed by these burr hole and deep well projects. Women are relieved of spending 3 hours a day obtaining water, and the village community can have better personal health, sanitation and hygiene, education, and economic development. Projects that deal with the root causes of disease should continue to be emphasized over programs directly targeting specific diseases, such as tuberculosis, malaria, and HIV/AIDS.

WARS AND REGIONAL CONFLICTS

Wars and regional conflicts are putting a strain on military, peacekeeping, and health care resources. With war there is an increase in trauma, malnutrition (as the chaos disrupts food supplies), infectious disease, and stress-induced illness, while resources are diverted away from health care toward arms and reconstruction. With improvements in body armor and vehicles, soldiers suffer fewer casualties but more serious injuries, which require more expensive, innovative, and complex care—and fewer physicians are attracted to the military to provide that specialized care. Even the turbulent transition from active military to the Veterans Administration for prolonged care has been fraught with problems.

CHANGING INTEREST IN INFECTIOUS AND CHRONIC DISEASES
Interest in infectious disease, chronic disease, and global surveillance of disease is changing. There has been a shift in attention and funding from acute infectious diseases (the biggest killers worldwide) to chronic diseases (the biggest killers in the United States) with the exception of greater funding for pandemic influenza, bioterrorism, AIDS, tuberculosis, and malaria. Six chronic disease categories (cancer, heart disease, hypertension, mental disorders, diabetes, and pulmonary conditions and stroke) account for $1.1 billion of the $2 trillion per year spent in direct and indirect medical costs in the United States.

Infectious diseases are continuing to damage developing economies. The World Health Organization (WHO) estimates that AIDS and malaria alone will reduce GDP in several sub-Saharan countries by 20 percent or more by 2010. This will set the stage for more political, social, and economic instability. This vicious cycle is occurring despite larger infusions of (mostly disease) targeted foreign aid. But this trend might change. In a report titled "Analysis: Wealth Brings New Health Threats," WHO concluded that:

> as the level of development worldwide increases, the greatest threats to health will shift from infectious diseases to noncommunicable health problems like smoking-related illness, obesity and depression. Economic growth and associated consumerism create diseases of affluence such as heart attacks, stroke, obesity and diabetes. As these illnesses are already rampant in the Western world, their increasing prevalence supports the notion of a reduced marginal rate of return on health expenditure, once basic public health measures (such as sanitation, safe drinking water and mass immunization) are implemented.

It should be noted that this view is not universally accepted.

There is also greater global infectious disease surveillance cooperation. Many international agencies are working together in disease surveillance and laboratory networks, including WHO, the World Bank, and many nongovernmental organizations. Better coordinated global surveillance will help us understand vectors, geography, and ecological conditions such as the impact of global warming on health. Climate change will cause disruptions that influence medical care with increasing floods, droughts, famines, and typhoons. New surveillance systems will help identify some of these patterns earlier and more accurately. Diseases associated with climate change include vector-borne diseases such as malaria, dengue, cholera, and yellow fever. Due to global warming, malaria is now present in a region of Kenya that never had it before. These trends also will intersect with migration patterns, water scarcity, and supply chains.

INSTITUTIONAL "KATRINAS"

Institutions are getting larger and more unwieldy, and there is an institutional disconnect between many of them, such as the Central Intelligence Agency and the Federal Bureau of Investigation; branches of the military; the military and the Veterans Administration; transportation, energy, and national security; and food supply and alternative energy. Alvin Toffler has called these "institutional Katrinas." Despite widespread publicity and more public and private initiatives, health care—and particularly infectious disease containment in the developing world—is being overwhelmed by a broken system of governance, corruption, and marginal economies.

Quality of life and political stability are correlated. Factors such as high infant mortality (due primarily to infectious diseases), low openness to trade (mainly a result of poor economic planning and corruption), and incomplete democratization (mostly due to corrupt and poorly educated politicians and citizens) may account for two-thirds of demonstrated instability. Malnutrition and disease go hand in hand with these factors. Major "headline" initiatives such as the Global Fund are focused on specific diseases and do not fully take into account underlying problems such as malnutrition, water quality, transportation needs to get to where health care is dispensed, diseases such as pneumonia, or even the inequity of payment to providers of health care involved in these initiatives compared to those who are not.

The Shocks

Many shocks can directly or indirectly affect the health care system, domestically and internationally, in both clinical medicine and public health. Shocks can occur as single isolated events, convergences, tipping points, or dominos. They can be slow, insidious, or sudden, and their effects may not be recognized until after the fact.

One potential shock would occur if a disaster were to overwhelm the surge capacity of the medical system. A natural pandemic affecting humans, plants, or animals; a bioterrorism or other weapons of mass destruction (WMD) event; or another disaster with mass casualties could surpass the capacity of the medical system to surge. Since the 1970s, new infectious disease threats have been identified at the unprecedented rate of one or more every year, meaning that nearly 40 diseases exist today that were unknown just over a generation ago. Over the last 5 years alone, WHO experts verified more than 1,100 epidemics of different diseases. Thus, a completely new pandemic threat such as Severe Acute Respiratory Syndrome is real and could affect the entire world. This will add political instability and slow democratic development in sub-Saharan Africa, parts of Asia, and the former Soviet Union.

But this type of scenario has to be put into perspective. While working, most physicians are so overwhelmed with the daily practice of medicine that disaster preparedness and management are not on their radar. One might even ask if it should be.

A combination of fanatical determination, vicious hatred, and WMD resources makes an intentional attack on the continental United States almost inevitable. The most vulnerable developed world biothreat targets include enclosed stadiums and underground rapid transit systems. Even with the National Incident Management System, the Hospital Emergency Infection Control System, a National Response Plan, and a new agency (the Department of Homeland Security), current responses are woefully inadequate. What is the role of the military and the National Guard in all this? As we saw with Hurricane Katrina, the resources of the Federal Government, and especially the National Guard, were desperately needed but came too slowly. DOD has even more resources that could be utilized, taking into consideration Title 10 statutes.

Rapid economic or other change disrupts medical care with or without a defined external disaster, which also could constitute a shock. This can involve liability issues, a panic, or merely the transition to a single-payer or national health insurance system. There can be economic disruption of the "just-in-time" supply chain of equipment and supplies. The global supply chain is so interconnected and fragile that a major disruption can have broad effects in supplying the medical needs of hospitals with masks, ventilator supplies, or disposable operating room equipment, for example. In the transformation process, we could learn from the Canadians who, during the 1970s, suddenly went from a private fee-for-service medical system to a national single-payer health insurance plan.

A third shock would be a large-scale cyber, electrical grid, or other directed technological attack that inhibits the medical system from functioning efficiently. Large-scale cyber attacks have already occurred in Estonia, and China is reported to be developing cyber attacks as a military tool. Many intranets and Internet connections are wireless and easily hacked. Much of our medical equipment, including radiological tests and laboratory evaluation, is dependent on technology, often without adequate safeguards. A direct technological attack could cause a widespread shock to the system. Ironically, this is much less of a problem in the developing world.

A related shock would be the intentional assault on the medical infrastructure that severely disrupts the system. In conjunction with another attack or a natural disaster, terrorists could directly target hospitals, clinics, essential suppliers, first responders, and doctors. This has happened in Israel, where a second suicide detonation was directly aimed at first responders coming to the scene of a suicide bombing. On a larger scale, a WMD attack directed at a meeting of specialists, such as the American Academy of Orthopedics or the Infectious Diseases Society of America, could quickly wipe out a majority of specialists in a medical field.

With any of the above or on its own, fear could lead to a large-scale disruption in trust of the medical establishment. Natural events or intentional manipulation can cause great anxiety in the population. This can overburden the mental health care system, and possibly even divide public opinion. Fear is exactly what terrorists want. Natural and WMD disasters produce the "worried well" (not exposed, not infected) as well as post-traumatic stress disorder patients. Mental health authorities would be overburdened with patients whose fear is naturally or intentionally manipulated by a terrorist or government. If an intentional attack instilling fear is well orchestrated to happen suddenly, it would be a shock with psychological and fiscal ramifications. The handling of the "worried well" during a large-scale disaster may require more resources than handling those who actually become ill.

Fear may be triggered by a new and widespread toxicity (real or perceived) or an unfounded concern that becomes widespread through the Internet and the news media. In other words, unfounded panic, whether spontaneous or manipulated, can lead to disaster. Rumors or poorly thought out media reports can be very destructive. Examples are mothers irrationally concerned about thimerosol in vaccines causing autism; the Nigerian cleric who claimed that the polio vaccine makes Muslim women sterile, which caused a polio epidemic affecting 16 countries on two continents; or the panic that 22 cases of weaponized anthrax caused in 2001.

Conclusion

Einstein said that significant problems could not be solved with the same level of thinking that created them. The next 15 years will bring more patients (especially elderly), more costs, more technology, more information (overload), more innovation, more competition, and possibly more uninsured—and that is without a major shock. If a major disaster did occur, how would we handle the convergence of multiple, related or unrelated, natural or manmade factors, along with a possible mass institutional breakdown? What happens when bureaucratic inefficiency, corruption, an economic downturn, malevolent technology, fanaticism, and an immature unified civilian command structure all converge? We must think in terms of a medium-size disaster that "stretches" our resources, not a small disaster (which requires little extra planning) or a mega-disaster (which we cannot possibly plan for). We must start thinking "outside the box."

A natural disaster may be intentionally followed up with a manmade WMD disaster to magnify the impact. A terrorist group might be waiting for such an opportunity. Civilian borrowing of command and control policies and procedures from the military, heightened surge capacity, and dual-use initiatives would be very useful here. Responsibility must be shared among Federal, state, local, and private parties. What would all this mean for the national security institutions, particularly the military? They would be subject to new degrees of stress as well as opportunity. But there is not enough sound, long-term vision and too much short-term thinking. The enormous roles of poverty and poor education are underemphasized and poorly addressed. The health insurance system lacks transparency and gives consumers little choice.

Most everyone agrees on the need to improve preventive care, modernize medical computer systems, study medical outcomes, practice evidence-based medicine techniques, and improve health in the developing world—for security as well as health reasons. But change in the United States is reactive, not proactive. It is being driven by rising costs, the failure to provide universal coverage, consumer dissatisfaction, and the increasing recognition that the country has suboptimal life expectancy and high infant mortality despite spending far more per capita on health care than any other country.

Dedicating enormous resources to a project to solve a problem or deficiency could provide a positive shock to the system. Past large-scale initiatives have included the Manhattan Project to develop a nuclear bomb in the 1940s, the U.S. interstate highway system in the 1950s, and the moon landing during the 1960s. Even the Marshall Plan could be put into this category. This kind of approach, if well directed, can serve our interests in the future. Examples might include developing alternatives to carbon-based fuels, changing vaccine-production techniques and magnitude to develop an avian flu vaccine, or reshaping the American political landscape for education or health care. These kinds of monumental initiatives require enormous political will and capital.

A modernized, interconnected health care system is a national security necessity. Witness how we still respond suboptimally to disasters like Katrina. While we grapple for the latest technological innovations, our system is still a 1950s model of static paper records stored in filing cabinets, warehouses, and hospital basements. There are regulations and restrictions on costly equipment, caps on hospital budgets, and cumbersome and inconsistent regulations and protocols. Nonetheless, we have the best health care system in the world. Our technological capabilities are second to none.

Medicine is a fragile, interconnected, multidisciplinary, and desynchronized system. It is dying a slow death with too little effort made domestically and internationally to make it more efficient. Some are waiting for the technological miracle; others are waiting for political decisiveness. The resources and interest are there, but the innovation, coordinated thinking, and planning are not.

7

Nanotechnology

Neil Jacobstein

NANOTECHNOLOGY TODAY is focused primarily on objects and technologies that are less than 100 nanometers (10^{-9} meter) in size. At this size range, the chemical, physical, and electrical properties of materials change, with profound implications for the types and properties of materials available to the defense community. Potential applications span virtually all material areas of defense, including sensors, armor, weapons, ground transport, avionics, computing, energy, medicine, environment, and emergency management. The range of near-term nanotechnology application trends is broad, deep, and relatively certain. However, what is often underappreciated, or sometimes discounted as science fiction, is that the next generation of nanotechnology will alter our relationship with molecules and matter as profoundly as the computer transformed our relationship with bits and information. Specifically, the result will be the precise, inexpensive control of matter. The consequences for defense are game-changing opportunities and risks.

Research on nanosystems eventually will produce programmable molecular factory systems that can make useful nanostructured materials and devices as well as grow them to macroscale sizes. This will enable a new industrial and defense manufacturing base that can scale to produce both small objects and large systems precisely and inexpensively. These manufacturing capabilities are still in the early research and development (R&D) stages, but due to the compounding of scientific and technical knowledge in the field, their technical precursors are being developed at a rapidly increasing rate in research centers around the world. The prospects are controversial, not because they violate any physical or chemical laws, but primarily because of the fundamental nature of the claims regarding them, their shocking implications, and the experimental demonstration of only partial capabilities. The claims rest on two foundations: early experimental demonstrations of the ability to manipulate single molecules and construct custom molecular devices; and technical arguments that make use of accepted scientific knowledge but constitute a "theoretical analysis demonstrating the possibility of a class of as-yet-unrealizable devices."[1] Progress toward molecular manufacturing will occur through an accelerating series of target technical demonstrations and increasingly complex molecular devices.

The enabling technologies for molecular manufacturing will be developed over the next 10–25 years at an approximately linear 2007 pace of technological progress. However, technological progress in this knowledge-based field is on an accelerating exponential rate of advance. Thus, the elapsed time in linear years to achieve molecular manufacturing may be considerably compressed. Knowledge of this acceleration factor is prerequisite to making wise R&D investment decisions and to avoiding strategic technological surprise. Nanotechnology focused on systems of devices will confer unprecedented economic and defense competitive advantage on the sponsoring entities and will prove difficult to control and defend against. The lead time to the global development of a molecular manufacturing technology base should not be squandered. Utilizing this relatively short lead time effectively will require inconvenient intellectual honesty, the ability to deal with counterintuitive accelerating technical change, and courageous technical leadership.

Description

Nanoscale science and engineering has been defined as technology with a size range less than 100 nanometers (nm), or 100 billionths of a meter. Using that definition only, most of chemistry would qualify. Practitioners in the field would add that nanoscale science and engineering researches and exploits the unique properties of materials that occur in the less-than-100-nanometer size range. Most of the effort in nanotechnology today is directed at the development and exploitation of novel materials that derive their unique properties from their size and structure. For example, carbon nanotubes in that size range may exhibit a tensile strength greater than diamonds and act as an electrical conductor, insulator, or semiconductor, depending on their specific configuration. Overall, nanotechnology in the form of materials, devices, or, eventually, systems of devices provides the ability to get more product performance, functionality, and lifespan with less weight, size, maintenance, power, and cost.

Assessment

The nanotechnology field has two key components, one of which deals with the properties of materials at the nanoscale and the development of nanoscale devices. This is the current focus of the field. It has research programs throughout the world and many companies commercializing applications. The other part of the field holds the most potential and is the less developed. It is currently research on the ability to design and construct three-dimensional objects of arbitrary size, inexpensively, and with atomic precision. This capability has game-changing qualities for defense operations and will be addressed after reviewing the near-term nanoscale materials and applications trends.

Commercial nanotech companies sell purified nanotubes made of tubular lattices of carbon, soccer ball–like polyhedra made of 60 atoms of carbon called Buckyballs, dendritic polymers called dendrimers, and other nanoparticles in the less-than-100-nanometer size range. The commercial and defense applications of these nanomaterials are numerous and significant. They enable fundamentally new types of pharmaceuticals, electronic memory and semiconductor devices, sensors, renewable energy capture and storage systems, water purification devices, super-strong fabrics and materials, security and military components, and antipollution devices. The nanoscale material applications under development are already beginning to emerge and will gather momentum over the coming years. This section presents a summary of a few categories of materials and applications.

Nanoparticles are particles with at least one dimension smaller than 100 nanometers. They are a bridge between bulk materials and molecular structures. The properties of materials change as the percentage of atoms at the surface of a material becomes significant, as it does for nanoparticles. For bulk materials larger than one micrometer (10^{-6} meter), the percentage of atoms at the surface is tiny relative to the total number of atoms of the material. In contrast, nanoparticles have a very high surface area–to-volume ratio. Copper nanoparticles smaller than 50nm are super-hard materials that do not exhibit the same malleability and ductility as bulk copper. Nanoparticles often have unexpected visible properties because they are small enough to confine their electrons and produce quantum effects. For example, gold nanoparticles appear deep red to black in solution and can be used in sensors.

Carbon nanotubes are allotropes of carbon. A single-wall carbon nanotube is a 1-atom-thick sheet of graphite rolled up into a cylinder with a diameter of about a nanometer. The resulting nanostructure has a length-to-diameter ratio exceeding 10,000. Cylindrical carbon molecules have novel properties that make them potentially useful in many applications. They exhibit extraordinary strength and configurable electrical properties as an insulator, superconductor, or semiconductor, depending on their chirality, doping substances, and other characteristics. They have been used as single molecule electronic gates, switches, and memories.

Dendrimers are globular nanostructures precisely engineered to carry molecules encapsulated in their interior void spaces or attached to their surface. Size, shape, and reactivity are determined by the number of generations (or shell branching factors) and the chemical composition of the core, interior branching, and surface functionalities. Dendrimers are constructed with a set of repeating chemical synthesis procedures conducted under conditions that are easily performed in a standard organic chemistry laboratory. The dendrimer molecule's diameter increases linearly, whereas the number of surface groups increases geometrically. Dendrimers are very uniform and are commonly created with dimensions incrementally grown in approximately nanometer steps from 1nm to more than 10nm. Laboratory control over size, shape, and surface functionality makes dendrimers one of the most customizable nanotechnologies commercially available.

Buckminster Fullerene or Buckyballs are C^{60} carbon molecules in the form of a truncated icosahedron resembling a soccer ball. Fullerenes are similar in structure to graphite, which is composed of a sheet of linked hexagonal carbon rings, but they also contain pentagonal (or sometimes heptagonal) rings that prevent the sheet from being planar. C^{60} has many potential uses—in energy storage, drug delivery, and structural composites.

Quantum dots are as small as 2 to 10 nanometers, corresponding to 10 to 50 atoms in diameter and a total of 100 to 100,000 atoms within the quantum dot volume. Self-assembled quantum dots are typically between 10nm and 50nm in size. At 10nm in diameter, nearly 3 million quantum dots could be lined up end to end and fit within the width of a human thumb. In contrast to atoms, the energy spectrum of a quantum dot can be engineered by controlling its size, geometry, and confinement potential. In quantum dots that confine electrons and valence holes, the interband absorption edge is blue shifted due to the confinement, compared to the bulk material of the host semiconductor material. As a consequence, quantum dots of the same material, but of different sizes, can emit light of different colors. They have superior transport and optical properties and are being researched for use in diode lasers, amplifiers, and biological sensors.

Quantum dot technology is also being evaluated for use in solid-state quantum computation. By applying small voltages to the leads, one can control the flow of electrons through the quantum dot and thereby make precise measurements of the spin and other properties therein. With several entangled quantum dots, or qubits, plus a way of performing operations, quantum calculations (for example, encryption algorithms) might be possible.

Smart materials are similar to sensors in that they change their chemical or physical properties in response to stimuli. However, the response triggers a pervasive change in the material that alters its properties in response to the sensed environment. For example, self-tinting glass may change its opacity in response to sunlight, or air filters may change the size of their pores in response to sensed agents in the air. Smart materials may be used in systems that exhibit self-recognition and limited forms of self-repair (for examples, see table 7–1).

These nanoscale materials have been used in specific applications. For example, sensors are devices that change in some dimension in response to a target object or event. Nanoscale sensors may be as small as a single molecule. They often form weak chemical bonds in response to a substance and change their conductivity, color, fluorescence, or conformation in response. Biosensors for particular pathogens may target the organism's specific DNA. Nanosensors are currently being developed to detect anthrax toxin, nerve agents, bacteria, and viruses. They may be deployed alone or in combination in a lab-on-a-chip configuration that attempts to analyze a broad array of potential threats and provide information on effective countermeasures.

Table 7–2 captures a sample of early nanotech applications in a variety of areas relevant to defense and some of the organizations sponsoring the work.

Nanoscale materials can be sensed by an increasing array of tools, including scanning probe microscopy, spectroscopy, electrochemistry, and electron microscopy. There is now an inventory of fabrication methods to produce nanostructured materials, including dip pin lithography, E-beam lithography, molecular synthesis, self assembly, nanoscale crystal growth, polymerization, nanobricks and building blocks, DNA and protein engineering, and scanning probe mechanosynthesis.

Nanotechnology Trends

The United States currently appears to be ahead in R&D on nanoscale materials and applications. The ability to stay ahead in this increasingly fast-moving, interdisciplinary field is entirely dependent on the supply of creative and technically

Table 7–1. Nanoscale Materials, Properties, and Impact

NANOTECH MATERIAL	SIZE	PROPERTIES	IMPACT
Nanoparticles	1–100 nanometer (nm)	Small size and immense surface area—yields much greater surface area. Note: Size-specific industrial hygiene controls needed to prevent exposure; sunscreen and food could be a problem—nanoparticles cross the blood brain barrier	Used in plastics, paints, clothing, food, sunscreens, energy, sports equipment. High-surface-area particles can be exploited for chemical catalysts and munitions—higher energy density explosions
Carbon nanotubes (single wall)	1nm x 50,000	Carbon nanotubes are 60 times stronger than steel, harder than diamond, lighter than aluminum, more conductive than copper, and a good semiconductor	Many structural and electronic component applications, programmable electronics
Buckminster Fullerene (C^{60})	1nm	Enclosed carbon "soccer ball" made of pentagons and hexagons; high tensile strength	Can be used to encapsulate material, possible batteries, H energy storage applications
Quantum dots (CdSe)	8nm	Nanoscale particles that change their properties with addition or removal of an electron	Can be used as a sensor suite for subtle effects and small concentrations of material
Dendrimer	1–10nm	Multiple configurations of rigid and flexible scaffolding provide polyvalent interactions between surfaces and bulk materials	Applications such as adhesives, surface coatings, drug delivery, catalysts, or polymer cross-linking
Smart materials	Variable	Changes shape when heated or automatically responds to a specific change in the environment	Combines sensor and effector in one material

Table 7–2. Early Applications of Nanotech

NANOTECH APPLICATION	SYSTEM	ORGANIZATION
Sensors	Lab-on-a-chip	Various, National Institutes of Health, Defense Advanced Research Projects Agency
Armor	Light, bulletproof vest and health monitor[1]	Massachusetts Institute of Technology Center for Soldier Technologies[2]
Weapons	Lightweight conventional devices and unconventional devices. Potential 4th-generation nuclear weapons: pulsed trigger, limited yield[3]	Various in United States; possibly some activity elsewhere
Ground transport	Nano coatings, stronger but lighter materials	Almost all auto companies
Avionics	Carbon composites for airplane wings	Boeing
Space	Air filters for National Aeronautics and Space Administration space flights that screen viruses like Severe Acute Respiratory Syndrome	U.S. Global Nanospace, Inc. (TX)
Computing	Ultra-dense, low-power, lower cost memory chips for microelectronics	Zettacore, Denver
Photovoltaic energy	1. Semiconducting particles of titanium dioxide coated with light-absorbing dyes, bathed in electrolyte, and embedded in plastic film	Konarka
	2. assembling nanomaterials into precisely ordered architectures	Nanosolar
Medicine	Nanoparticle-based gene detection for use in medicine and biowarfare detection	Nanosphere, Inc. (IL)
Environment	Removes arsenic from public water supplies	Inframat (CT)
Emergency management	Sensors to detect weapons of mass destruction, such as anthrax	Integrated Nanotechnologies (NY)

1. Army Research Office, "Soldier Status Monitoring, Working Group Result," workshop on Nanoscience for the Soldier, February 8–9, 2001, available at <www.aro.army.mil/phys/Nanoscience/sec4soldier.htm>.
2. *MIT News*, "Army Selects MIT for $50 Million Institute to Use Nanomaterials to Clothe, Equip Soldiers," press release, March 13–14, 2002, available at <http://web.mit.edu/newsoffice/nr/2002/isn.html>.
3. Andre Gsponer, "Fourth Generation Nuclear Weapons: Military Effectiveness and Collateral Effects," 2007, available at <http://arxiv.org/PS_cache/physics/pdf/0510/0510071v5.pdf>.

well-educated R&D talent. Cross-referencing the known demographic trends in the United States and the world with respect to the production of scientists and engineers indicates that the United States may lose its preeminent position unless it can rapidly grow or import sufficient talent to keep up with demand. It appears that other populous countries, such as India and China, could over the next 20 years outstrip the science and engineering talent base of the United States.

There currently is no substitute for science and engineering talent. If the assumption is that the distribution of genius is roughly equal in different populations in the world, then India and China will each have approximately a four-to-one advantage in this regard. They may not be as efficient in developing their human resources, but the demographic and educational trends are relatively clear—and are often taboo to discuss openly. Appeals to the idea that only U.S. scientists and engineers can be creative and others are just imitators are based on notions that are outdated and unlikely to be supportable as globalization penetrates into the R&D sector. Reports by the National Science Foundation and the National Academy of Sciences have addressed the seriousness of this problem. In 2007, Congress passed legislation supporting the American Competitiveness Initiative to increase R&D funding dramatically for nanotechnology and other areas, but it did not actually follow through with the funding.

In addition, for a variety of reasons, the United States may not keep up with the rest of the world in tackling molecular manufacturing. The factors include discounting the possibility that molecular manufacturing could be developed within the next 25 years (of linear progress), concerns about risks of accidental or deliberate abuse, and religious concerns about intervening with death and the natural scheme of things. Three analogies are relevant in this context.

First is the inability of biochemists to take nonlinear rates of accelerating exponential technology improvement into account in their own field. When polled in 1990 on how long it would take to complete the sequencing of the human genome after completing about $1/10,000^{th}$ in a year, the consensus opinion was that even with reasonably aggressive advances, it might take 100 years or more. In fact, it only took 13 years! Semiconductor improvements occur on this kind of curve, but this sort of nonlinear exponential thinking has yet to penetrate most assessments of technological progress outside that field.

Second was the inability of the Detroit auto companies to listen to the statistical quality control advice of W. Edwards Deming. The Japanese did not have that problem and embraced Deming's methods wholeheartedly. Detroit is now a shadow of its former glory, and Toyota has become the world's largest auto company, with an extraordinarily high customer satisfaction rating in its Lexus and Prius lines.

Third is the recent fate of stem cell research in the United States. Due to a largely misguided set of concerns and assumptions, the United States has lost both talented researchers and its competitive edge in this critical area of biological research. A similar fate could occur with next-generation nanotechnology unless there is a concerted effort to prevent this scenario. Unfortunately, this loss of competitive edge scenario would be a continuation of inconsistent support for science education and R&D in the United States rather than a shocking discontinuity.

Nanoscale technology is now being pursued worldwide and is showing no signs of slowing down. Moore's law predicts a reduction by half in semiconductor device feature size every 18 months; conversely, packing density doubles (see figure 7-1).

Figure 7–1. Trend in Minimum Feature Size of Semiconductors

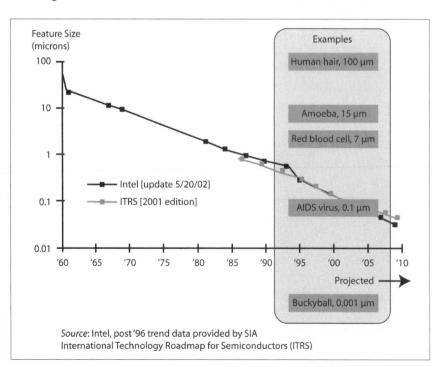

Source: Gordon Moore, "No Exponential Is Forever," available at <http://download.intl.com/research/silicon/Gordon_Moore_ISSCC_021003.pdf>.

This trend will continue on an accelerating exponential curve, fueled in part by the compounding of "know-how" knowledge that Ray Kurzweil[2] calls the Law of Accelerating Returns. Capabilities growing on an exponential curve actually accelerate due to the positive feedback effect of increasing knowledge. The outcomes of this trend in knowledge-driven technologies are counterintuitive. The effect in new knowledge-based technological fields will likely become "obvious" after the facts and examples accumulate and the compression factor becomes more extreme. Any attempt by experts in the field to assess the timing of molecular manufacturing without taking these factors into account is doomed to be too conservative, and could squander the competitive opportunity.

Nanomaterials and nanoscale devices likely will continue to reduce the volume of materials required by industry. Know-how drives miniaturization, which delivers better products at lower prices. Consider a laboratory in a building with delivery times in days, a laboratory in a box with delivery times in hours, and a lab-on-a-chip with delivery times in minutes. R&D in nanotechnology accelerates the flexibility, quality, and cost trends in manufacturing dating back centuries or more. Figure 7–2 shows how DuPont Corporation has observed that until recently, its revenues were a function of the physical volume of goods sold. Now revenue is a function of the know-how or knowledge intensity of its products, and the physical volume of goods sold is decreasing.

The ultimate limits to nanotechnology are dictated by basic physics and economics and may be defined simply in terms of what is possible:

- flexibility: arranging atoms in most of the ways permitted by physical law
- quality: getting almost every atom in the right place (greater than 7 sigma quality)
- cost: manufacturing at increments above the expense of raw materials.

If the United States could manufacture large-scale products with high flexibility, high quality, and extremely low feedstock cost, it would possess an economic driver and defense capability much larger than the whole of computing technology in the last quarter-century. This is not an exaggeration, nor is it a description of a "free lunch" in economic terms. It is the recognition of a technical, economic, and defense opportunity that will accrue to any country that develops nanotechnology-enabled molecular manufacturing first. It is also important to note that given the inherent multiple uses of the technology, attempting to develop it as a military-only technology would probably not fare well in the

Figure 7–2. How Knowledge Intensity Affects Volume of Goods Sold

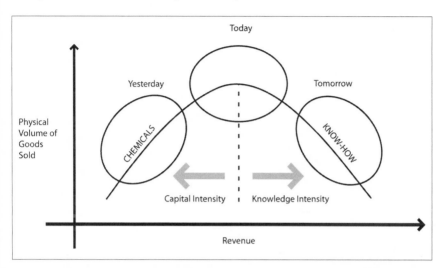

Source: James C. Romine, "Opportunity and Responsibility," presentation at fall 2003 meeting of Commercial Development and Marketing Association, available at <www.cdmaonline.org/uploadedFiles/Member_Area/MeetingProceedings/CDMAMeetings/Fall03/Romine Presentation.ppt#273,4,Slide 4>.

worldwide Darwinian competition driven by decentralized R&D investments and market economics.

A few technical objections have been raised to the possibility of molecular manufacturing.[3] These objections and their rebuttals are summarized in table 7–3.[4]

Molecular manufacturing is currently a research area of nanotechnology that will eventually produce programmable systems that can build atomically precise, inexpensive, three-dimensional products of arbitrary size. These systems may take 10–25 years to develop and mature. The projected timing may seem compressed, but it is due to exponentially increasing technology acceleration. These systems will be qualitatively different from nanomaterials in their technical characteristics, application economics, and risks. The defense implications are immense, but they likely have not yet been fully comprehended. There are a variety of additional potential outcomes that have been described in the Foresight Guidelines[5] for the responsible development of advanced nanotechnology. These guidelines are just a start on what may eventually be required for responsible development and utilization of the technology.

Table 7–3. Feasibility of Molecular Manufacturing

INFEASIBILITY CLAIMS	EVIDENCE AND RESPONSES
Fat fingers problem—not enough room for atomic control	Ho and Lee[1] bound cobalt and iron via scanning tunneling microscopy; key is effective control for precise product
Sticky fingers problem—atoms of the manipulator hands will adhere to the atom that is being moved	Voltage can be applied between a manipulator tool and the workpiece (see Ho and Lee)
"We don't know *anything* about designing self-sustaining, self-replicating systems."	See Moshe Sipper[2]
How could artificial nanomachines be powered?	Primitive artificial nanomotors have *already been constructed and fueled*[3]
How could molecular factories store and process information for programs to build more copies?	Significant progress in molecular electronic devices, also off-board memory and security broadcast schema
Pincers must be smaller than atoms in order to manipulate atoms with dexterity	Tools much larger than atoms can manipulate atoms with precision; transfer ribonucleic acid manipulates amino acids

1. Wilson Ho and Hyojune Lee, "Single Bond Formation and Characterization with a Scanning Tunneling Microscope," *Science* 286 (November 26, 1999), 1719–1722, available at <physics. uci.edu/~wilsonho/stm-iets.html>.
2. Moshe Sipper, "Fifty Years of Research on Self-Replication: An Overview," *Artificial Life* 4 (Summer 1998), 237–257. See also Moshe Sipper, "The Artificial Self-Replication Page," available at <http://lslwww.epfl.ch/~moshes/selfrep/>.
3. T.R. Kelly, H. De Silva, R.A. Silva, "Unidirectional rotary motion in a molecular system," *Nature* 401(September 9, 1999), 150–152.

DOD may be a follower of commercial investment in nanoscale material science, but it will have to lead with the rest of the National Nanotechnology Initiative in order for the United States to stay in the lead for molecular manufacturing capabilities. The Productive Nanosystems Technology Roadmap[6] and the associated Working Group Proceedings[7] from Battelle, Foresight, Institute for Molecular Manufacturing, and others outline several ongoing trends and viable pathways to achieve productive nanosystems manufacturing capabilities.

The most straightforward infrastructure for manufacturing will be built with special-purpose molecular fixtures and components. These systems are analogous to macroscale factory components that produce devices that are inherently incapable of replication. Special-purpose manufacturing systems will eventually be able to manufacture very large structures by scaling specific components and subsystems.

The simplest, most efficient, and safest approach to molecular manufacturing or productive nanosystems is to make specialized nanoscale tools and put them together in factories big enough to make what is needed. People use simple tools to make more complex tools, from blacksmiths' tools to automated machinery. The convergent assembly architecture developed by Ralph Merkle[8] describes how small parts can be put together to form larger parts, starting with nanoscale blocks[9] and progressing up the hierarchy to macroscopic systems. The machines in this would work like the conveyor belts and assembly robots in a factory, doing similar jobs. If one of these machines was pulled out of the system, it would pose no risk; it would be as inert as a light bulb pulled from its socket.

The eventual applications of these special-purpose manufacturing systems include the ability to build almost any mechanical device cheaply and in large quantity. This is why molecular manufacturing will eventually do for our relationship to molecules and matter what the computer did for our relationship to bits and information. The computer enabled an ever-expanding number of people to access billions of dollars' worth of information. Dual-use productive nanotechnology may enable an ever-expanding number of people to enjoy significant material wealth, based on carbon dioxide (CO_2) feedstock, which currently is in overabundant supply in the atmosphere. This capability could buy an enormous amount of goodwill around the world. It also may produce the technical infrastructure required to address effectively many of our most pressing transportation, environmental, medical, and global warming issues. However, there is no guarantee that the political and technological leadership required to make this happen will be sufficient. In addition, the technology could be abused and might one day have to be defended against. This is one of the reasons for the Foresight Guidelines mentioned above.

The primary risks of molecular manufacturing enabled by productive nanosystems concern what is manufactured, not the manufacturing infrastructure itself. Special-purpose molecular manufacturing systems can be designed to be safe and reliable. They could be made to build a wide range of devices cheaply, in place, and on demand. These products could include components for large-scale buildings, computing, mass transit systems, energy storage, and spacecraft. They could also construct tiny new security devices and large quantities of inexpensive and super-strong conventional weapons systems.[10] However, developing molecular manufacturing likely will prove difficult. It requires a time perspective beyond the usual commercial and industrial R&D horizons. It will be a dual-use technology, but it will take long-term R&D funding that is focused on specific performance objectives. This fits the high-risk, high-reward profile for Federally funded R&D. However, unlike projects that are essentially "science experiments" with unknown outcomes or performance objectives, we already know that molecular manufacturing of large objects at little more than the cost of raw feedstock is technically feasible—because it happens in nature. For example, trees are solar-powered molecular manufacturing systems that convert the raw feedstock of atmospheric CO_2, water, and soil minerals into tons of low-tensile-strength wood. Nanotechnology-engineered systems could produce a macroscale carbon product from CO_2 with a tensile strength that is 50 times that of titanium.

Metrics to confirm or disconfirm the trends outlined for molecular manufacturing would require monitoring the field for specific progress in:

- moving molecules with atomic precision
- building blocks or systems of nanoscale components
- molecular assembly and positioning devices
- systems designs for achieving scalability
- control and communication systems for molecular manufacturing
- energy and materials transport mechanisms
- embedded controls and safeguard systems
- high-value molecular manufacturing application systems
- technical and social control regimes to contain risks.

Potential Shocks

Given the trends nanotechnology is following, a number of potential shocks are possible:

- rapid deployment of nanomaterial applications: surprising exploitation of early nanoscience in military innovation by other countries
- nanotechnology-enabled massive economic influence: inexpensive, green manufacturing of massive quantities of material goods for the developing world
- molecular manufacturing of conventional military technology: in situ utilization of solar energy and carbon dioxide for the inexpensive production of conventional military technology using high-tensile-strength carbon compounds

- molecular manufacturing of radical military technology: in situ utilization of solar energy and carbon dioxide for the inexpensive production of radical new military technology enabled by programmable materials and high-tensile-strength carbon compounds
- nanotechnology arms race: inexpensive production of fundamentally new military technology leads to positive feedback cycles of defensive and offensive weapons development
- nanotechnology-enabled opening of space frontier: rapid production of high-tensile-strength materials and reduced price per pound to launch payloads, enable space-based industries, energy production, and a new defense frontier
- nanotechnology-enabled intelligence explosion: accelerating exponential increase in computational power surpasses human brain processing[11] and continues to evolve machine intelligence by several orders of magnitude.

These shocks, and their general likelihoods, time frames, and consequences, are summarized in table 7–4.

Table 7–4. Shocks: Consequences and Indicators (in linear years)

SHOCKS	CONSEQUENCES	PROBABILITY	TIME FRAME (YEARS)	INDICATORS
Rapid deployment of early nanotech by other nations	Defending against our own early innovations would be costly	Medium	5	• Controls slow adoption in United States • Evidence of other nations' early adoption • Competitive disadvantages in the field
Molecular manufacturing of conventional military technology	Faster, cheaper, higher quality, in situ deployments	High	15–20	• Industrial Molecular Manufacturing demos • Requests for proposals for radical reductions in cost, time, and product defects
Nanotechnology-enabled massive economic influence	More effective than warfare for antiterror	High	20–25	• Massive increase in ability to deliver necessities to developing world • Government programs to buy influence this way
Molecular manufacturing of new military technology	Breakaway defensive and offensive capabilities	High	15–25	• Explosion of new military concepts and designs • Rapid product innovation cycles • "Game over!" scenarios on battlefield
Nanotechnology-enabled arms race	Fast, unstable positive feedback cycle, eats resources with little incremental or positive return. A scenario to avoid by focusing on cooperative operations other than war	Medium	10	• Predator-prey cycles of weapons development • Must have defensive capabilities • Absence of effective arms control framework, and other worthy and competitive applications ensures this scenario
Nanotechnology-enabled opening of space frontier	Routine access to space environment; huge new energy and material resources	High	20	• Nanomaterials used in spaceflight • Rapid decrease in cost per pound of space payloads
Nanotechnology-enabled intelligence explosion	Computational power equal to, then exceeding, that of humans; extreme strategic and design power amplification	High	15–20	• Computers hit 10^{16} operations per second • Computers hit 10^{26} operations per second • Software that learns and improves continuously

8

Cyberspace

Gregory J. Rattray

A Construct for Analyzing Trends and Shocks in the Cyberspace Environment

THE TERM CYBERSPACE has acquired numerous meanings. Usually attributed to science fiction writer William Gibson, the term came into heavy usage during the early 1990s. Many commentators at that time discussed how cyberspace was fundamentally different from the physical world. However, this analysis treats cyberspace as a physical environment resulting from the connection of systems and networks orchestrated by rules established by software and communications protocols.[1] Discussion of cyberspace in the national security realm largely evolved from the interest in information warfare, particularly computer and network warfare.[2] As of fall 2007, the United States was increasingly stressing the concept of cyberspace as an operating environment. The U.S. Department of Defense (DOD) has defined cyberspace as "a domain characterized by the use of electronics and the electromagnetic spectrum to store, modify, and exchange data via networked systems and associated infrastructures."[3]

The cyberspace operating environment includes a wide range of activity. At the core, most analyses focus on the Internet and computer software applications, but a much broader set of networks, protocols, and electronic transmission media must be considered—traditional circuit-switched networks and protocols such as SS7, microwave networks, long-haul fiber, and satellite networks utilizing ATM and synchronous optical network protocols to carry digital signals. Cyberspace includes the use of analog signals and transmissions from air traffic control radars and air defense systems to supervisory data and control systems based on proprietary algorithms and protocols for power grids that drive their use. Supporting elements of cyberspace include systems such as the global positioning system for timing information and telecommunications hotels that house the switching/routing infrastructure that interconnects them.

Cyberspace comprises physical and logical systems and infrastructures governed by laws of physics as well as rules of code. The key physical laws governing cyberspace are those related to electromagnetism and light. The speed at which waves propagate and electrons move creates huge advantages and challenges for directing activities in cyberspace. Global communications across cyberspace can happen nearly instantaneously. Vast amounts of data can rapidly transit vast distances often unimpeded by physical barriers and political boundaries. This movement at rates beyond normal comprehension creates challenges for individuals, organizations, and states to use cyberspace for advantage while simultaneously avoiding the creation of unintended weaknesses that can be exploited by adversaries.

Of crucial import is that cyberspace interactions are governed by hardware and software that is manmade. Therefore, cyberspace is much more mutable than other environments in terms of its geography. Mountains cannot be moved or oceans drained, but portions of cyberspace can be turned on and off with the flick of a switch or effectively moved through insertions of coded instructions in a router or switch. Air and space environments also require manmade technologies for transit, but actors cannot establish or remove whole new regions of the environment through use of technological tools. Cyberspace is effectively unique in this regard, but it is not infinitely malleable as some claim. Limits to the pace and scope of change are imposed by physical laws, properties of code, and the capacity of organizations and people. The number of actors and communities who play a significant role in cyberspace is also a distinguishing feature. Key groupings include:

- producers of software, hardware, and algorithms that make up cyberspace
- operators of long-haul telecommunications networks, Internet service providers (ISPs), and a wide array of supporting services, such as timing and domain name services
- ISPs, domain name registrars, Web hosts, cellular providers, and others who provide digital services that enable use of the Internet and other communications mediums in cyberspace
- users ranging from global multinational corporations running extensive cyber infrastructures with top-notch cadres of expertise to individuals with little to no technical knowledge

- governments at all levels that establish and enforce legal, regulatory, and policy frameworks for activity in cyberspace
- nongovernmental stakeholder organizations whose activities range from establishing agreements on protocols, to assignment of Internet addresses, to advocating the privacy rights of users.

The complexity of interactions between individual actors and the communities they form means that cyberspace is best analyzed as an ecosystem. Understanding outcomes requires understanding many factors in the environment and a multitude of actors in complex nonlinear interactions. Behavior in the cyberspace ecosystem has aspects of equilibrium and stability. Dramatic change has resulted from getting outside boundary conditions, such as the explosion of use resulting from breakthrough interfaces in the form of the World Wide Web applications in 1995 and system outages from outbreaks of worms and viruses dating back to 1988. As a manmade system, the characteristics of cyberspace are driven by cooperative and competitive behavior of human actors in a way that can be managed. The challenge will be to develop the capacity to understand the behavior and leverage points in this complex system.

Key Trends in the Cyberspace Environment

TECHNOLOGY AND DEMOGRAPHICS

The most stable trend for the next two decades is likely to be growth in use of cyberspace. Over 1.1 billion users are estimated to be on the Internet globally, a 225 percent rise in the last 7 years.[4] E-commerce has reached $3 trillion a year and is expanding rapidly. Closely related to growth, the ever-growing convergence of use of the Internet as a basis for transmission of data between systems and applications and the development of easily implemented, high-bandwidth, wireless transmissions standards has enabled increasingly ubiquitous access and ease of connection. This increased connectivity also has raised the importance of setting up boundaries and control over cyberspace use by governments such as the People's Republic of China (PRC) and Saudi Arabia. Governments have long jammed radio and TV broadcasts they deemed undesirable. Such nations now employ software filters and other techniques to similarly limit the information that reaches their citizens.

In the early phases of Internet growth, concerns were raised regarding the development of a "digital divide," a term used to describe the potential for the Internet and other advanced technologies to exacerbate the gaps between rich and poor. Deployment and effective employment of cyberspace connectivity and associated user technologies require financial and intellectual capital that is unevenly distributed. Dramatically declining costs and increasing maturity of wireless and other technologies to enable access have fostered hopes that properly crafted government and nongovernment programs may be able to rapidly close this gap. Another hope is that the open source movement in software development will reduce control by large corporations and lower the costs of systems. However, the problem is complex and tightly interwoven with other development challenges, in particular, development of technological skills, user education, and basic managerial acumen. The outcome of this phenomenon will be important in how cyberspace impacts development dynamics. Most likely, the impact on development will be uneven, providing important leverage for some areas in overcoming development challenges while potentially deepening problems for others based on such conditions as the educational system, government policy, and other institutional factors.

Cyberspace, with its associated connectivity and computing power, also underpins other breakthrough technologies of the early 21st century, especially those associated with nanotechnology, biotechnology, and neurological developments. The engineering of devices at the molecular level, the analysis of the genome, and tracing pathways in the brain only can occur with high-power computing, often linked in a distributed fashion, and collaborative analytic efforts of scientists and laboratories across the globe. The enabling nature of cyberspace will result in contributions to the increasing general health of populations who can leverage these technologies, as well as deployment of advanced systems on the battlefield down to the individual soldier.

Most of these trends have two-edged implications for the United States and DOD. The evolution of the United States into the sole superpower in the early 21st century has been significantly enabled both politically and militarily by cyberspace. The global spread and penetration of cyberspace will continue to fuel a growth in the soft power potential of the United States as people around the world see and discuss alternative models of economic activity and government and social dialogue. Many cited the importance of communication with the outside world in the demise of the Soviet Union. Similarly, the growing penetration of the Internet into the PRC stands to be a major force in changes to the political system and already is of clear concern to the communist rulers of that country. American military campaigns waged in the former Yugoslavia and the early stages of wars in Afghanistan and Iraq have leveraged technological and operational advantages provided by cyberspace. The precision attack, dominant situational awareness, and future hopes for net-centric modes of warfare stem from its ability to take advantage of this environment. The United States should continue to leverage these aspects of cyberspace.

However, the enabling power of the technology will also allow more state and nonstate actors to compete more effectively with the United States economically and pose asymmetric security threats. In doctrinal writings, the PRC increasingly sees cyber war conducted by the masses as a means for conflict with the United States. Corporations worldwide can use the leverage that cyberspace provides to advantage. Nonstate actors also can more effectively compete in this operating environment than others dominated by the international regimes and military forces established by states.

The volatility of the growth of cyberspace is low in terms of increasing global numbers and penetration to increasingly remote regions. However, the speed at which growth may occur is more variable, and the technical direction that communications pathways or user applications might take is likely to be as variable in the near to mid-term as it has been for the last two decades.

ECONOMICS

The capacity of the Internet and associated technologies to reduce transaction costs and barriers to entry into many markets has become a major, if not the dominant, driver of economic growth and innovation in the world economy. Cyberspace enables and utilizes a global supply chain. Major corporations use global connectivity to place customer service, engineering design, and other operations overseas. Those technology providers of the software and hardware products that comprise cyberspace increasingly conduct all activities from research and development to software coding to component production and assembly through continuous global processes involving large numbers of partners across the globe. The degree of leverage and control over these partners varies widely. Modern enterprises leverage global talent to design and architect systems and drive efficiencies in logistics systems. Ever-increasing competiveness and globalization in most markets will continue to motivate more off-shoring of information technology (IT) activities and the extension of supply chains in many industries across national borders. Generally, the United States has fostered conditions that strengthen and leverage this trend and will want to continue to do so.

The effectiveness of IT in reducing operating costs also has resulted in a dramatic growth in how increasingly open, accessible networks underpin key functions across advanced societies. Organizations in competitive markets and constrained budgets have aggressively used cyberspace as a means to reduce overhead costs and automate operations. Major corporations continue to consolidate networks and facilities responsible for digital processing of operational transactions, employee records, and customer data. The U.S. military increasingly builds modern weapons, such as the Joint Strike Fighter, DDG-1000 *Zumwalt-* class destroyer, and ground-based future combat systems with development approaches that leverage multiple, international partners joined through cyberspace to engineer systems that depend on automated logistics systems involving multiple organizations that transit public networks. The deployed systems require complex software processing vast amounts of information traveling through a variety of cyberspace mediums to provide navigational, threat warning, and targeting capabilities fundamental to their combat effectiveness. Similarly, in advanced societies, critical infrastructures such as airlines, electric grids, and water systems, as well as telecommunications systems themselves, have leveraged cyberspace to increase efficiency. Systems for automated control of dams and power substations have moved increasingly to widely available commercial software that uses the Internet to transmit data and commands. Also, reduced costs for transporting data and desires to interconnect networks have led to a consolidation of key communications facilities. Over the past two decades, the major U.S. long distance telecommunications companies have consolidated their major routing and peer interconnection points into fewer than a dozen facilities in a handful of major cities.

Additionally, the same connectivity and ease of access that empowers e-commerce, electronic banking, and automated inventory systems also lower barriers for malicious actors to achieve their objectives. Myriad terrorist, dissent, and extremist groups now utilize the Internet for a wide variety of purposes from recruitment to fundraising to the promulgation of information on how to conduct bombings and whom to target.[5] Steve Coll and Susan Glasser have observed that "al Qaeda has become the first guerrilla movement in history to migrate from physical space to cyberspace."[6] Extremely worrisome is the growth in cyber-related skill sets within organized crime, currently focused on fraud, but potentially available to be leveraged by both state and nonstate actors to achieve disruptive effects. Additionally, the skill and costs required to craft disruptive cyber tools, such as worms, or to find vulnerabilities in operating systems have declined dramatically. Markets have formed in an Internet underground to facilitate the cheap transfer of modules of code used to build worms and of already hacked networks of computers, known as "botnets." Such malicious networks now can involve a million or more machines that are used for spamming to facilitate phishing and fraud and to conduct massive disruptive denial-of-service attacks.

CONFLICT AND GOVERNANCE

The growth in human activity in cyberspace also has created an operating environment that permits a range of competitive activities from protest to crime to espionage to disruptive attacks. Many ways exist to access, corrupt, and disrupt networks and systems in cyberspace. Attention over the last decade has been focused on digital hacking and the presence of computer viruses and worms that transit the Internet, but the longstanding ability to disrupt communications paths and signals in the electronic spectrum also must receive continued attention. A crucial question for analyzing trends and shocks is whether the rising levels of malicious activity observed in cyberspace, particularly on the Internet, are reaching a point that will upset the ecosystem's equilibrium, especially as regards its utility in conducting military operations. The 2006 U.S. National Defense Strategy notes, "Successful military operations depend on the ability to protect information infrastructure and data. Increased dependence on information networks creates new vulnerabilities that adversaries may seek to exploit."[7] The trend toward growing vulnerability and malicious activity in cyberspace noted above has increased geometrically in scale over time. The Computer Emergency Response Team Coordinating Center at the Software Engineering Institute reveals a growth in reported vulnerabilities from 417 in 1999 to 8,064 in 2006 and in reported computer security incidents from 9,859 in 1999 to 137,529 in 2003, the last period covered.[8]

The trend likely results both from the general increase in use and accessibility of cyberspace, particularly the Internet, and more frequent efforts by actors to gain advantages in the operating environment. The growing ease of creating and using technologies to conduct illicit monitoring and control of systems in cyberspace and to disrupt their operation also are contributing factors. In general, the trend has advantaged offensive action in overcoming efforts to defend assets in cyberspace. The economic pressure for ever-growing connectivity and ease of access is likely to continue this trend.

Most states currently do not, or cannot, control cyberspace to the same degree as they can control land, sea, and air. In the United States and many other areas of the globe, the myriad providers of devices, connectivity, and services are brought together in loosely woven networks with open standards that governments would have extreme difficulty in controlling across the full spectrum of their activities. Managing conflict in the ecosystem has proven difficult, and all trends point to it becoming increasingly so. A central challenge in the cyberspace environment has been developing governance models that go beyond the traditional approaches to managing international conflicts centered on the role of the state.

As noted, the environment now includes actors such as terrorist groups using cyberspace to facilitate activity and criminal actors extending lines of business such as extortion and fraud into cyberspace. The emergence of more purposeful, sophisticated, malicious actors in cyberspace also has created a challenge of identifying the most threatening activity, such as espionage that occurs within a growing volume of other illicit activity. The growing significance of nonstate actors in general makes their ability to leverage the disruptive potential of cyberspace a key trend that must be addressed. Such actors are likely to pursue conflict strategies, such as guerrilla campaigns, in an environment where "hit and run" activities are enabled by difficulties with attribution of malicious acts to specific actors.

The potential to hold nation-state actors and key components of the cyberspace ecosystem itself at risk is also now becoming increasingly real. In the spring of 2007, a weeks-long series of attacks against Estonian government, banking, and other activities resulted in public calls for assistance from the Estonian president.[9] The core Internet Domain Name Services have come under attack. Such attacks started in 2002 and have continued to grow in scale.[10] So far, the attacks have been of limited duration and effect, but those responsible have not been identified. A real possibility exists that these events have been test runs for use of Internet attack capabilities in the context of conflict with an economic or political objective. Unfortunately, the technological offense-defense imbalance likely will continue. Additionally, the United States must be prepared to address new alliances between malicious actors seeking to quickly raise threats from groups that previously have been seen as disinterested or lacking capability.

Potential Shocks in the Cyberspace Environment

Cyberspace has been a rapidly evolving sphere of human activity over the past century, and particularly the last two decades. Revolutionary developments—networking based on Internet protocol, ease of use based on Web applications, emergence of self-propagating malicious code, and social networking, for example—continue to enter the environment regularly and cause significant and even dramatic change in patterns within the ecosystem. Speculating on future shocks for this analysis is therefore viewed more as a means of illustrating possible situations that might challenge current trends than as any effort to predict even a range of possibility.

TECHNOLOGY

The emergence of ubiquitous, easy-to-use security within the ecosystem, particularly the Internet, is growing. Encryption and authentication systems have become easy to implement; and algorithms to characterize abnormal, malicious activity have become highly precise and effective. Breakthroughs in computing and communications hardware, software, and protocols that ensure users of control over information and establish transparency regarding who was using cyberspace for what purposes would dramatically shift the dynamics of many behaviors of the ecosystem, especially in conflict and governance. In terms of conflict, such breakthroughs could enable actors to severely limit unauthorized malicious activity. Cyberspace would no longer present a haven for criminal and terrorist activity and could enable a broader and stronger reach for central authorities. A collateral effect likely would see further strengthening of the incentives to transfer economic activity to cyberspace, if risks from fraud and other illicit activity were largely eliminated. Such a technological future also would make espionage in this environment difficult. Very significantly, depending on the types of implementation and the policy of states, such technologies also could contribute to Orwellian outcomes in terms of severe limits on personal privacy and increased visibility into the behavior of individuals by corporations and the state. Such a scenario seems unlikely in the face of recent history and current technological trends. A technological breakthrough may occur rapidly, but implementation of new technological approaches across the breadth of cyberspace in a way that significantly raises the bar for the conduct of malicious activity may be slow.

DEMOGRAPHICS

Dropping costs and ease of use by most individuals, even with limited resources and education, allow for rapid economic and institutional development in disadvantaged regions. Extension of the reduction of transaction costs and barriers to entry that cyberspace can enable would take hold in remote areas and underdeveloped markets. These areas also would create visibility into, and dialogue with, the greater global community. The governance effects of this effort likely would vary considerably, potentially reducing the degree of crisis and conflict flashpoints where improved economic development reduced political strains resulting from wide gaps in income and increased social dialogue fostered strengthening of governance institutions.

The likelihood of this scenario having a positive effect will be highly variable, depending on a variety of contextual factors in different cases. From the point of view of the United States, a special case would be the potential for rapid development of forces for political change in states with authoritarian regimes, such as the PRC, Cuba, and North Korea. Such change could occur in a fashion similar to the end of the Cold War in Eastern Europe and the former Soviet Union, but could also result in political crises that destabilize regimes and increase potential for conflicts at local, regional, and even global levels.

Conflict 1: Malicious activity on the Internet becomes so pervasive that it no longer is a viable means for handling sensitive data, performing economic transactions, or conducting social dialogue. The growing incentives for criminal use, the prevalence of egregiously offensive material, and the ease of subverting transactions or threatening extortion on an increasingly converged set of digital networks reach a tipping point. The pervasiveness of identity theft, economic competition through disruption of competitor networks and data, and spoofed information in political campaigns causes a crisis of confidence. Individuals demand alternative ways to conduct activities. Companies and markets follow, with government adapting more slowly. Some large institutions endeavor to create more secure cyber environments within which to conduct activities with far more limited numbers of trusted players.

Vibrant technology innovation is undermined, as are the speed and breadth of transactions in many spheres of economic activity, negatively impacting economic growth. Military capacity to leverage cyberspace for network-centric warfare is degraded as the commercial backbone grows more slowly, as does capacity to leverage technology development based on far-flung networks of enterprises linked through cyberspace. Governments in most cases endeavor to exert much greater control over cyberspace in all spheres—military, economic, and social—reinforcing the power of autocratic governments. The likelihood of such events coming to the fore is medium to high. The pace of loss of public and institutional confidence may be high as well.

Conflict 2: In the first successful, large-scale prosecution of cyber war in a political conflict, the use of cyberspace to gather intelligence, corrupt adversary information flows, disrupt military operations, and directly conduct digital strikes against critical infrastructures, such as finance, power, and transportation, allows victory by a small nation or nonstate actor against a major power. Offensive advantages in cyber conflict make deterring and countering such attacks, especially by nonstate actors, very difficult. States may leverage groups and individuals outside the traditional national security organizations to conduct cyber warfare.[11] Recognition grows within and outside the United States of its vulnerability to such attacks. Political dissent groups turn to cyberspace as a means for achieving their goals via disruptive attacks like those directed against Estonia. Terrorist and extremist groups such as al Qaeda and Aum Shinrikyo see the value of nonkinetic modes of mass disruption as a major path to achieving their fundamental goals of undermining the Western way of life. Such groups seek to leverage the technological and operational prowess developed by organized crime in malicious cyberspace activity. Long-term guerrilla campaigns targeted at economic and political disruption become a constant feature of the cyberspace environment.

The onset of such constant cyber political conflict would involve significant short-term disruption to the targeted parties. In this scenario, the long-term withdrawal of activity from cyberspace to mitigate military, economic, and social vulnerabilities seems likely. These conditions also could raise substantially the probabilities for physical conflict in situations where the attacked party looked for some means to punish transgressors and resolve the conflict on more advantageous turf. The likelihood is medium to high. As with cybercrime becoming rife, the technical conditions for this scenario are already in place, meaning endemic cyber wars could emerge quickly.

Conflict 3: The modes of cyber conflict beyond the battlefield expand dramatically from manipulation of digits to the disruption of electromagnetic means of transmission. Disruptive effects—through a range of directed energy effects from pinpoint failure of specific systems to capacity for broad-area, nonnuclear, electromagnetic pulse—become viable. This development could occur in conjunction with either of the conflict shocks discussed above. The likelihood of such developments is low to medium but increases over time. Such means of waging cyber conflict likely would be less widely accessible to a spectrum of actors given the technological sophistication and financial means needed, although this condition may not last. The barriers to entry also will likely slow the rate at which such developments become a major national security concern.

GOVERNANCE

State-driven "walled gardens" may emerge. The stagnation of progress in Internet technical evolution and governance regarding security, stability, and resiliency combines with national objectives regarding political dialogue and capacity for cyber defense resulting in most governments striving to exert control over cyberspace networks and systems within their borders. The Internet is no longer assumed to be a global resource managed as a commons. Governments increasingly assert rights of sovereignty and territoriality across the full range of Internet governance forums such as the Internet Engineering Task Force, the Internet Corporation for Assigned Names and Numbers, and the United Nations. For example, the PRC already has engaged in a multifront approach of controlling public Internet access, developing proprietary operating systems for national use, and endeavoring to influence global standards evolution with the next version of the Internet protocols, IPv6.[12] The technological, interoperability, cooperative focus of activities surrounding the development of Internet and other cyberspace architectures is supplanted as key governments push organizations such as the International Telecommunication Union to control the evolution of cyberspace as the purview of governments. Issues such as making cyberspace a controlled environment because of security concerns, even to the level of agreements regarding cyber weapons and limits on cyber attacks, would come to the fore.

The impact on globalization and economic growth would be detrimental. Similarly, the scenario would likely strengthen the ability of governments to control social dialogue. For those concerned with national security, this future may allow for more effective, large-scale cyber defenses and possible coordinated responses, especially against nonstate actors that challenge the interests of the majority of governments. The U.S. Government and DOD will face conflicting interests in terms of how to engage in global governance debates, as desires for more direct control will have to be weighed against conditions that would undermine broader objectives of fostering global markets and democratic dialogue. While the likelihood of this development is low, the probability of this scenario would rise if controlling conflict in cyberspace were to become a major concern. The onset rate of such change would likely be slow, as dialogue and decisions would play out over many years.

Broad Vectors for DOD Efforts to Address Cyber Trends and Shocks

Given the growing significance of cyberspace and the possibilities for discontinuous change, DOD must push for more mature national mechanisms to determine strategy and set policy. The challenge is to synchronize economic, military, diplomatic, and informational activity in cyberspace to achieve synergy with national values and goals, particularly the ability to pursue free trade in global markets and freedom of political choice. DOD will need to play a leading role in these efforts.

National policy can influence the international, national, organizational, and individual use of cyberspace. Strategic choices exist. The PRC is focused on tighter control of individual rights in cyberspace and is endeavoring to establish a more separate national cyberspace enclave with controlled access to foster political control and improve the ability to defend national cyber assets against malicious activity. The United States has taken a more laissez faire approach. U.S. national regulation and positions in international forums stress the economic benefits of loose control in empowering innovation and access by all to services provided via the Internet and other cyberspace mediums. This approach entails risks in terms of limiting understanding of the potential weaknesses of the overall system and the ability to orchestrate coordinated activity across systems and infrastructures if required. The impact of different national approaches on the ability to manage strategic conflict in cyberspace is not clear. A loosely controlled, diverse, but robust network infrastructure may fare better than a centrally managed infrastructure with mandated barriers and defense, but retaining a limited capacity for rapid adaptation in the face of new threats seems imperative.

We must develop the methods and intellectual capital to analyze and answer such questions. A key concern will be how to manage cyber security risks posed by the increasingly global production, operation, and ownership of key IT and communications that underpin the ability of the U.S. military, other government, and critical infrastructure operations. Establishing such capabilities will require dedicated programs employing significant financial resources and intellectual capital over the long term as part of strategies to mitigate risk at all levels from weapons programs to national cyber infrastructure evolution.

The United States must constantly seek to understand shifting opportunities and vulnerabilities embedded in the evolving foundations of cyberspace and aggressively manage its equities across the range of social, economic, and military concerns. To establish a better protected cyberspace, we should pursue redundancy and diversity in undersea cable, satellite ground stations, and fiber-optic routing generally to avoid chokepoints in the key infrastructural hubs and physical connectivity. We can worry less about precise mapping of all potential vulnerabilities, which has been a focus of many Federal Government efforts, given the constantly morphing cyberspace environment.

Public and private sector actors who operate and use cyberspace for key national economic and security purposes should conduct regular scenario analyses and exercises jointly to focus investment and develop migration strategies to establish a more robust cyber infrastructure. In the past 2 years, the Defense Department has demonstrated increasing concern for the eroding security dynamics related to the Internet. The main barrier to DOD preparing for a shock that stems from such trends may be the institutions and culture that manage information and network security programs. These programs are dominated by an ever-larger effort to engineer impregnable castle walls. The resulting programmatic focus extends over very long periods, even decades. The community responsible for devising and implementing solutions to the balancing acts required must be much more agile in terms of thinking along adaptive systems solutions to response and recovery, and nimble in terms of employing resources programmatically.

In managing the evolution of the logical cyber environment, the United States should more aggressively engage standard setters the way competitors, such as the PRC, have increasingly chosen to do. National policymakers must understand the significance of the evolution of security and control over standards and assets for IPv6, Border Gateway Protocol, and Domain Name System to make informed choices about how to pursue their objectives. Choices about open versus closed systems and more defensible versus more accessible cyberspace systems at the national level will depend on the ability to balance intelligence, military, law enforcement, commercial, and social objectives. Research and development efforts to develop more secure, robust protocols and systems may allow for more options in pushing the evolution of networks to be both open and trusted. Choices such as the need to invest in a separate, more securable government network for sensitive unclassified information may be the consequence of a desire to limit government control to enable economic growth and social dialogue by encouraging growth of networks that emphasize accessibility and innovation. Major progress in technological solutions, operational art, and intelligence capabilities to attribute the origin of malicious activity must be a major focus of DOD and national cyber security efforts, both to combat the rise of cyber crime and to hold at risk terrorist and state adversaries who might try to conduct hidden operations in cyberspace.

The United States and its partners also should seek more robust mechanisms for cooperation in the governance of a global commons. While notions of arms control agreements to pursue international control over information warfare have surfaced, the more appropriate approach for the United States will be securing freedom of passage, similar to regimes governing the seas and space. U.S. efforts to seek a "culture of cybersecurity," and private sector leadership over the evolution of the Internet in the past 10 years, have been largely successful.[13] DOD should continue to support these efforts.

To be able to adapt to shocks to the system, DOD must ensure it has a highly capable cadre of people at all levels—tactical, operational, and strategic. The centrality of human expertise requires competing globally in creating, attracting, and retaining the right human capital to effectively construct, utilize, and engage in conflict in cyberspace. These personnel must be capable of analyzing the changing opportunities and risks present in the environment, operating and protecting the large enterprises and infrastructures that sustain cyberspace, and performing specific tasks ranging from developing new modes of sharing information to providing actors the capacity for disruptive attack. For the U.S. military, the challenge is nurturing a strong cadre of cyber experts similar to the naval, air, and space leaders and operators who have enabled success in other realms. The issue is one of vision and will to pull limited resources away from traditional military missions and invest in the core capabilities that will enable pursuit of more important objectives through operating and controlling the cyber environment. The intellectual challenges are interdisciplinary, and the effort must engage the best minds beyond the techno-elite.

Conclusion

Cyberspace will remain a dynamic environment that will continue to challenge those who want to harness its opportunities. The convergence of information, biological, and nanotechnologies is likely to cause the eruption of unforeseen challenges and complexity. Economic, political, and military conflicts are increasingly spilling into this environment, and cyberspace probably will become a central playing field for this activity. In the near term, U.S. leaders must develop policy mechanisms to engage more holistically the range of social, economic, and security concerns arising in cyberspace to make effective tradeoffs. Over the longer term, a national effort must include the ability to shape economic and technological drivers to enhance the resilience and transparency of the cyberspace fundamentally important to the United States and its global partners. We cannot leave to faith that a cyberspace environment facilitating access, innovation, and security will emerge on its own. We must have the political will, expend the fiscal resources, and develop the human capital to shape our future opportunities to leverage cyberpower.

We must understand the limits to our crystal ball but have confidence in engaging the opportunities and risks presented by cyberspace. As in other Darwinian struggles, the fittest will survive and prosper. The lesson of biology is that survival does not necessarily advantage the biggest, strongest, or meanest, but rather the most adaptable. The ability to learn, cooperate when fruitful, and compete when necessary will provide the fundamental strengths of those actors seeking cyberpower.

9

Life Sciences

Robert E. Armstrong and Mark D. Drapeau

IN THIS CHAPTER, we discuss four trends within the field of life sciences and potential shocks that may disrupt these trends. Our first topic is pandemic influenza. We discuss the ecology underlying the annual evolution of the influenza virus and how this relates to animal farming practices in rural China. Centuries-old farming practices promote diversification and spread of novel strains of bird flu. The Chinese leadership is in a difficult position, as it is required to choose between being responsible for the origin of the next flu pandemic, with potential severe economic consequences, or proactively creating rural societal disruption to promote global health, and possibly creating instability and losing political power in the process.

Next, we discuss a growing trend toward diffuse, networked threats, which include traditional terrorists and contemporary computer hackers. Advancements in biotechnology and global communications allow strangers with common interests to collaborate on bioengineering projects—and will enable traditional terrorists to more easily create and use advanced biological materials as weapons. More worrisome, however, is a distinct scenario: amateur biohackers conducting benign research could inadvertently help criminals or terrorists obtain sophisticated biological agents that can be used as weapons. This could occur through hijacking or copycatting of research. Alternatively, disaffected biohackers could undertake criminal missions after adopting an ideology related to scientific research.

The third area we explore is the trend of civilian and military human performance enhancement via interactions of the body with both biological and inert technologies. A potential shock here—perhaps foreshadowed by the contemporary political and scientific debate over stem cell research—is that a myriad of ethical concerns may delay U.S. advancement in this area, while potential enemies may not similarly restrict themselves. As a result, an emergent

131

power may be able to use the life sciences as an asymmetric force multiplier. More importantly, we may be forced to alter our societal values to meet such a threat.

Our final section takes the very long view of advances in genetics, genomics, proteomics, and advanced technology—including DNA sequencing, gene "chips," and advanced information-sharing—that make the biological research possible. We discuss general trends in biotechnology intersecting with the seemingly disparate worlds of traditional agriculture and advanced engineering. In the long view, applying new biotech to old problems will most likely result in a bio-based economy (rather than a petro-based one) in which everyday objects will be manufactured from renewable biological resources. Potential shocks associated with this trend are an attenuation of urbanization trends due to building of regional biorefineries, primarily in rural areas, and hot or cold conflicts over access to biological resources arising between the gene-rich/technology-poor countries along the equator versus the gene-poor/technology-rich countries of the more developed world.

As a next step beyond this chapter, we are interested in answering two fundamental questions. First, what defense strategies can shape the environment and hedge against major risks or shocks? Secondly, how can we synthesize trends and shocks from different areas to use them to the competitive advantage of the United States?

China's Farming Practices and Bird Flu

TRENDS

Pandemics recur periodically yet unpredictably and are invariably associated with high morbidity, mortality, and great social and economic disruption.[1] The likelihood of pandemic outbreaks grows with increasing human-animal and domesticated animal–wild animal contact, particularly in the setting of nonindustrial, unregulated agriculture. The U.S. National Intelligence Council recently proposed that pandemic disease poses the greatest overall threat to the world economy.[2]

More worrying is that even the best public health systems may not be able to deal with a pandemic emergency. As Peter Katona points out in chapter 6 of this book, the world is clearly overdue for a major pandemic. Simultaneously (in the United States, at least), the number of patients (including the uninsured), overall medical costs, and the already vast amount of medical technology and knowledge are all expected to increase during the next 15 years. These trends could result in a pandemic influenza overwhelming both domestic and military health care systems, with serious downstream effects on social life and economics.

In recent years, highly pathogenic H5N1 influenza (also known as avian influenza or bird flu) has swept through poultry populations in large swaths of East and Southeast Asia, creating the potential for a pandemic. China has been identified as the principal reservoir for influenza and southern China as the influenza epicenter. China's role as an incubator of influenza viruses can be traced to the first domestication of the duck, which occurred about 2500 BCE, near the beginning of Chinese recorded history.[3]

Studies suggest that wild aquatic birds—ducks—are the principal hosts for influenza in nature. The two primary habitats of ducks are on lakes in the far reaches of Siberia and in the rice paddies of southern China. Migrating ducks, hosts to great numbers of flu viruses, "seeded" southern China with the viruses as they moved south, and the virus took hold in domesticated ducks. Although ducks were domesticated 4,500 years ago, it was not until the early years of the Qing dynasty, in the mid-17th century, that Chinese peasants began keeping ducks together with wild waterfowl in rice paddies.

Throughout history, the connection between birds and the flu has spawned epidemics in Asia, especially in southern China. Dense concentrations of humans and livestock have left few of China's original migratory habitats intact.[4] Birds find it difficult to locate quality places to land as they make their migration every year between southern Indonesia and the Arctic Circle of Siberia. Consequently, they land on farms and compete with domestic animals for food and water, thereby introducing new viruses into farms and spawning epidemics in China.

The country is estimated to have 640,000 to 1 million villages where fowl are raised in close proximity to humans and which annually raise about 13 billion chickens, 60 percent of them on small farms. Unfortunately, China's agricultural practices have not changed appreciably in any of the peasant areas where birds live with humans—birds are treated as pets by peasant children—and infection control measures for farming are not only disregarded but also mostly unknown.

The critical link in the spread of flu viruses to humans is the swine population in the farming areas where wild and domesticated fowl interact. Typically, avian viruses do not pass directly to humans. (When they do, they are usually extremely lethal.) In the annual development of flu viruses, the avian viruses normally pass through the swine population before reaching the human population. Additionally, an avian virus can enter the pig population, then recombine with a human virus that also has been passed to pigs. The result is a dangerous avian virus that can infect humans.[5]

Understanding and interacting with China requires understanding its culture. In general, because of ever-increasing global economic interdependence, culture is becoming a more important consideration in U.S. national security policy. Culture, broadly defined, encompasses a learned or shared way of life, and the way in which common information (values, beliefs, norms, language, and artifacts) is constructed and communicated within a society. A significant disruption of a politically significant (sub)culture may constitute an important cultural shock of consequence to the United States. Furthermore, as Dale Eickelman points out in chapter 10 of this volume, while cultures and identities may be unlikely to cause trends or shocks by themselves, underestimating their effects dooms one to avoidable mistakes and obstacles.

Traditional Asian methods of raising, buying, slaughtering, and cooking meat make it difficult to track the spread of an influenza virus. In Asia, consumers prefer to buy live animals at the market and slaughter them at home. Asians thus have a high level of exposure to potentially disease-carrying animals, both in their homes and as they pass through the markets that line the streets of densely packed urban centers. In general, the farming practices in southern China are seen as dangerous, and they received wide coverage during the Severe Acute Respiratory Syndrome (SARS) outbreak.[6] For example, it is not uncommon for chickens to be raised in cages above pigs, with the chicken waste being deposited into the pig trough as additional feed.

The choices that Chinese officials make profoundly affect their ability to manage future epidemics.[7] Decentralization and underfinancing of public health services have significantly undermined China's ability to mount an effective, coordinated response to potentially pandemic infectious illnesses.

The best prospects for containing avian flu start with using vaccines appropriately in conjunction with public education, rigorous surveillance, quarantines, escape-proof poultry coops, and disinfection of poultry handlers and their equipment. Unfortunately, low budgets and weak infrastructure hinder such common-sense measures. China has not yet truly invested in a public education campaign regarding personal hygiene and public health practices that could possibly nip future epidemics in the bud.

Peter Katona notes two global health trends of importance in chapter 6. First, with societies increasingly crowded, industrialized, and urbanized, disease is more likely to spread faster and be more dangerous than we have experienced in the recent past. Second, while a worldwide, integrated disease surveillance system is most likely a decade or so away, international cooperation on disease surveillance is growing. This cooperation includes organizations such as the World Health Organization and the World Bank and could reduce the effects of epidemic flu or similar incidents.

SHOCKS

We see two potential first-order shocks with regard to China and pandemic influenza. In the first shock scenario, a deadly influenza epidemic breaks out in Asia. Millions of people become sick, and many die. Researchers are able to trace the origin to China, and expert commentators discuss trends in farming practices that led to the devastating result. Measures to reduce risk to the United States lead to a backlash against China, and trade and travel are greatly reduced, with wide-ranging effects on world economies.

In a corollary scenario, an influenza epidemic breaks out in Asia; for some reason it does not have the potential for worldwide distribution (some biological limitation in transmission or a very rapid time-to-death post-infection, for instance). But governments outside the outbreak region err on the side of caution when dealing with China and nearby nations. The shock is that within Asia, or even within China (for example, between Guangdong and Hong Kong), import-export and hygiene officials suspend trade of items like live birds, eggs, and other meat, such as pigs, until the "problem is cleared up."

Downstream effects of this policy shift include a generally decreased confidence in Asian agricultural products, reduced futures trading of these commodities, and migration of farmers from China to other regions where they can ply the only trade they know. These developments in turn could have economic or general regional stability consequences for the United States and other countries that trade with China. Also, Chinese health officials, in the course of broadcasting the news, may affect regional travel in and around China with second- and third-order effects.

All of these potential effects are significant when one takes into account that despite the fact that only 10 percent of China's land is suitable to farming, approximately half of China's labor force works in the agriculture industry, contributing 13 percent of the nation's gross domestic product (GDP).[8] China is a major trading partner of numerous countries and exports significant amounts of food products. Approximately 3.4 percent of Chinese exports are agricultural.[9]

A strategic shock may occur when a naturally occurring pandemic intersects with an inadequate or poorly prepared public health system. Here, pandemic flu (or numerous other ailments like SARS, tuberculosis [TB], or plague) overwhelms the surge capacity of the health system. Reasonable predictions by the U.S. Centers for Disease Control (CDC) are that a flu pandemic in the modern era would come in three waves over 12–18 months. The pandemic would greatly affect agricultural production, general commerce and trade, and travel.

(Similar consequences could result from a more severe, weaponized flu virus. Unconfirmed media reports state that North Korea, for example, has attempted such a weaponization.)

In another primary shock scenario, the Chinese government adopts a counterculture strategy, anticipates a pandemic and its wide-ranging effects, and alters farming practices, disrupting centuries-old cultural traditions, displacing people, and forcing them into new lifestyles and careers. While avoiding the moral and economic backlash of scenario one, here we have a conflict between world health, Chinese culture, and social structure. What will the farmers do if they are unable to sustain business? Where will they live? This scenario has wide-ranging consequences in the areas of demography, culture, identity, economics, and globalization.

China is a demographically interesting nation, and some of its quirks may have consequences for U.S. national security. The country may grow old before it grows rich, which has the potential to increase internal instability. China is on track to be the world's fastest aging state after its population peaks around 2030. Also, skewed sex ratios resulting from China's one-child policy may result in approximately 40 million unmarried Chinese men. Finally, China is undergoing massive urbanization while remaining a relatively rural country. Experts disagree on the results of these trends, with some predicting increased unrest, while others anticipate adjustments in policies to deal with changing demographics.

In the short term, China's immense population growth will help to fuel its economy via a supply of labor and talent, but after 2030 there may be unintended, and possibly unpredictable, consequences. First, a growing divide between rich and poor—primarily poor, rural elderly and relatively prosperous, young urbanites—may undermine the legitimacy of the communist party regime, if members of a poor majority feel their leaders are not providing security and stability. Second, an aging and shrinking workforce may be unable to sustain high economic growth.

With regard to the weighing of foreign culture in U.S. national security considerations, Dale Eickelman notes the importance of identity or a sense of belonging to a group. Components of identity include profession, tribe, and class, all of which may be relevant in discussing Chinese farmers versus more prominent—and possibly more politically influential—urbanites. Because identity is fundamental to what it means to be human, it drives behavior and, therefore, conflict, and may contribute to tensions inside China.

Identity also relates to governance. Shifts in identity of relevant social groups could result in a lack of governance of the group (hence, a "shock in governance," wherein a group does not accept the authority of the government). In combination with new media imposing state transparency and accountability, and empowering opposition groups in general, such a situation could result in a hot or cold conflict within China between "rich yuppies" and "poor farmers."

Additionally, low-wage, disaffected workers like the farmers, who are not benefiting from globalization, may seek an alternative identity from the one they perceive as being imposed upon them. (As an analogy, this is not unlike the reaction we currently see among young, single males in the Middle East.)

With regard to U.S. national security interests, the consequences of curtailed trade with China to reduce risk from infectious disease are obvious. Economic prosperity could suffer in both countries, which in turn could create instability, particularly in China, and could have unintended consequences that include confrontation. Such developments could contribute to instability—or distraction—within China's leadership, also producing unintended consequences globally.

As Robert Ross comments in chapter 12 of this book, the U.S.-China relationship is now the most important great power relationship, affecting not only U.S. and Asian security but also the stability of the global economy. With regard to China, this is for three main reasons: geopolitical advantages, economic dynamism, and global economic importance.

Long-term, stable U.S.-China strategic competition is dependent on a number of trends continuing, such as Chinese domestic stability and economic growth and sustained U.S. economic prosperity. All of these are potentially affected by a pandemic flu outbreak. One or both nations could suffer an economic collapse. Alternatively, China could adopt national security policies that increase tension with the United States.

Peter Katona points out that a pandemic and its downstream consequences will be greatly affected by general international trends. Approximately 2 million people cross borders weekly, often between developed and developing countries. About 60 million Americans are international tourists yearly; millions of foreigners visit the United States each year. Shutting down air traffic for only a brief time would have major economic consequences. These trends in international travel increase the dangers of global spread of disease.

Finally, something specifically of interest to the Department of Defense (DOD) is that the U.S. military may be called on to respond to mass migration caused by an epidemic or pandemic. This possibility combines trends and shocks in security, international relations, disease, and demography.

A caveat is that a different kind of shock would be produced if a "universal immunity or decontaminant" based in new biotechnology were to be found and widely utilized, which would lower the damage caused by the breakout of any particular infectious disease.

IMPLICATIONS

As judged by attendees at the September 2007 Trends and Shocks workshop, pandemic disease (naturally occurring or manmade) is a huge concern, across all topic areas and caveats/considerations. It was voted one of the most important shocks, whether judged by overall impact or general likelihood. To put the ranking in perspective, its closest contenders were scenarios such as a global economic collapse, loss of control of the global commons, and the use of nuclear weapons in conflict. Overall, pandemic disease was rated the second most important of all shocks considered, placing after nuclear/radiological terrorism. Pandemic disease had twice the score of such shock items as disruption of the U.S. oil supply or a U.S.-Iran crisis. Furthermore, when judged whether it was likely to happen relatively soon, pandemic disease also was ranked high among all potential shocks.

Even more significant are potential interactions of a pandemic disease with other highly ranked shocks. Just below it on the overall list is "during a pandemic, limited/no prophylaxis/therapeutics available." Slightly further down the list but still highly ranked is "mass casualty event overwhelms a medical system's surge capacity." The possibility of "genetically modified/synthetic organisms used in an act of terrorism" was also highly ranked. (The topic of "biohacking" is explored further later in this chapter.) The cumulative effect of these possibilities, whether natural or manmade, is that a pandemic will not only have direct health effects but is also likely to have second-order effects on the health care system more broadly—doctors and other health sector workers will be ill or for other reasons will not report for work, medical countermeasures will run out, or people will not know where they are. This in turn will result in even more disease spread.

Finally, interactions may occur due to effects of climate change (which could affect disease transmission or various aspects of the biology of animals, such as the timing of migrations); various national security problems including a clash with China over Taiwan or the Chinese leadership taking a hard line in foreign policy and national defense; and molecular manufacturing of fundamentally new military technology (which could include entirely novel biological weapons, such as a "nanobot" that carries the flu virus directly into the lungs). All of these are "modestly ranked" shocks by impact and likelihood.

Decentralized Biohacker Networks

TRENDS

Information technology (IT) as a field has grown over the last 15 years from consisting of the presence or integration of computers into mission requirements to revolutionizing how missions are performed. IT includes computers, communications, digital control systems, and information storage and retrieval. Command, control, communications, computers, intelligence, surveillance, and reconnaissance (C⁴ISR) is part of military IT, and the U.S. military is the world leader in this area, with U.S. companies dominating in the private sector.

While better IT promotes free movement of knowledge, it also creates vulnerabilities that aid the enemy, especially in asymmetric confrontations. Increasing U.S. dependence on IT also creates novel weaknesses that can be exploited in both primitive ways (such as bombing communications systems) and sophisticated ways (such as computer hacking). As Greg Rattray indicates in chapter 8 of this volume, the wonderful commercial developments in IT—including e-commerce, e-banking, and electronic shopping and inventory—also have lowered barriers for malicious activity by terrorists and criminals. These parties can use the same tools for recruitment, marketing, psychological operations, and fundraising.

Vast improvements in global communications technology in the last decade have contributed to the growth of decentralized threats to U.S. national security. While nation-states are still potential enemies in a traditional form, new foes have arisen, and their threats are mainly diffuse and unconventional. This trend is likely to continue.

Three general categories of emerging decentralized challenges to the United States are global terrorism, organized crime, and customized weapons proliferation. To some extent, these have been a problem for a long time. What is changing is not their names but rather their essence. The recent competition along ideological lines versus those of nation-state borders, in combination with increasingly accessible and sophisticated communications and networking, has resulted in a previously unobtainable level of decentralized organizational structure. We now see this organizational feature in such seemingly different threats as al Qaeda, cyberwarfare, and biohacking.

A useful biological metaphor—the starfish and the spider—describes two broad categories of organizational structure seen among threats to national security.[10] Hierarchical spider organizations, such as militaries and corporations, have a central command and control (head) and dependent parts (legs). It is easy to devise a strategy for attacking and destroying even a strong spider organization; survival is futile without a head.

Starfish organizations, on the other hand, have little central command and control. They typically have an inspirational leader—a catalyst—and a decentralized, hyper-mutable, and amorphous organizational structure. When a leg is cut off a starfish, the base will regenerate the limb, which can grow into a new starfish. The same holds true for starfish organizations, such as al Qaeda. Overall strategy is laid out by an inspirational catalyst, but operations and tactics are largely left to a network of modest-sized, sporadically networked groups. With such a diffuse and fluid structure, it is difficult for outsiders to gather accurate intelligence on individual group size and location, and on intergroup relationships.

The starfish metaphor applies to other national security threats besides al Qaeda. A recent "cyber-riot" effectively shut down the networked computer systems of North Atlantic Treaty Organization member Estonia—the most networked country on Earth—with targets that included government communications, large banks, and international media. The riot was caused not by an attacking nation-state, but by a coordinated but decentralized network of Russian computer hackers with an axe to grind and a good deal of sophisticated talent. Identifying distributed cyber attackers is difficult at best, and defeating them using strictly military forces is impossible.

A more futuristic but still reasonable threat concerns synthetic biology—building things partly or completely from biological parts—and "biohacking." Analogous to the first computer hackers of the 1980s, the hackers of the future will be able to tap into increasingly available biological information and tools to create novel organisms.

Three trends in the life sciences make this threat possible: predictive biology (information management, computational modeling, advanced analyses, data mining); systems biology (modeling complex systems, including whole organisms, *in silico*); and synthetic biology (creating artificial molecules, organisms, or systems). These trends may result in personalized medicine—for example, personal risk profiles, noninvasive testing, biomarker disease indicators, and advanced drug delivery. Combined, these three trends can lead to medical benefits, but also to sophisticated and dangerous drugs.

Currently, with minimal effort and cost, a curious and intelligent individual can acquire used biological laboratory equipment (on the online auction site eBay), whole-genome organism sequences in free government databases (like the National Center for Biotechnology Information Web site administered by the National Institutes of Health), and biology toolkits that enable the user to combine simple parts in a fashion akin to building with Legos (such as the BioBricks curated at the Massachusetts Institute of Technology). As with computer hacking, Web sites and discussion groups, such as DNAHack.com and *Biotech Hobbyist*, already have sprouted where common interests and goals are discussed and information will be shared across a diffuse, leaderless starfish network.

In the not-so-distant future, novel organisms will be created by youthful amateurs. Where computing led, biotechnology may follow with both beneficial and destructive novel agents generated in home workshops.

SHOCKS

Benign advances in science and globalization will empower a huge range of actors to create and employ biological weapons (BWs). Additionally, new abilities to biohack will overturn the conventional notion about weapons of mass destruction of "intent drives capability" (for example, our nation needs biological weapons, let's make some), resulting in an atmosphere in which "capability drives intent." Actors may initially carry out bioresearch simply because they can do so with no harmful intent—in other words, out of pure curiosity. Later, the results of such research may drive intent—what we might call "curiosity killed the enemy."[11]

As medical researchers continue to describe key molecular circuits for every bodily function, terrorists may use freely available information for evil. For example, research on brain function may allow an individual to develop an agent that can cause amnesia, violence, or depression. Such an agent obviously would be extremely dangerous to warfighters and civilians alike. The key dual-use challenge of this research is that the materials will be widely available and have many conceivable purposes; malicious research could be conducted in legitimate laboratories; and tools for combating the effects of the agents will most likely be unavailable.

In sum, novel, synthetic biological organisms may be utilized as synthetic biological weapons (SBWs). It is important to note that synthetic biology and biohacking are about more than merely making known diseases like anthrax, flu, TB, or plague more dangerous; they are about creating entirely new forms of biological threats. In chapter 2 of this book, Michael Moodie uses the term *advanced biological agents* to describe these threats and distinguish them from, say, modified anthrax, which would be termed a *genetically modified traditional agent.* Advanced "designer" SBW, such as binary weapons that only work when two independently safe parts are combined, or "stealth" BW, which lie dormant until triggered, are particularly worrisome for obvious reasons.

While the shock of garage-crafted SBWs is unlikely today, it could occur in the next 10–15 years, not only in American suburbs, but also in crude facilities in the "disorderly spaces" around the globe that Michael Moodie describes.

The argument has been made that terrorist groups might be unable to exploit biological technology for a host of reasons, including an inability to manipulate biological material properly to make advanced synthetic organisms. However, even a modestly advanced biological agent would be adequate to meet a group's goals and may be very destructive.

Copycat variations on the garage SBW shock are exceptions to this argument as well. With both computer hacking and biohacking, the goals of most people involved might be completely innocent. Perhaps more likely than terrorists or a transnational criminal organization conducting biotechnology research, however, is a potential shock where a network of benign overseas biohackers is infiltrated by terrorists or criminals who wish to steal and use inventions against the United States or its allies. They could do this either by spying on the group from a distance (for example, reading their email correspondence) or by physically joining it undercover.

A different shock would occur if a decentralized group of biohackers intersected with an attractive, violence-promoting ideology. For example, U.S.-based biohackers may in general be strong advocates of research and therefore have a natural tendency to disagree with social conservatives who, on religious grounds, do not support advanced research on stem cells and similar advancements. Rather than terrorists becoming geneticists, might geneticists become terrorists? If they feel strongly enough about an issue, some may feel compelled to act, targeting groups opposed to the scientific research they fervently believe in. These smart, capable, and financially secure people have deadly weapons at their disposal and the know-how to craft additional sophisticated threats.

The inventions of these home-based biohackers are not limited to organisms that target humans; an increasing amount of research is being done on anti-materiel organisms. Such biotechnology is potentially dual-use with both benign civilian applications (bacteria that eat oil from tanker spills) and offensive military uses (bacteria that eat tanks or airplanes).

The applications of this kind of technology are innumerable. Possible targets include petroleum products, explosives, plastics, adhesives, and metals.

According to retired Army colonel John Alexander, "We came to understand that there was almost nothing in the world that some organism will not consume."[12] Peter Katona points out that agroterrorism and natural agricultural disruption should be considered a potential shock because the general centralization of food resources (grain silos, chicken coops, and so forth) can make them a tempting target. Biological threats in this arena include mad cow disease and foot and mouth disease.

The most innocent researcher developing genetically modified bacteria to consume human waste can have the technology co-opted by other forces that are threats to national security. The technology does not change—only the intent of the user.

The threat can be made more complicated. Besides biological material being relatively easy to obtain—from nature, by purchase, or via laboratory theft—it can also be rendered time-delayed relatively easily. Freeze-drying or another stabilizing treatment could allow a biothreat to be planted and then not used for months or years (one of the "stealth" threats mentioned earlier). It would be very difficult to identify the perpetrator.

A more far-flung shock could result from a synthetic organism lying effectively dormant that could over time colonize an ecosystem, competing with naturally occurring organisms for food resources. Such an organism could have (possibly unintended) consequences for the local environment (animals, soil, vegetation) and also would be difficult to eradicate, even if discovered and understood. This shock could occur because of deliberate action, but perhaps more likely because of inadequate control by amateur experimenters (there are analogies with computer codes meandering their way through cyberspace).

Michael Moodie explains that any kind of biological threat might be used not merely for an "incident" but for a "campaign" of multiple interconnected incidents.[13] Here, the additional shock is that the system is largely poised to respond to a single mass incident. Imagine if the 2001 anthrax attacks had been followed by similar events in state capitals up and down the U.S. east coast. Many people deployed to Washington would have been unavailable to respond in their home states.

IMPLICATIONS

Attendees at the September 2007 Trends and Shocks workshop ranked a "genetically modified/synthetic organism used in an act of terrorism" 10th in terms of impact and 13th as to likelihood. Genetically modified organisms are a serious concern. Of even greater concern is that unlike nuclear materials, which individuals have few reasons to possess or work with, there are many legitimate reasons for using biological material and even conducting biotechnological experiments. Moreover, it is nearly impossible to distinguish between biotechnology laboratory equipment, orders placed at supply companies, or literature searches in databases being used for "good" or "bad" purposes, and biotechnology laboratories are easily hidden from imagery intelligence assets like satellites. Finally, SBWs can be expected to circumvent conventional biodefenses like sensors and vaccines, which may be rendered less effective or completely useless.

An incident utilizing SBWs would likely intersect with other highly ranked shocks. First, such an attack could cause a large epidemic or worldwide pandemic. Numerous secondary effects, including economic disruption, travel disruption, and social disorder, are possible. Second, whether localized or more widespread, an SBW attack is likely to overwhelm the already at-capacity health care system in the area of attack. Finally, SBWs could intersect with advances in nanotechnology (as discussed by Neil Jacobstein in chapter 7). One of Jacobstein's modestly ranked shocks is the "molecular manufacturing of a fundamentally new military technology." But there is no reason to assume that only the formal military apparatus could invent such a technology with military applications, and there is no reason to believe that biohackers would necessarily limit themselves to biology.

In a worst-case scenario, traditional engineering is used for a container and delivery system, biotechnology is used to engineer an infectious threat, and nanotechnology is used to facilitate delivery of the threat. This project would most likely be accomplished by a small team—a technology cell.

There are also intersecting shocks that involve more steps or assumptions. Peter Katona points out that a cyberattack on the power grid would have a drastic effect on medical services. If the attack were combined with an infectious SBW attack targeting humans, the resulting chaos and positive feedback would be devastating—sick people would overwhelm medical services, medicine would be inhibited by powerless machines, power would not be restored because utilities employees were sick, and so on.

A second possibility pointed out by Katona, possibly combined with an ideological struggle, is that of a direct attack on the medical establishment itself—hospitals, clinics, doctors, nurses, or technicians, for example. This is not as far-fetched as it sounds, considering that U.S. doctors have been widely targeted during violent abortion protests. Taking the possibility a step further, it is not hard to conceive of an infectious SBW spreading through a hospital. Typically, approximately 100,000 people die every year in the United States from an infection caught while under hospital care.

In a variation, a widely advertised conference of medical specialists in a major convention city could be targeted. There, a "traditional" attack like a bomb could kill many of the leading infectious disease specialists in the country (or world) and be followed by an infectious SBW attack, simultaneously overwhelming the public health system and robbing the government of expert advisors. The opposite is also possible: in the aftermath of a novel biological attack, a campaign of traditional attacks occurs, which we are unable to respond to after dedicating media, health care, and military resources to the novel attack.

To end on a somewhat positive note with regard to biotechnology interacting with potential cyberspace shocks, Greg Rattray posits that ubiquitous, easy-to-use Internet security may emerge that would result in more user transparency, easily characterized malicious activity, and better information control. Reducing the availability of cyberspace as a terrorist/criminal haven might decrease the likelihood of terrorist/criminal infiltration of a biohacker network. (However, this would not affect the shock of geneticists becoming terrorists.)

Ethics of Military Transhumanism

TRENDS

The term *biotechnology* encompasses medical technology, pharmacology, molecular biology, and the genetic sciences. Robotics and the man-machine interface include programmed, remote, and direct human control of machines, human-machine intelligence, and hybrid systems. In biotechnology, the U.S. private sector leads the global markets, and in robotics and the man-machine interface, DOD is far ahead of all others—which leads to unique advantages and vulnerabilities. There are many implications of such technology. The most serious, for our purposes, is the potential for dual use—for example, medical research used for nefarious ends. Because of the so-called light footprint of biotechnology, it is very difficult to assess the intentions of researchers from the outside.

There are many defense implications besides threats. Among them, human performance gains could have dramatic impacts on operations of various kinds. A two- to tenfold performance enhancement involving sleep, cognitive performance, and similar human attributes would be a huge shock to warfare. An interesting trend, or set of trends, would be that social/cultural norms in the United States (but perhaps not other nations) may limit some applications of basic research and technology development.

Jonathan Moreno, a professor at the University of Virginia and the author of *Mind Wars: Brain Research and National Defense*, has observed that "the human being is the oldest instrument of warfare and also its weakest link." Technological advances to strengthen this weak link are rapidly accelerating on many fronts. The so-called Nano-Bio-Info-Cogno-Socio interface is increasingly allowing the modification of human beings. Initially, this was seen as a means to repair "problems," such as tumors or genes at the root of disease. Now, however, it is also seen as a conduit to "improving" humans, whether in a military or civilian context.

A good deal of research is being done regarding the "post-human future."[14] Designer drugs made in biotechnology laboratories can interact with the brain in a genotype-specific manner to improve memory or decrease the effects of sleep deprivation. Research on the brain-machine interface is leading to improvements in such human senses as hearing and vision. Exoskeleton suits allow soldiers to carry 200 pounds and bound large distances with little effort. Custom replacement organs will soon be generated from one's own stem cells. New prosthetics containing microprocessors are being used to repair warfighters wounded in Iraq.

The trend toward transhumanism[15] is likely to continue, if only because of general advances in cross-disciplinary technologies that intersect with the study of human anatomy and physiology. For example, in a recent article in *Science*, 10 prominent academic and government researchers called for a transdisciplinary "Decade of the Mind" initiative. The proposed research would "reach across disparate fields such as cognitive science, medicine, neuroscience, psychology, mathematics, engineering, and computer science."[16]

Not everyone is a fan of endowing humans with novel abilities. In a sense, the futuristic advances described above are no different from accepted alterations to humans, such as repairing a broken hip with metal rods and pins, using a hearing aid, or taking aspirin for a headache. But this comparison is similar to that between genetic modification of crops and livestock and the breeding selection traditionally practiced in agriculture. At least in the near future, because of the normal uncertainty associated with new technologies, and presumably high costs, people will generally take advantage of standard mechanisms of human alteration while being wary of the new Nano-Bio-Info-Cogno-Socio interface.

This latter attitude is summarized in a 2003 study by the President's Council on Bioethics, chaired by Dr. Leon Kass.[17] The council's members asked not only the obvious question—"What is biotechnology for?"—but also the less obvious one—

"What *should* biotechnology be for?" Briefly, the group concluded that society should try to draw a line between human therapy and human enhancement. (They also admitted that this is a difficult line to draw.)

SHOCKS

Despite obvious advantages of human performance enhancement to U.S. warfighters, future leaders and authorities, using ethical, moral, and legal arguments, may limit the ability of U.S. Government, academic, and/or private researchers to work on research that might be classified as transhumanism. It is also possible that, while basic research in these areas continues, companies will be prohibited from developing downstream technologies that fundamentally alter human abilities. Citing other arguments on this side of the debate, Francis Fukuyama contends that the post-human future comes with a "frightful moral cost" whose first victim may be equality.[18]

There is a legitimate concern over the ethical and legal implications of technology that blurs the line between living and nonliving and thus approaches the "cyborg" of science fiction. This anti-transhumanism viewpoint may be logically defensible, but other nations will not necessarily follow this ethical, moral, or legal trajectory. They may in fact see this area of scientific and technological progress as something they can harness to improve their military strength, to the disadvantage of the U.S. Armed Forces.

At this juncture, many delicate ethical issues need to be carefully considered. Advances in biotechnology can contribute greatly to combat success, while simultaneously complicating the field of bioethics. Here, at the intersection of science, technology, culture, and identity, we offer three of many possible examples of ethical complications arising from advances in biotechnology affecting the military.

First, new biotechnology has altered the application of an answer to a classic military ethical question: how many soldiers should put their lives at risk to try to rescue a fallen comrade? New biosensors may, for example, monitor vital signs, such as the heartbeat, of a wounded soldier. If a military physician observes that a soldier's pulse is falling due to blood loss, this will enhance the urgency to attempt a rescue. This raises the question of whether a rapidly falling heartbeat should be a criterion for a rescue attempt being made (or not made), and if it should, how much weight it should be given.

Second, current biotechnology, in combination with other technologies, could also better determine exact locations of fallen friendly and enemy soldiers, allowing more precise calculations of rescuers' likely risks. During the heat of battle, commanders can best decide what risks to both fallen soldiers and rescuers are warranted. Hence, a major ethical implication of new biotechnology with regard to the ethics of rescuing fallen soldiers is that there will be a greater need for commanders and physicians to find better ways to work together.[19] Another point of view on this ethical dilemma is that, independent of preserving the maximum number of soldiers' lives, trying to save the wounded also respects the dignity of soldiers.

Third, genetic screening is a complicated issue both in and out of the military. Performing such screening on soldiers and excluding some from combat or other missions on the basis of the results would violate soldiers' privacy and violate equity by requiring other soldiers to take disproportionate risks.[20] Both concerns also would be more ethically problematic if more "genetically vulnerable" soldiers have a greater likelihood of having combat fatigue.

Numerous other instances can be cited in which genetic screening could be used to reduce servicepersons' risks. For example, soldiers with genes that make them more vulnerable to heat could be withheld from deployment to deserts or tropical areas. Key considerations in determining whether this kind of screening is justifiable are the magnitude and probability of harm to soldiers genetically at risk. Unless this harm is most substantial and/or likely, the inherent violation of soldiers' privacy and dignity would tend to preclude such screening.

Biotechnology may alter traditional cultural and societal roles within and outside the military. The use of material from spider webs, particularly from the black widow, holds the potential for more effective but much lighter body armor.[21] In the past, heavy armor offered additional protection but slowed soldiers down. A significant effect of the new armor could be to open additional combat opportunities for women. This would raise anew the question of the extent to which women can and should serve in the same combat roles as men.

By way of a shock, countries that are potential enemies of the United States with even fledgling programs in biotechnology, computer science, or nanotechnology may decide that pursuing transhumanism as a military objective, within the framework of a U.S. (Government and/or public) aversion to it, would provide an asymmetric advantage in a cold or hot war.

One factor limiting transhuman research is its cost in both financial and human capital. Not only are the experiments expensive, but the finest researchers and facilities in the world are necessary for significant progress. Taking only medicine as an example, a number of countries that are infrequently allied with the United States are doing a good deal of research that could be applied to transhumanism.[22] Cuba hosts bioresearchers from more than 75 countries. China created the first licensed gene therapy. Indian patent awards have increased about tenfold over the last decade. Israel spends more than twice the U.S. percentage of GDP on research and development (R&D). China now graduates more science and engineering PhDs per year than the United States.

Assuming arguments against transhumanism are legitimate—even for warfighters—and also assuming there is a reasonable chance a potential enemy will pursue this technology, are there arguments to be made for conducting this R&D, at least within the defense community?

Consider thermonuclear weapons and intercontinental ballistic missiles. These are surely terrifying inventions that can cause immense amounts of death and destruction. Ethical, moral, and legal arguments have been made against their development and use. Nevertheless, the United States created many of them under the philosophy of mutual assured destruction.

We return to the question of, "What *should* biotechnology be used for?" It is true that arguments can be made for applying biotechnology only to curing disease and other ailments and against pursuing research for human enhancement and transhumanism. However, it may be more morally costly *not* to pursue human enhancement because of the risk that another nation will do so and therefore threaten U.S. national security.

IMPLICATIONS

As judged by participants at the September 2007 Trends and Shocks workshop, this shock did not score in the top 25 by either impact or likelihood. However, a recent study commissioned by the DOD Office of Force Transformation sees a major policy issue in human enhancement of warfighters intertwined with significant legal and ethical concerns.

We also note that numerous shocks related to developments in nano-technology scored very high. There is a clear trend toward the development of novel technologies at the interface of nanotechnology and biotechnology. How is this related to transhumanism shocks?

The highly rated shock of "molecular manufacturing of fundamental new military technology" might include unique nano-tools that can contribute to tremendous human enhancements. Whether alone or in combination with medical resources, such as pharmaceuticals, they might, for example, improve memory capacity, help heal wounds, or deliver more oxygen to muscles. These nano-biotechnology tools for human enhancement will most likely act internally and be a combination of living and nonliving material.

Petro to Agro: The Coming Age of Biology

TRENDS

Biotechnology will have applications far beyond medicine, pharmacology, and genetics. A broad-ranging, long-term view of biotechnology's influence on the future U.S. military includes intersections with materials science and manufacturing, trending away from a petroleum-based society and toward a bio-based economy. This, in turn, likely will affect how, where, and why our military fights.

For much of the last century, and particularly since the end of World War II, petroleum has been the primary raw material for the world's economy. The U.S. consumption of petroleum is typical of worldwide trends. The bulk of it consumed in the United States meets energy demands, with approximately 90 percent going to gasoline, diesel, and other fuels. Since 1949, however, the industrial consumption for nonfuel uses in the United States has increased nearly sevenfold. The chemical industry, for example, relies on petroleum for more than 90 percent of its raw materials in the manufacture of products ranging from plastics, refrigerants, and fertilizers to detergents, explosives, and medicines.

As the 20th century was ending, Michael Bowlin, then-president of the American Petroleum Institute and then-chief executive officer of ARCO, told industry executives the world was entering "the last days of the Age of Oil." Estimates of the remaining life of oil reserves vary widely, but many experts agree that worldwide production will peak between 2010 and 2020. Even if there is agreement with those who posit that the petroleum supply may be "renewable," environmental pressures and economic incentives will remain to drive us to newer technologies, which will no doubt replace petroleum.

Prominent among replacements are products developed from biological sources. Using biomaterials obtained from plants and animals as raw materials for fuels and industrial and consumer products is not new. Before the rise of cheap oil, agriculture was the dominant source of raw materials. Indeed, when the U.S. Department of Agriculture was established in 1862, its motto proclaimed, "Agriculture is the Foundation of Manufacture and Commerce." As recently as 2002, about 8 percent of the U.S. corn crop went to industrial uses rather than directly to meeting food or feed requirements.[23] Indeed, the agricultural industry offers the most cost-effective way to manufacture large volumes of biologically based raw materials. In its vision statement for the 21st century, the National

Agricultural Biotechnology Council—a consortium of leading agricultural research universities in the United States—forecasts agriculture to be the source of not only our food, feed, and fiber but also our energy, materials, and chemicals.[24]

As the bio-based economy matures and issues of production and processing are improved, the demand for new products will grow. New products will require new raw materials. In a bio-based economy, the basic raw material will be genes, and novel genes will be the source of novel products. Thus, as we shift from an economy based on geology to one based on biology, the basic unit of commerce will shift from the hydrocarbon molecule to the gene. Just as we currently demand assured access to sources of hydrocarbons, in the near future we will demand assured access to a broad-based, diverse supply of genes. This demand has the potential to cause international conflict in the diplomatic, economic, and military arenas.

As with any resource vital to our economy, the location of large supplies of genes will be important to our national security. Petroleum is found worldwide in nearly all climate regions; genes are concentrated in the equatorial regions for physical and biological reasons that give rise to what biologists call the "latitudinal density gradient." A consequence of this is that equatorial regions may become more important to our nation's energy security.

The primary issue in the development of the bio-based economy is the cost of processing the feedstock into materials that can be further refined and used in manufacturing. The cost of the conversion process—turning biomass into energy, materials, and chemicals—is, roughly speaking, not competitive with the costs of using petroleum. Even with the recent rise in oil prices, petroleum-based products are generally less expensive than bio-based products. One difficulty in making cost comparisons is that the production costs are based on existing manufacturing processes designed for petroleum feedstocks. When processing biomass, some of the end products can be made through direct physical or chemical processing; others can be produced indirectly through fermentation (using microbial agents) or by enzymatic processing. Existing facilities typically do not take advantage of advanced microbial agents specifically designed for processing biomass.

"Biorefineries" are needed.[25] Like an oil refinery, a biorefinery would take carbon and hydrogen and produce desired products. The biorefinery's economic advantage will emerge from its dual capability. Along with the intended end products, foods, feeds, and biochemicals could be produced. Biorefinery prototypes already exist in our industrial base in the form of corn wet mills, soybean processing facilities, and pulp and paper mills. While the prototypes of full-scale biorefineries are mostly in the planning stage at the moment, two facilities designed for specific bio-based end products have been operating in the United States for the past few years.

One of the largest biomaterial facilities in the world is operated in Tennessee under a joint venture between DuPont and Tate & Lyle BioProducts. In mid-2001, DuPont announced that it had successfully manufactured a key ingredient in a new clothing polymer (now known as Sorona™) from corn sugars instead of petrochemicals—previously the only source for the polymer.

For the last 4 years, NatureWorks, LLC, a wholly owned subsidiary of Cargill, has been manufacturing a biodegradable plastic made from sugars derived from cornstarch. The manufacturing takes place in a $300 million plant in Nebraska specifically built for the production of bio-based products. The plastic, polylactide acid (PLA), already has been incorporated into products for large food sellers, including Coca-Cola and McDonald's. PLA can be incorporated into a number of products that replace current petroleum-based polyesters, polyolefins, polystyrenes, and cellulosics—for example, fibers, nonwovens, films, extruded and thermoformed containers, and emulsion coatings.

NatureWorks also manufactures Ingeo™, the world's first artificial fiber completely constructed from renewable resources. The fiber is stain-resistant and is being used in items ranging from pillows to carpeting to padded outerwear. A most interesting application of Ingeo™ was revealed at the first European bioplastics conference in Brussels in November 2006: a biopolymer-based wedding dress created by a famous fashion designer and sponsored by a major European agricultural organization.[26]

An Internet search on the words *bio-based plastics* yields nearly a quarter of a million entries. Many new partnerships are being forged. Clearly, a trend toward a biobased economy is emerging.

SHOCKS

Biorefineries will revolutionize how business is done in the energy sector. Delivering feedstock to biorefineries is unlike delivering petroleum to current refineries, because the amount of energy contained in each molecule of petroleum is considerably higher than that found in the biomass that will supply the raw material for biorefineries. Thus, while we can economically transport petroleum to distant refineries, with biomass the economics of transport begin to fail after about 350 miles. Initially, with currently envisionable technology, biorefining will have to be done close to the source of the biomass.

Biorefining conducted near the sources of biomass will cause the construction of biorefineries in and near numerous rural areas, resulting in the creation of local jobs that could slow migration to urban areas. This gradually occurring shock will have numerous cultural, economic, and demographic consequences, not just in the United States, but around the world in places with significant bioresources. Local biorefineries will provide local products while meeting their own energy needs through new technology being developed at the intersection of a few fields of study that currently are mainly separate.

Energy security is a major concern of DOD that will be addressed to some degree by the bio-based economy of the future. Trends toward nanotechnology, robotics, and IT should make possible the manufacture of goods—including energy products—in a "distributed and configurable" way within the next 30 years. With regard to U.S. national security, whereas now large distribution centers and shipping lines are targets, an increasing number of smaller manufacturing and distribution centers will comprise a harder target overall.

In a bio-based world, international relations with gene-rich Ecuador will be more important than those with Saudi Arabia. At this early stage in the bio-based economy, it would be wise to consider what controversies could arise over another nation's genetic treasure and how best to secure access and provide compensation to the regional owners.

Conflict, hot or cold, could arise between the gene-rich, technology-poor countries along the equator and the gene-poor, technology-rich countries of the more developed world. Conflict could be caused by disputes over bioresources between governments, or between governments and large corporations, resulting from bioprospecting in gene-rich countries for resources to be used for drugs or other products. For example, a gene-rich nation might sign an exclusive treaty unfavorable to the interests of the United States with a large foreign nation or corporation, thereby cutting the United States off from a new class of renewable natural resources—genes.

IMPLICATIONS

As judged by participants at the Trends and Shocks workshop, the impact or likelihood of the gradually occurring proposed shock of an increasingly bio-based economy and dependence on genes as a renewable energy resource is not high. However, participants were limited to considering the next 15 years.

A bio-based economy is a likely trend, but a long-term one. A trend toward a bio-based economy would create its own shocks and interact with other shocks, some of which were highly ranked in the workshop. For example, the transition to a bio-based economy could be accelerated by a disruption of traditional oil supplies, which would accelerate research on materials made from renewable resources. Three such shocks that were highly ranked by impact, likelihood, or both were "global economic collapse," "new nuclear power," and "United States-Iranian crisis." Finally, the shock termed "nation's need for critical resources is outpaced by its ability to procure it" also might accelerate research on and the use of renewable natural resources.

On the other hand, if a comprehensive settlement in the Middle East—a shock ranked high by workshop participants—were to result in a reliable supply of petroleum, it might act as a disincentive to research into renewable energy, postponing U.S. energy independence.

Another highly ranked shock, "effects from global warming," could slow the development of a bio-based economy. Global climate change could result in severe effects to the natural environmental sources of a bio-based economy and therefore negatively impact relevant bioresearch. It is also possible due to the melting of snow and ice that new fossil fuel resources will be discovered (for example, in Siberia), which in turn could also delay a bio-based economy.

Finally, because of the importance of genes to the emerging bio-based economy, the United States should strive for good strategic intelligence on the gene-rich, equatorial nations of Latin America and cultivate close political and economic relationships with them.

Part II: Regional Trends

10

Culture and Identity in the Middle East: How They Influence Governance

Dale F. Eickelman

> One cannot make culture with politics,
> but perhaps one can make politics with culture.
> —THEODOR HEUSS (1884–1963)

AN UNDERSTANDING of the importance of *cultural* ideas of authority, loyalty, trust, and responsibility is not recent, nor is it confined to scholars alone. A month following the U.S.-led invasion of Iraq in March 2003, a mid-ranking Army officer who had been working on tribal and local leadership issues prior to the invasion convened an assembly of Iraq's major tribal and religious leaders, both Sunni and Shia, with the intent of having them meet "Shaykh" Paul Bremer, as he was known to influential Iraqis at the time. The meeting never took place. A subordinate of Bremer's, described as "a 26-year-old recent M.A. graduate in international studies from [a Washington-area university]," told the officer who had organized the meeting that such "feudal" leaders were just the sort that the United States intended to disenfranchise.[1] A later attempt to organize a second meeting failed, having occurred after the disbanding of the Iraqi army in spite of pre-invasion assurances that officers who did not resist the U.S.-led invasion would be "taken care of." Such actions contributed to the erosion of trust in anything that the Coalition Provisional Authority (CPA) subsequently said.

This massive failure was not the fault of individuals alone. The main reason for it is the culture-deficient concept of "modernization" that took hold among many social scientists and policymakers from the mid-20th century until the recent past. The example above illustrates that incorporating thinking about culture and identity, often considered the "soft" side of political and military action, is as important as the "hard" issues of developments in nanotechnology, nuclear weapons, climate change, epidemics, and other more conventional areas of focus.

Underestimating the need to comprehend how religious, tribal, and ethnic identities shape and constrain understandings of authority—and how U.S. actions in the Middle East and elsewhere have inadvertently exacerbated ethnic and sectarian conflict—is already sharply containing the U.S. ability to act effectively on the world stage. Far from receding in significance, as predicted by most versions of modernization theory in the mid-20th century, sectarian, ethnic, tribal, and religious identities are re-emerging as causes for which people die. In the Horn of Africa, the lands bordering the Sahara, Iraq, Afghanistan, Pakistan, Lebanon, Palestine, or the Balkans, such divisions already profoundly affect areas of the world of concern to U.S. interests. Between economic crises, population movements caused by inadequate water and other resources, and other shocks, such conflicts are likely to increase in the next 5–10 years. Globalization, once thought to lead to a homogenization of culture and politics, instead is leading to a strengthening of culturally and religiously based "ties that bind." It is likely to increase the ability of ethnic and sectarian groups to act locally and globally. In the case of the U.S.-led invasion of Iraq in 2003, the postinvasion disarray provided a shock that dismantled the remains of the Iraqi state and forced Iraqis to rely on ties of sect, tribe, clan, ethnic group, and local community.

Developing an ability to recognize the changing shapes of organizational effectiveness and loyalties of religious groups, tribes, ethnicities, sects, and religious groups is a skill that the Department of Defense (DOD) needs to operate in Iraq, Afghanistan, and many other parts of the world. Language and cultural training cannot be inculcated overnight. Indeed, most of the recommendations of the DOD-financed Lambert Report of 1984 remain unimplemented. These recommendations included how to make the parallel systems of language instruction in government agencies and on campuses more mutually supportive, especially in raising the level of skills in the less commonly taught languages, as well as improving on-campus and government agency area competencies. Especially needed was support for long-term research and training not constrained by short-term policy shifts, and efforts to retain the high-level complementary competencies offered by universities and some government agencies.[2] In 1996, Lambert led a follow-up study that proposed the creation of a National Foundation for International Studies.[3]

Localities and Loyalties in the Age of Globalization

Technological advances mean that small groups such as al Qaeda can regularly field professional-quality audio and video releases that reach large, dispersed audiences as they are inevitably picked up by a multitude of media and "viral" communications (including word of mouth among the like-minded).

New communications technologies enable small ethnic and sectarian groups and others with similar views to act effectively from widely dispersed locations in support of a homeland or religious cause. Negative events affecting Yerevan or Nagorno-Karabakh are instantly relayed to organized groups in California, and small ethnic groups in northern Mali (and Malian refugees in Libya) rapidly can share their plight with their compatriots and supporters in Europe and elsewhere. Similarly, photographs taken with a humble cell phone camera by a guard at Abu Ghraib can be flashed around the globe and incorporated into a variety of narratives that devastatingly undermine official stories of why the United States is engaged in Iraq, render ineffective the U.S. Government public diplomacy apparatus, erode our allies' confidence in U.S. military and diplomatic capabilities, and serve to justify direct attacks against U.S. facilities and those of governments that support U.S. goals and interests.

The Dynamics of Culture and Identity

States, even failed states and those unable to control their own territory, continue to be major international actors, but the United States is now operating in an international landscape in which tribes, ethnicities, and affinities based on linguistic, religious, and sectarian identities cannot be ignored. This situation is not a new one. Such identities have been there all along, but now they are more evident. Sub-state groups based on these identities, whether in Pakistan or Chechnya, increasingly act not just in localized and remote localities but also on a regional and global scale.

The notions of tribal, sectarian, and ethnic identities—once thought of as primordial, incapable of flexibility and renewal, and doomed to extinction—are an integral part of modernity and the modern world and can be a force for good if properly understood, or at least can be held in check if recognized for what they are. As parts of the world face the collapse of effective state governance, the breakdown of order, climate change, major demographic shifts, water shortages, threats of disease, or other threats that can come from small groups, an increasing number of people will rely on more familiar bonds of trust. Put quite simply, those bonds work—and to date, they have been poorly understood by the world powers that sometimes intervene in regions where effective action requires understanding how these loyalties work. These bonds can encompass the highly educated (such as the U.S.-trained Radovan Karadzic of Serbia) as well as the downtrodden and oppressed. Identities of tribe and sect are not fixed; they can incorporate new elements and be integral parts of the "modern," globalized world.

When states and invading forces become unpredictable, tribes, extended families, ethnic groups, and other ties invisible to the wider world will take up the slack. Indeed, it can be argued that U.S. actions in Iraq since 2003 have inadvertently contributed to polarizing the Sunni-Shia sectarian divide—among other Iraqi fault lines—creating sharp schisms where, in the recent past, frontiers had been relatively benign, engendering a huge refugee problem in neighboring countries, and accelerating the exodus of educated and middle-class Iraqis, thus further destabilizing and forcefully rallying those left behind. Efforts to recognize how and why Iraqis place trust in sectarian and tribal leaders instead of a flawed and often destabilizing central government necessarily involve thinking of tribes, ethnicity, and sectarianism as having the potential to play positive roles in modern societies and not just negative ones.

The Modern Meaning of Culture

Culture refers generally to a set of implicit, widely shared assumptions about how things work in a society and how they ought to work—at least for one's group of reference. Shared cultural understandings—of trust, obligation, loyalty, family, faith, and hierarchy, for example—have no sharply drawn territorial, ethnic, or religious boundaries. They are contested and emerging concepts, so policies based on assumptions that shared cultural understandings of tribe, for instance, are "fixed" and static—a prevalent view in the early 20th century—are bound to fail. Such notions are largely implicit and shared, not explicitly articulated. In the politics of organizations, as in those of states, one ignores such cultural understandings, including those of religion and ethnicity, at the peril of effectiveness.

Understanding how culture influences politics and security requires making sense of not just the dynamics of other people's cultures and histories, but also prevalent U.S. and European understandings of drivers important to political thought and change. An article by Lisa Wedeen concerns only how ideas of culture have evolved in U.S. political science, but by analogy it indicates how rapidly subnational groups can take on a life of their own and assume prominence in state societies.[4] Effective action requires not just understanding others, but incorporating culture, and indeed historical knowledge, as an antidote to seemingly persuasive "one size fits all" ideas of governance and social cohesion.

Politics is not just who gets what, when, and where; it also concerns the struggle over people's imaginations.

The Return of Religion

Post–World War II modernization theory[5] mistakenly held that religion had become marginal to the modern world. Iran provides an example of how mistaken that theory was. Of all the Third World countries, Iran was a society that had undergone enormous modernization prior to 1978–1979. Nonetheless, the shah's greatest challenge emanated from the growing urban middle classes, those who had benefited the most from modernization. Revolution, not political stability, was the result. It was religious sentiment and leadership, not the secular technocrats, that gave coherence and force to the Iranian revolution.

Some Iranian scholars go ever further. Fariba Adelkhah[6] argues that the real Iranian revolution is taking place only now, with the coming of age of a new generation of Iranians who were not even born in 1978–1979. This new generation is creating and participating in an Iranian "religious public sphere" (*espace public confessionel*) driven from below and not by the state, in which politics and religion are subtly intertwined, and not always in ways anticipated by Iran's established religious leaders. Reaching this group requires a policy more subtle than seeking to undercut the existing regime.

Latin America offers another major contrary example to the conventional wisdom of modernization theory. In Peru and Guatemala, among other countries, new networks of trust, confidence, and organizational capacities arose with religious change in the 1980s, as groups of clergy inspired by liberation theology, including progressive Catholics in Peru and evangelicals in Guatemala, created a social capital in which "'stability' is created from below, not imposed from above."[7] These movements did more to bring an end to autocratic regimes than any external, top-down U.S. efforts. The United States provides another example of religious congregations, hierarchies, and special interests contributing significantly to ongoing debates over collective values. Likewise, one cannot explain Poland's powerful Solidarity movement without explaining the role of religion. All of these "revolutions from below" also suggest the limits to outside intervention by military force alone.

The Legacy of the "West versus the Rest"

It is easy to be critical of Samuel Huntington's "West versus the Rest" argument. His aim in the early 1990s was to produce "a simple map of the post–Cold War world,"[8] one that emphasized a coming "clash of civilizations." Nevertheless, Huntington spurred other political scientists as well as international relations theorists to reemphasize the role of culture and tradition in political and international relations.

Huntington's simple map and the equally dated "end of history" argument[9] notwithstanding, tradition is not a residual concept that can uniformly describe the premodern values of all civilizations and cultures. For the premodern era, as for today, it is difficult to see civilizations and cultures as sharply demarcated and closed.[10] Traditions are clusters of cultural concepts, shared understandings, and practices that make political and social life possible. Such pervasive cultural understandings play a crucial element in constituting what we now recognize as "multiple modernities," the notion that there can be trajectories of modernity distinct from those of the West, together with the important capacity of continual self-correction.[11] Multiple traditions coexist with and shape the experience of modernity. In this sense, ethnicity, caste, sectarianism, and clientelism can be as distinctly modern as—and compatible with—the idea of individual choice and personal responsibility.

A principal difficulty with Huntington's "West versus the Rest" formulation is that having reintroduced culture and religion to thinking about politics, it overstated their coherence and force, in addition to treating the Muslim world as a monolithic bloc. To use the language of political science, culture became an independent variable. The view of religion as a stark alternative—either an independent or a dependent variable—can be avoided by adopting an approach to understanding politics that goes beyond power relations and interests alone. Approaching these issues in a more effective way also requires an understanding of the shared, often implicit, ideas of what is right, just, or religiously ordained— ideas upon which individuals in a society or from different societies base cooperative relations. Such background understandings are common to adherents of religion, be it Islam, Christianity, or Hinduism. Evolving doctrinal considerations are only one factor among many, and often not the most important, in contributing to the creation of frameworks of practices and understandings, and adherents to religious traditions are far from monolithic in their use of these frameworks.

In addition to being a struggle over the control of population and resources, politics is equally a struggle over people's imaginations, a competition about the meanings of symbols. It encompasses the interpretation of symbols and the control of institutions, formal and informal, that produce and sustain them. This interpretation of symbols is played out against the backdrop of the implicit, taken-for-granted understandings against which the beliefs and practices in any given society are formulated. More broadly, politics can be conceived as cooperation in and contest over symbolic production and control of the institutions—formal and informal—that serve as the symbolic arbiters of society.[12]

Islam and Ethnicity

The Muslim-majority world remains feared by those who regard it as the last outpost of the antimodern, although the concept can be applied equally to sub-Saharan Africa, Southeast Asia, and regions of Latin America with significant indigenous populations. In all these cases, the growth of higher education, the increasing ease of travel, and the proliferation of media and means of communication are rapidly transforming the "ties that bind." The *hawala* system of transferring money and messages throughout the Middle East, including remote parts of Afghanistan, Iran, and Pakistan, may be regarded with suspicion by some, but its flexible combination of modern and traditional means of reliable communication sustains life in remote villages and enables migrants and refugees to support those left behind in a way that no central authority or international aid organization has managed to do on its own.[13]

Muslims say that commitment to Islam supplants ties of ethnicity, the ways in which individuals and groups characterize themselves on the basis of shared language, culture, descent, place of origin, and history. Yet from the first Muslim conquests in 7th-century Arabia, as Muslim armies spread forth from the Arabian Peninsula to peoples who neither spoke Arabic nor could claim Arab descent, issues of ethnicity and descent frequently surfaced in practice.

As elsewhere in the world, Muslim notions of ethnicity are cultural constructions. For this reason, it is difficult to find a specific counterpart in Middle Eastern and other languages for the English term *ethnicity*. Ethnicity is an observer's term, although those who assert ethnic ties often regard them as fixed and natural. Ethnicity is often thought to be a matter of birth, but exceptions are common. The social and political significance of ethnic and religious identities alters significantly according to historical and social contexts. For example, take the term *qawm* (people) in Afghanistan. Depending on context it can mean a tribe or a subdivision of one, a people sharing a common origin or region of residence, or more generally a shared religious and linguistic identity. Moreover, since the latter half of the 20th century, the experience of large-scale migration in search of wage labor—Pakistanis to Saudi Arabia, Turks and Kurds to western Germany, and North Africans to France—or as refugees—Afghans to Iran and Western

Europe and Bosnian Muslims to Austria and Germany—has had a major impact on changing the significance and political implications of ethnic identity.

In the Arabian Peninsula, claims to ethnic or tribal identity—the two notions are almost indistinguishable in countries such as Saudi Arabia, Oman, Yemen, and the Gulf states—are usually framed in genealogical terms as descending from one of two eponymous ancestors. "Northern" Arabs claim descent from an eponymous ancestor called Adnan; "southern" Arabs, including those who speak Semitic languages other than Arabic, claim Qahtan as their ancestor. The possibility for some groups of claiming either Adnan or Qahtan as eponymous ancestors allows for flexibility in making descent claims, although genealogies are considered fixed. Indeed, since the 1960s, groups such as the Sindhi-speaking Shi'i Liwatiya of coastal Oman also have claimed Arab descent, explaining their "temporary" loss of Arabic and tribal identity by centuries of residence on the Indian subcontinent. Ex-slaves (*khuddam*) attached to tribes and ruling families throughout the Arabian Peninsula, and other groups lacking tribal descent, have traditionally had an inferior social status, as shown by occupation and the lack of intermarriage with other groups. Modern economic conditions are rapidly eroding some of these distinctions. Visible African descent might suggest slave descent to some traditionalists on the Arabian Peninsula, but it also might imply descent from one of the ruling families in which slave concubines were common in earlier generations.

Contemporary Arab identity suggests how historically and contextually diverse ethnic claims can be. Many Arabs assert that they are a race, although for centuries populations have mixed and intermarried throughout the Arab world. Although divided politically, despite the first claims to Arab unity in the early 20th century, made as the Ottoman Empire weakened, Arabs are unified by language and culture. Nonetheless, many of the regional Arabic dialects are mutually unintelligible. For example, Arabs from Saudi Arabia and the Gulf states understand colloquial Moroccan Arabic only with difficulty. The spread of mass higher education throughout the region since the mid-20th century contributed to widening the appeal of Arab nationalism and pan-Arabism and, of course, facilitated communications among Arabs from different regions able to converse in a common "educated" Arabic modeled on classroom and the broadcast media. Still, major differences of dialect and situational identity remain. One is not just Muslim in the Middle East or elsewhere, but also Arab (and there are not only Christian and Muslim Arabs, but also Arabic-speaking Jews in Israel and North Africa), Berber, Nubian, Circassian, Hui, Malay, Sindhi, Sumatran, or Fulani.

Since ethnic and religious considerations are only two of several attributes shared by persons and groups in the Middle East, it is crucial to consider how such social distinctions figure in the overall context of social and personal identity and not to stop at a mosaic-like enumeration of ethnic group, sect, family origin, locality, and occupation. In North Africa, for example, the peoples of the region claim both Berber and Arab descent, and these claims to ethnic identity are based on language and cultural characteristics.

Arabic is the dominant language of North Africa, and Arab civilization is pervasive, but so is the rising tide of a distinct Berber identity not only in remote oases and mountain valleys, but also in urban areas. In Morocco, nearly half the population speaks one of the several Berber dialects, although most Moroccan Berbers, especially men, speak Arabic as a second language. Since the mid-1990s in Morocco, television news has been given in the major Berber dialects, as well as in Arabic and French, and since 2005 a unified Berber language based on spoken *tashilhit* has been used in schools in Berber-speaking regions and on state television. Faced with the civil war in neighboring Algeria and the specter of a Berber separatist movement in Algeria, by the mid-1990s Morocco's King Hassan II decided that accepting a Berber cultural movement would diminish the appeal of separatism.

In Morocco, the categorizations *Arab* and *Berber* are often situational. People stress different aspects of their identity depending on context. Identity as Arab or Berber is best thought of as a continuum rather than as a sharp distinction. Diverse patterns of occupation, residence, marriage, urban and rural origin, and other factors show that the ethnic distinctions of Arab and Berber in North Africa lack the all-pervasive typification that ethnicity takes in contexts elsewhere, including being Kurdish in northern Iraq or Muslim in Bosnia.

Assertion of an ethnic identity is often a political claim. In Afghanistan, opposition to the Soviet-dominated state that took power in 1978 and to the 1979 Soviet invasion came largely from tribally organized ethnic groups, for whom attachment to Islam served as a common denominator. In Pakistan, especially after the secession of Bangladesh in 1971, the country's ruling Punjabi elite viewed other ethnic groups with suspicion, including Sindhis, Pashtuns, Muhajirs (Muslim refugees who migrated after 1947 from what is now India), and Baluch. The Pakistani state emphasizes Islam as an identity more important than the common ethnic ties of its minority groups, including the Baluch, who from 1973 to 1977 fought for regional autonomy. The insurgency was unsuccessful, but contributed to a heightened Baluch national consciousness that cut across tribal divisions.

Ethnic and sectarian tagging involves shared notions concerning the motivations and attributes of the members of other ethnic groups and what can be expected of them, as well as those of one's own ethnic group. Ethnic identities, like those of language, sect, nation, and family, can be comprehended only in the context of more general assumptions made in a given society concerning the nature of the social relationships and obligations. Such understandings can be benign, as in most Arab-Berber relations in North Africa, or they can menace civil society, as in Bosnia and Iraq. Nor are they confined to the less educated. Radovan Karadzic, whose medical studies included postgraduate training at Columbia University, is a poster child for malignant ethnic identity.

Modern notions of ethnicity emphasize how such distinctions are generated, produced, and maintained in society. Ethnic identities are constantly adjusted to changing requirements, even if some advocates of ethnic nationalism maintain that ethnic identities are irreducible and self-evident.

The Kurds are a case in point. How Kurds construct their ethnic and religious identity—or have the label "Kurd" applied to them by others—indicates the difficulties involved in treating ethnic identities as primordial givens or as locally held aggregations of collective interests. Most Kurds live in Turkey (15 million, perhaps 20 percent of the country's population), although several million live in neighboring Iran and northern Iraq, with smaller numbers in Syria and elsewhere, including western Germany. The importance of the de facto autonomous Kurdish region of northern Iraq indicates the volatility and transnationalism of ethnic identities.

Contemporary ethnic and religious identities in the new states of Central Asia and the Caucasus merit special consideration. During the Soviet era, Joseph Stalin created ethnic identities—"national" identities in the political language of the former Soviet Union—to weaken the possibility of resistance to Soviet domination. Beginning in the 19th century, Russian imperial expansion led to the forced migration of the Muslim populations of the region, creating hostility against Russians. Subsequently, those speaking Turkic languages, including the Turkmen, Kazakh, and Kirghiz (whose traditional lifestyles involved pastoralism), and the Uzbeks, primarily agricultural and urban, were considered separate for administrative purposes, as were the Persian-speaking Tajiks. The frequent displacement of populations, heavy Russian immigration to the major towns and to certain regions (such as northern Kazakhstan), and frequent shifts of language policy, including changes of alphabet and the substitution of Russian for the Turkic languages and Persian in schools, served to fragment ethnic identities. The newly independent republics rapidly reversed this situation. In Azerbaijan, for example, schools shifted in the early 1990s from the Cyrillic to the Latin alphabet and to Azeri Turkish instead of Russian as the language of instruction. Uzbekistan and Kazakhstan have made similar moves. In all cases, the demise of the Soviet Union has led to a growth in ethnic consciousness and ethnic conflicts linked to competing claims over land, water, and other national resources. Because the various ethnic populations often live side by side—many Tajiks, for example, live in Uzbekistan, and a significant minority of Uzbeks lives in the neighboring republics—the possibilities of conflict are enormous. Their right to cultural self-expression has varied considerably in the past and continues to do so.

There is a subtle interplay between ethnic and religious identities throughout the Muslim world. The intercommunal tensions between Hindus and Muslims in India, a formally secular state, parallel in many respects the interplay of religion and ethnicity between Hindu Tamils and Buddhist Sinhalese in neighboring Sri Lanka. In Malaysia, claims to ethnic identity are inextricably linked to religion and, since the Islamization movement of the late 1970s, have led to economic, educational, and legal preferences and entitlements. Some 40 percent of Malaysia's population is non-Muslim, yet the country's constitution is confusing and contradictory regarding the relationship between religion and the state. In neighboring Indonesia, in contrast, the official ideology, the *pancasila*, encompasses general principles from several world religions, including Islam—at least 90 percent of Indonesians consider themselves Muslim—and the government frequently limits the participation of religious organizations in politics. Nonetheless, international corporations and organizations often impute leadership skills to personnel based on ethnic origin. Batak and Ambonese, for example, are sometimes favored over Javanese because of their reputation for being good administrators and for not favoring their relatives. The depletion of resources in some regions also leads to strong and often uncontrollable ethnic conflict.

Ethnic identity is now more intensely transregional and transnational than it was in the past, and contacts between homelands and diasporas can be immediate. The Yemeni grocer in Brooklyn, New York, serves as a link for others from his tribe and village in Yemen—and possibly as a link in *hawala* transmissions—and the Turkish factory worker in Germany, or the Moroccan domestic servant in Spain, facilitates the adjustment for others from his or her home region or country to life in a foreign land, and his or her remittances make life bearable for those left behind. Similarly, in times of ethnic conflict, these transnational lines can ease the flow of money and arms across international frontiers, as they did for the bombing at Madrid's Antocha train station in March 2004.

Ethnicity, like language, is embedded in a system of shifting social meanings, an element of social identity among others. Yet ethnicity and sectarianism are products of global economic and political circumstances that encourage, thwart, or stigmatize the formation of such identities, which are then used for obtaining political and economic advantage for some and denying it to others. Understanding claims to ethnic identity entails attention both to constructed collective meanings and to the economic and political contexts in which such identities are created and sustained. Ethnic distinctions, like those of region, sect, gender, language, and even tribe, are not being erased by modern conditions, as an earlier generation once assumed would happen, but rather provide the base from which newer social distinctions are created and sustained.

Even when there is a popular consensus or a desire among intellectual and political leaders to facilitate the reshaping of identities and responsibilities, either to mute the importance of divisive ethnic or sectarian identities or to emphasize them, ethnic identities must be taken into consideration. Some governments and political leaders, like their religious counterparts, often seek to ease possible tensions that arise from making such group definitions by officially denying their existence, but it would appear more reasonable to recognize them for what they are and constructively to seek to harness them. Shared notions of community by ethnic group or region often can provide the basis of trust and solidarity necessary for the effective functioning of and participation in modern society. Unfortunately, they can also be used to intimidate and to destroy.

The Special Place of Tribes and Clans

The term *tribe* refers to a group of persons forming a community and claiming descent from a common ancestor. In the Middle East and North Africa, unlike many other parts of the world, claiming tribal affiliation often positively affirms community, identity, and belonging. In the mid- to late 20th century, nationalist leaders in some regions rejected claims to tribal identity as "primitive" or potentially divisive to national unity. In present-day Morocco, Yemen, and Jordan, tribal affiliations figure implicitly in electoral politics in many regions, although other aspects of personal and collective identity also come into play. Anyone who has seen lists of the security details that accompanied Jordan's King Abdullah or his uncle, Prince El Hassan, will note a perfect balance of Jordan's dominant tribes, clans, and minorities. In Iraq, under Saddam Hussein (1979–2003), the mention in public of one's tribal identity, outlawed in the 1980s in an effort to forge national identity, crept back into common usage and regime practice by the mid-1990s in order to sustain legitimacy. Their importance has been belatedly recognized by the U.S. Government presence in Iraq, and tribal identities remain important in many regions of the Middle East. Tribes and clans provide the basis for many forms of communal and political solidarity, although never exclusive ones, in many parts of the Arabian Peninsula, Iraq, Jordan, Syria, among Arabs in Israel, and in the Palestinian areas.

Tribal identity, like other bases of social cohesion, including kinship, citizenship, and nationalism, is something that people (and sometimes ethnographers and state officials) create, and it changes with historical and political context. Often there is strong resistance to efforts to write down genealogies or claims to tribal descent because writing, by fixing the relationships among groups, distorts the ongoing process by which groups rework alliances and obligations and "reimagine" the past to legitimate actions in the present.

Socially and politically dominant individuals use ideas of tribe and lineage to fix political alliances with members of other tribal groups and to enhance their own position vis-à-vis state authorities and their followers. Ethnographers working in tribal societies have frequently based their accounts of kinship relations and tribal organization on information provided by such socially and politically dominant individuals. In contrast, the notions of tribal identity maintained by ordinary tribesmen, not to mention tribeswomen, often differ significantly from such formal ideologies of politically dominant tribal leaders.

Another notion of *tribe* is based on its use as an administrative device in contexts as varied as the Ottoman Empire, Morocco, Iran, and other countries prior to, during, and after colonial rule. Administrative assumptions concerning the nature of tribes are generally based, to some degree, on locally maintained conceptions modified for political purposes. Thus, administrative concepts of tribe frequently assume a corporate identity and fixed territorial boundaries that many tribes do not possess and give privileges and authority to tribal leaders that are dependent on the existence of a state organization and not derived from leadership as understood by tribal people themselves. In cases such as Morocco and Sudan, colonial authorities formally promoted tribal identities and developed tribal administration to a fine art in an attempt to retard nationalist movements. In reaction, the postcolonial governments of these and other countries signaled an ideological break with the colonial past by formally abolishing tribes as an administrative device, although such identities remain politically significant.

A third meaning of *tribe* refers to the practical notions that tribal people implicitly hold as a guide to everyday conduct in relating to their own and other social groups. These notions emerge primarily through social action. Tribal people do not always articulate such notions in ordinary situations because they are so taken for granted and because the social alignments based on these notions frequently shift. Practical notions of tribe and related concepts of social identity implicitly govern crucial areas of activity, including factional alignments over land rights, pastures, and other political claims, marriage strategies (themselves a form of political activity), and many aspects of patronage. In Jordan and among Palestinians in the occupied West Bank and in Israel, for example, Arabic newspapers are filled with announcements indicating the settlement of disputes among lineage and tribal groups precipitated by disputes or even automobile accidents resulting in personal injury in which tribal leaders mediate a settlement.

What Can Be Done

In his proposal for an agenda for the National Foundation for International Studies, Richard Lambert wrote: "In a curious variant of the Heisenberg principle, intelligence agency sponsorship of overseas academic research can make it impossible to gather the information it is designed to collect."[14] There is, Lambert writes, a long tradition of government agencies other than intelligence supporting research on international topics of direct interest to them. Private foundations establish research agendas of their own, and at one point in the late 1980s, the MacArthur Foundation invested more in international security studies—in an effort to encourage scholars to move beyond disciplinary frontiers and explore new perspectives—than was available from all other private and Federally funded resources combined.

Effective defense planning must involve recognition of the complementary institutional settings for effective foreign language training and foreign area-based research. As the Lambert report indicated, only some of this training can be optimally done within government settings. The other part requires renewed investment in public and private universities to sustain strong training in critical languages and international area studies.

To provide only one example, even the early al Qaeda video productions show a highly sophisticated and contemporary awareness of popular culture in the areas in which they operate. The use of *nashid*s, or male chants without musical accompaniment, in al Qaeda videos is a case in point. Most are not specific to al Qaeda but are part of wider cultural trends. By accent, some of the *nashids* appear drawn from Syria, Lebanon, and Palestine. Others are from Egypt and Iraq. Here, for example, is a *nashid* of apparent Levantine origin:[15]

> *Give me my kit, supplies, and ammunition*
> *Three days, three mines, and let me go*
> *I'm not asking you to accompany me; protect my back, O brother*
> *And don't let evil hands run after me*
> *Give me my arms and my men and take care of my children*
> *Take my possessions and leave me*
> *You don't have to accompany me; beware*
> *And we will show you what these men can do*
> *They fight the war and won't come back to you.*

Like rap music in the United States, the portrayal of violence in popular musical expression does not necessarily parallel life on the streets, but al Qaeda's al-Sahab Institute for Media Production shows an ability to draw on the implicit cultural understandings and popular culture of the areas in which they work. Like the "Army of One" video advertisements in the United States, al-Sahab's producers create an aura of familiarity on which more specific communications can be built. Discerning this commonality takes more than a passing schooling in languages and cultures and cannot be acquired through short-term "targeted" training alone.

Language often is the key to "active" ethnic identities. As early as 1993, at a meeting involving a number of government agencies and academics, a major concern was the high level of sophistication of transnational organized crime engaged in drug and arms trafficking as well as money laundering in exploiting globalization. Criminal groups centered primarily in China, Nigeria, and Israel were highlighted as ones that used languages and coded communications that drew on dialects almost unknown to law enforcement authorities, or that could be understood only months after the information was needed or by asking for the assistance of people who might be linked to the targets. Even in the cyberspace of the early 1990s, these groups constantly altered their communications to stay one step ahead of their pursuers. Their ability to change not only codes but organizational patterns demonstrated more flexibility than that of the U.S. Government offices tasked with tracking transnational organized crime.

Language is just one part of the picture. Attention also should be given to asking better questions and not assuming that religious and ethnic identities, or the constantly shifting themes and concerns of popular language, are at the margins of politics. Whether it is a Nigerian tribal group claiming a share of the country's oil revenues, an ascendant regional movement in Waziristan, or a coterie of urban Moroccans training for fighting in Iraq and then returning home to continue what they see as a parallel battle, learning to listen and assess requires a willingness to question and to take the shifting faces of religion, ethnicity, tribe, and other markers of identity seriously.

A final issue concerns the social organization of political knowledge. In figuring out what military capabilities the United States will need 5 to 15 years from today, it is reasonable to assume that parts of the DOD establishment are already scrambling to address the need for better cultural proficiency. Since 2003 we have seen that a real threat to our military effectiveness is the inability of using existing cultural knowledge within the U.S. Government and within the DOD establishment itself. Understanding other cultures and societies also requires understanding the organizational impediments within DOD to make effective use of such knowledge.

11

Africa

William M. Bellamy

There is a tsunami every month in Africa. But its deadly tide of disease
and hunger steals silently and secretly across the continent. It is not
dramatic, and it rarely makes the television news. Its victims die quietly,
out of sight, hidden in their pitiful homes. But they perish in
the same numbers.
—*Report of the Commission on Africa*, 2005

Both figuratively and literally, the struggle of impoverished millions
to reach higher ground will be the dominant trend in Africa for the next two
decades and probably beyond. This struggle, in which some African societies may
succeed while others fail, will produce shocks requiring careful responses from
the United States. Though few of these shocks are likely to pose serious threats to
the security or fundamental economic well-being of the United States, American
policymakers will find it hard to resist demands, both domestically and more
broadly within the developed world, for humanitarian and developmental interventions in Africa. Such interventions will consume resources and incur risks
that may be disproportionate to America's actual strategic interests in Africa.

Likely trends in Africa over the next 20 years can be tracked along two axes.
Along the first, labeled "poor Africa," key trends would include widespread and
seemingly intractable poverty, the prevalence of infectious diseases, accelerating
environmental degradation and resource depletion, and weak and ineffective
governance. Some of the main effects of these trends are likely to be rapid and
chaotic urbanization, increased human migration and capital flight, and a
continuing risk of civil strife and interstate conflict. Any requirement for U.S.
developmental, humanitarian, and/or military intervention in Africa would
come as a result of shocks along the "poor Africa" axis.

Along the second axis, paradoxically labeled "rich Africa," the key trend is increased investment in and exploitation of Africa's rich resource base. Because of its oil and mineral wealth, Africa will elicit much greater commercial attention and a larger number of international suitors in the future. However, it is unclear that African governments will succeed where thus far most have failed: in transforming this wealth into sustainable development.

Partly as a result of its growing relative commercial importance, Africa will emerge more confidently in coming years as a collective of some 50 nation-states seeking to coordinate policy and speak with a single voice. China is already well aware of Africa's potential usefulness as a critical mass of opinion in a competitive, multipolar world and is organizing its soft power diplomacy accordingly.

Poor Africa: Trends
POVERTY

Until relatively recently, Asia was thought to present harder developmental challenges than resource-rich sub-Saharan Africa. Thirty years ago, average per capita incomes in sub-Saharan Africa were twice those of East and South Asia. Since about 1980, however, average per capita incomes across Africa have steadily declined. In 2004, most African countries were actually poorer per capita (in constant 1995 dollars) than in 1980. The number of Africans living on less than a dollar a day has doubled since 1981 to 314 million, or almost half the continent's total population. Of the world's 48 poorest nations, 34 are in Africa. Of the 32 nations ranked lowest on the United Nations Development Program human development index (a calculation based on life expectancy, education levels, and income), 24 are African.

Many factors contribute to Africa's stagnation and poverty, though there is no agreement on which matter most. There is, however, a growing international consensus that Africa's situation—whereby a sizeable percentage of mankind moves in the opposite direction of overall global economic trends—must be addressed as a matter of urgency. The "Make Poverty History" campaign launched in 2005 is the latest international effort to mobilize global resources to address African poverty.

Some solace can be found in recent data (see The World Bank, "Africa Development Indicators, 2007") showing that growth sustained over several years has lifted Africa as a whole, even if only temporarily, back into the global mainstream. Diverse factors have contributed to this trend, including better economic policy and performance by governments. Average growth of 5.4

percent in 2004 and 2005, and strong growth since then across most of the continent, means that African economies are, for the first time in three decades, moving in step with the world economy. Will this trend continue? The World Bank notes that *volatility* of growth—an outcome of conflict, governance, and world commodity prices—has historically been greater in Africa than any other region. Past surges of economic growth rarely have been sustained, and ensuing downturns have inevitably erased previous gains.

If Africa's new position within the global economic mainstream proves more durable than before, governments will have new options for confronting the challenge of persistent poverty.

DISEASE

Infectious diseases have exacted a fearsome toll in Africa in recent years. While AIDS is the fourth leading cause of death worldwide, it is the leading cause in sub-Saharan Africa. Sixty-three percent of all persons infected with HIV/AIDS—25 million—live in Africa. Of the estimated 2.9 million persons who died of AIDS in 2005, 2.1 million were in Africa. Malaria, tuberculosis, and other infectious diseases kill another 3 million Africans annually. Infectious diseases are estimated to cost Africa about 1 percent of gross domestic product growth per year.

Primarily because of AIDS, life expectancy across Africa has fallen to 49 years. In the most severely affected countries, the results have been worse. In Lesotho, where one in four adults lives with HIV/AIDS, life expectancy went from nearly 60 in 1995 to 36 in 2007.

The long-term impact of AIDS in Africa is still unknown. What, for example, is the likely long-term damage—social, economic, and psychological—caused by the orphaning of an estimated 40 million African children by 2007? How will large numbers of deaths today in the 29 to 40 age group—mortality patterns that have severely distorted the age-sex structure of many African societies—affect future economic prospects? Little about the AIDS pandemic is linear. What is predictable is that the impacts of the disease will continue to be felt for years and that the situation will get significantly worse before it gets better.

ENVIRONMENTAL DEGRADATION

In the next two decades, Africa will suffer the same effects from climate change, environmental degradation, and resource depletion as the rest of the planet—only sooner, with greater severity, and with fewer chances of successful mitigation.

Although rapidly urbanizing, Africa is still predominantly rural. Most Africans survive on subsistence agriculture, despite the fact that the continent's climate and soils are not particularly conducive to farming. The marginal existence eked out by African agriculturalists is highly vulnerable to small year-to-year changes in rainfall or growing conditions. Drought is a recurring (and apparently worsening) reality throughout eastern and southern Africa. Given these already difficult conditions, and the inability of most African governments to do anything about them, Africans will be among the first to experience significant impacts on their livelihoods from human-induced climate change.

Even if climate change is discounted as a factor over the next 20 years, environmental degradation linked to human activity will have a profound impact on African societies. An estimated 20 percent of Africa's vegetated land already is degraded, and two-thirds of that is considered severely degraded and unsuitable for productive use. More than half of Africa's nations will experience serious water scarcity in the next 20 to 30 years. The disappearance of Lake Chad is the most visible example of a generalized drying up of lakes, rivers, streams, and aquifers across the continent. Water levels in Lake Victoria, the world's second largest body of fresh water and the source of the Nile, have dropped alarmingly in the past 5 years. Nobel laureate and environmental activist Wangari Maathai frequently points out that "every Kenyan can tell you of a perennial river that existed in their childhood that is today seasonal, if it still exists at all." Deforestation is one cause of increasing water scarcity and soil depletion in Africa. In Kenya, for example, only 5 percent of the nation's forest cover is still intact. This is partly because most Kenyan households—70 percent by most estimates—still rely solely on firewood for domestic energy use.

Competition for increasingly scarce resources—water, charcoal, pasture, farmland—has long been a source of intercommunal conflict in Africa. Accelerating resource scarcity, coupled with the advent of cheap automatic weapons, has given this conflict a dangerous new dimension. As environmental pressures continue to mount, the escalation of conflicts to the interstate level cannot be discounted. One obvious example would be disputes concerning management of the Nile.

GOVERNANCE

There is general agreement today that Africa's persistent backwardness is due in part to the deficiencies of African governments. Even if poor governance is not accepted as a major historical cause of underdevelopment, good governance is widely acknowledged as an essential prerequisite for future improvement in Africa's economic and social outlook. The prognosis in this regard is mixed.

Africa experienced a wave of democratization in the 1990s as militaries withdrew from politics and democratic elections became the continent-wide norm. Yet this was a decade of unprecedented violence (genocide in Rwanda, state collapse and civil wars in West Africa, wars in Sudan and the Democratic Republic of Congo [DRC]). It was also a decade of economic decline and escalating human misery. "Democratization" in the narrow sense of legitimizing civilian governments through periodic elections clearly produced few socioeconomic dividends for most Africans.

However, a consensus has emerged within Africa and among Africa's major donors about the importance of accountable government and improved public policies. There is a growing demand across the continent from civil society—itself the product of the wave of democratization of the 1990s—for improvements in governance as an indispensable prerequisite to the reversal of Africa's socioeconomic slide.

It is too early to tell if this new ethos marks a real break with the past. There is a temptation in many Western capitals—especially among the government agencies and their nongovernmental organization partners that run development assistance budgets—to interpret several consecutive years of economic growth, relative peace (compared to the turmoil of the 1990s), and increased political freedoms as signs that Africa has reached an important crossroads, or that, as the Commission for Africa puts it, "a singular moment has arrived for Africa."

Unfortunately, good governance is still more of an aspiration than an accomplished fact in most of Africa. While political freedoms have expanded and elections have occurred in many states, examples of effective governance are still few, because of either official corruption or lack of institutional capacity. A fundamental weakness of many African governments is an inability to maintain public order and guarantee security within legal frameworks.

Poor Africa: Effects

URBANIZATION

Africa is 37 percent urban, but its urban growth rate is the highest in the world, at 4.58 percent per year. By 2030, Africa will be 53.5 percent urban, and that population (748 million) will be larger than the total population of Europe. Unfortunately, Africa's slums are growing as fast annually (4.53 percent) as its cities.

The loss of rural livelihoods, often due to environmental degradation, accounts in part for the rapid pace of African urbanization. Rather than escaping unemployment and poverty in the countryside, however, vast numbers of Africans are simply becoming urban, or rather slum-dwelling, poor. This has provoked concern that Africa is witnessing an *urbanization of poverty* that will result in slums gradually becoming the predominant form of human settlement.

Lagos, Nigeria, the fastest growing megacity in the world, is in many ways the prototype. In 1950, fewer than 300,000 lived in Lagos. Today it is the world's sixth-largest city. By 2015, it will be the third largest, behind Tokyo and Mumbai, with 23 million inhabitants. It is a city without piped water or sanitation, with little in the way of functioning schools or hospitals—without, in fact, a single working traffic light. It is a place where millions of urban poor improvise an existence and regulate themselves as best they can with only occasional governmental intervention.

Lagos presents the example of a densely populated, heavily polluted, and essentially ungoverned urban space. In this environment, diseases incubate and spread more effectively than in rural areas. Criminality thrives, sometimes as a necessary way of life, beyond the reach of government. It is a place, as well, where terrorist activity can be concealed relatively easily. For many if not most African governments, comprehending and managing the effects of rapid urbanization, such as has occurred in Lagos, could prove to be an insurmountable challenge over the next two decades.

MIGRATION

Lack of opportunity has for many years motivated educated Africans to emigrate. This brain drain has continued and intensified in recent years. An estimated 80,000 highly educated or highly skilled Africans now emigrate permanently each year, many to North America. This has resulted, for example, in a situation where half of all Nigerian-born MDs and PhDs now live in the United States. For South Africa, a nation with a strong scientific infrastructure and a history of knowledge generation, emigration since 1997 is estimated to have cost the economy $7.8 billion.

More recently, Africans at the other end of the socioeconomic scale have begun emigrating as well, often in extremely precarious circumstances. Almost all of this emigration is born of desperation and of hope for employment elsewhere. The smuggling of human cargo in open boats across the Mediterranean and through the eastern Atlantic has not yet reached epidemic proportions, although an estimated 30,000 illegal African migrants arrived in Spain alone in 2006. Smaller but significant numbers also reached Malta and Italy. Africa's proximity to Europe, coupled with the near certainty that conditions now driving emigration are likely to intensify over the next two decades, means this trend will continue to develop. Faster-than-expected climatic changes or other sudden shocks to the already marginal economic existence of many Africans could result in an upsurge of the human outflow from Africa. Fleets rather than individual boats, possibly organized by governments or even militant activist groups, are a possibility. Europe would be the obvious destination, although flows could target the United States as well.

CONFLICT

Since the end of the Cold War, Africa has been ravaged by conflicts rooted in scarcity, poverty, and poor governance. Except for the long-running Angolan civil war (1975–2002), which was a legacy of the Cold War, almost all rebellions, insurgencies, and civil wars in Africa can be traced to the grievances of marginalized or disenfranchised communities and to the failure of central governments to either address these grievances or muster the strength to suppress the revolts that issue from them.

One of the more extreme cases of a government without either carrots or sticks was that of Sierra Leone in the late 1990s. Corrupt, dysfunctional, and deaf to the demands of neglected rural populations, the central government finally gave way in 2000 to bands of armed and rampaging young men, the so-called Revolutionary United Front, whose much-publicized brutalities shocked the world. This conflict generated more than 500,000 refugees, spilled over into and destabilized neighboring Guinea, generated the rebellion that eventually led to the overthrow of Charles Taylor in Liberia, and inspired the instigators of the rebellion in Côte d'Ivoire that split that country into two warring camps. At the time, many analysts believed the Sierra Leone/West African crisis was a harbinger of a trend of widespread state collapse across Africa.

A less extreme but potentially more significant example of conflict comes from the oil-producing Niger Delta region of Nigeria. Communities in this region have profited little from the oil extracted there. Many have lost their livelihoods due to widespread environmental damage. Largely as a response to official neglect, activist groups have grown violent and succeeded over time in seriously disrupting the operations of oil companies in the area. The Nigerian government has been unable to find a formula that would allow it to suppress this violence without inflicting unacceptably high numbers of civilian casualties. As a result, up to one-third of Nigeria's oil production is "shut out" at any one time.

The dilemma faced by the Nigerian government is a familiar one to many African states. While governments formally may possess a monopoly of coercive power, they are often unable to consistently maintain law and order in wide swathes of their territory. Even in the case of Kenya, where there is no violent resistance of any kind to governmental authority, borders are mostly unprotected and large stretches of the country are beyond the effective reach of police or military forces.

The inability of many African governments to either adequately address grievances or suppress violent opposition at acceptable cost suggests that the potential for conflict will remain high. This is especially true given that the many problems fueling popular dissatisfaction, problems related to underdevelopment, are not likely to be resolved in the foreseeable future.

The risk of state-on-state conflict in Africa also is increasing. Examples of such conflict were, until recently, extremely rare. The Rwandan genocide of 1994 may have broken this taboo. Rwanda was largely responsible for the subsequent overthrow of Mobutu Sese Seko in Zaire. The resulting civil war in the newly formed DRC involved armies from seven African states and numerous Congolese factions.

While tensions exist elsewhere—most notably between Ethiopia and Eritrea, which fought a conventional land war in the late 1990s—the main risk of state-on-state conflict in Africa probably comes from the spillovers of internal struggles. The crisis in Darfur, for example, has resulted in Sudan and Chad waging a low-level war against each other through guerrilla proxy forces.

Rich Africa: Trends

Africa's importance as a supplier of hydrocarbons and raw materials will continue to increase over the next two decades. In 2004, Africa accounted for 11.4 percent of global oil production and held 9.4 percent of proven reserves. North Africa and sub-Saharan Africa accounted for 18.7 percent of U.S. oil imports in 2005 (compared to 17.4 percent from the Middle East). By 2015, Africa's production will have doubled, and its share of U.S. imports will have climbed to 25 percent.

Sub-Saharan Africa is particularly important to the independent oil companies (IOCs) because it is one of the few remaining resource-rich areas fully open to significant foreign investment. (Of the world's proven oil reserves, 80 percent are controlled by national oil companies that do not permit equity access to the IOCs.) Because sub-Saharan Africa is open to competition, it has become a field of growing activity for new global players, notably China.

China's consumption of oil doubled from 1995 to 2005, to 6.8 million barrels per day. It will double again by 2025, with imported oil accounting for two-thirds of this growth. Africa already supplies China with 30 percent of its imported oil. In the past decade, China has aggressively pursued opportunities in Africa, investing an estimated $15 billion in 20 oil-producing or potential oil-producing African states. China has been willing to overbid and take economic losses in the African market to nail down long-term positions meant to guarantee energy security. Profit is a secondary consideration.

China's surge into Africa is not limited to obtaining hydrocarbons. The quest for commodities to sustain rapid industrialization has taken Chinese companies into every part of the continent in the past decade, seeking copper from Zambia, cobalt from the DRC, manganese from Gabon, iron ore from South Africa, platinum from Zimbabwe, diamonds from Sierra Leone, timber from Equatorial Guinea, Congo-Brazzaville, Cameroon, and Gabon, and cotton from Burkina Faso, Benin, and Mali. China's entry into the African market has provoked fears of a new scramble by the world's industrialized powers for resources and influence on the continent.

China will not be the only future competitor in Africa. Corrupt governments and weak institutions have attracted a range of nonstate actors to Africa. Some of the more spectacular recent examples involve large-scale stripping of resources— notably, timber, diamonds, and coltan, an ore that contains niobium and tantalum—during the Congolese civil war, activities carried out by neighboring governments, or elements of those governments and their armies, in collaboration with international brokers and buyers. The arms-for-diamonds traffic that fueled civil wars in West Africa in the 1990s involved elements as disparate as Russian and Israeli crime figures and expatriate Lebanese representatives of Hizballah.

A worrisome potential longer term trend will be the tendency of governing elites to strike bargains with rogue states or, more likely, with rogue nonstate actors for the purpose of consolidating or prolonging their rule. These bargains would typically entail bribes and clandestine or criminal services provided to governing elites in exchange for protection of the nonstate actors' illegal activities. The prospect of weak African states serving as sovereign enclaves for criminal or terrorist activity of concern to the United States is one of the principal future trends that bears close watching.

Attempts to deepen pan-African integration will continue over the next two decades. These efforts will be reinforced by a growing sense of Africa's geopolitical importance because of its resource wealth. While the African Union (AU) has had little success thus far promoting economic development or functioning as a regional peacekeeping organization, it has worked reasonably well as a coordinator of African positions on important international issues. The AU and its member states see bloc voting at the United Nations and in multilateral fora as an important means of maximizing Africa's international clout. This trend will continue. In a multipolar world, the United States cannot afford to take lightly a bloc of 50 like-minded developing nations. China already has recognized this and has matched its quest for resources in Africa with a soft power diplomatic offensive that is far more ambitious than anything yet contemplated by the United States.

POSSIBLE SHOCKS AND SOME RESPONSES

As predictable trends develop further and generate intersecting effects over the next two decades, shocks that might require a U.S. response include the following.

A heightened risk of diseases spreading from Africa. Obvious possibilities are pandemic flu, extensively drug-resistant tuberculosis, and malaria. While the threat from Africa may be no greater than that from Asia, Africa merits special concern because of its general lack of public health infrastructure and limited ability to detect and contain outbreaks of infectious diseases. The United States is increasing its public health presence in Africa. A focus of U.S. action in the future should be to build the surveillance and reaction capacity of African public health services. The United States also should step up its research efforts in Africa to develop vaccines against HIV/AIDS and malaria.

Unmanageable levels of illegal migration from Africa. This scenario, should it materialize, is far more likely to affect Europe than the United States. However, the emotional impact on American audiences of legions of poor Africans desperately launching leaky boats and heading to Europe—a Haitian or Cuban migration multiplied several times and sustained over a long period—should not be discounted.

A cutoff of African oil exports to the United States. While it is difficult to envision African states wielding energy as a weapon, it is easy to foresee cutoffs of oil supplies to the United States due to factors beyond governments' control. Unrest in Nigeria already has periodically "shut in" up to a third of Nigeria's output and had an impact on world oil prices. The correct U.S. response to such risks is probably the same in Africa as it is in any other oil-producing region, which is to develop national policies that promote energy efficiency and reduce our dependence on imported oil.

The capture of a sovereign state by criminal or terrorist groups or other forces hostile to the United States. There are obvious complementarities between weak and corrupt African political elites on the one hand, and powerful international criminal organizations on the other. Weak states will be tempted to trade sovereign protection for money or services; criminal organizations need protected enclaves in which to operate. Examples of such partnerships abound in Africa. A significant example was Charles Taylor's rule in Liberia, which was largely financed by a combination of diamond and weapons smuggling and illegal timber exports. What has not yet occurred is the formation of an enduring partnership at the highest levels between a governing elite in Africa and an international criminal or terrorist organization. The appropriate U.S. response to such an occurrence is likely to involve a combination of diplomatic, intelligence, and law enforcement tools, and concerted action with other concerned governments.

The Need to Intervene

More likely than any specific trend or event in Africa to require a strong U.S. response is an occasional requirement for intervention to alleviate human suffering. On one level, this will take the form of highly visible, possibly dramatic development initiatives, similar to the 2003 launch of President George W. Bush's 5-year, $15-billion emergency plan for AIDS relief. The challenge will be to find the right balance among the actual needs of recipient countries, the activities of other donors, and the priorities of Congress and U.S. interest groups.

On another level, there will be occasions over the next 20 years when U.S. military assets are required to address security emergencies or humanitarian crises in Africa. In almost every conceivable case, such interventions will be more effective if they form part of a concerted, international response or are at least carried out under multilateral auspices. The ideal case for any U.S. military intervention in Africa is one in which U.S. forces are seen to be acting not unilaterally but with African nations or organizations and in support of host-country counterparts.

12

China

Robert S. Ross

CHINA IS AMERICA'S most important great power competitor, and the U.S.-China relationship is the most important great power relationship in the 21st century. The course of this relationship will determine not only American security but also the strategic stability of East Asia and global economic stability. Even should Russia regain some of its Cold War military strength, the importance of China to the United States is likely to be paramount.

Its geopolitical advantages and economic dynamism, and the global economic importance of China and East Asia, place China in direct competition with the United States. This strategic reality guarantees that Washington and Beijing will not be able to develop a friendly or even primarily cooperative relationship over the next 15 to 20 years. The two dominant great powers in international politics are never friends or strategic partners. They are always competitors. But within the parameters of U.S.-China strategic competition, there is considerable room for variation. Great power strategic competitors do not necessarily fight wars, nor are they always locked into Cold War–style animosity characterized by polarized alliances, economic blocs, nuclear crises, trade wars, arms races, and proxy wars. The issue for the United States is not whether a rising China will be a friend or foe. Rather, it is what kind of strategic challenge China will pose to U.S. interests and what the implications will be for U.S. security, the U.S.-China relationship, and regional and global stability.

On the other hand, there is no guarantee that current U.S.-China trends will continue. China may fail in its great effort to modernize its economy of 1.3 billion people. The experience of many developing countries suggests that successful modernization is not a sure thing; many countries have failed to sustain the political and economic policies necessary for success. Similarly, there is no guarantee that the United States will be able to maintain its relative economic competitiveness over the next 25 years. Unequal rates of change among the great powers can contribute to an unexpected decline of status quo powers.

The Baseline: 2008

The baseline for understanding China's future development and the development of the U.S.-China relationship is China's 30 years of nearly uninterrupted economic growth at approximately 9 percent per year. Should other things remain constant, China can be expected to maintain this rate of growth for an additional 20 years. It possesses sufficient low-income population and low-cost land to enable prolonged, low-cost manufacturing and high rates of growth. And China's remarkable 30-year preoccupation with infrastructure development will enable it to exploit these resources in its interior. But the past is not always prologue to the future. The issue for the U.S.-China relationship is whether shocks will derail the trend in Chinese development or alter the trend in the bilateral strategic balance in the context of sustained Chinese growth.

Throughout 2008, U.S.-China relations were characterized by a competitive strategic relationship that allowed for stability and cooperation. Since 1978 and the onset of the post-Mao reforms, and after nearly 30 years of 9 percent average annual economic growth, the economic transformation has enabled China to develop a wide range of new military capabilities. Ground forces possess far greater offensive capability than they had just 20 years ago and pose greater challenges to immediate neighbors. China's conventional ballistic missile capability similarly has been heightened, enabling the People's Liberation Army (PLA) to extend its reach beyond the nation's borders. The air force, benefitting from Russian imports and indigenous production, has also improved, while the navy has benefitted from purchases of Russian diesel submarines and indigenous production of diesel submarines. These military advances have enabled the PLA to develop a limited power projection capability and an access-denial strategy in its coastal waters and to challenge U.S. forward positions on China's perimeter. The significant erosion of the U.S.-South Korean alliance, recent trends in Taiwan public opinion and electoral outcomes reflecting diminished interest in a formal declaration of independence, and the downward trends in Taiwan's defense budget and in purchases of weaponry from the United States similarly reflect the rise of China.

Washington's response to Beijing's advances has been dramatic expansion of the U.S. strategic presence in maritime East Asia. Since 1997, the United States has transitioned its military from preparing for war in Europe to preparing for war in East Asia. It has increased deployment in the region of attack submarines, bomber and fighter aircraft, and advanced destroyers and has enlarged its stockpile of cruise missiles in the Western Pacific. The most advanced U.S. weapons are first deployed in the Western Pacific Ocean, including the F–22 fighter aircraft, cruise missile submarines, and missile defense systems. The United States also has decided to deploy an additional aircraft carrier in East Asia. Washington has compensated for the erosion of the U.S.-South Korean alliance with significant expansion of U.S.-Japanese military cooperation, in part reflecting the growing "normalcy" of Japan and its correspondingly greater contribution to the alliance. The result is that U.S.-Japan military cooperation is stronger today than at any time since World War II.

The United States also has strengthened defense cooperation with Southeast Asian countries. Singapore's construction of the Changi aircraft carrier port facility has contributed to the significant expansion of U.S.-Singapore naval cooperation and permits expanded American forward maritime presence in Southeast Asia. The U.S. Navy also has benefited from expanded access to Malaysian port facilities in the Strait of Malacca. In the context of cooperating against terrorism, the United States has strengthened naval cooperation with the Philippines.

The challenges of the rise of China and the U.S. response have generated the foundation of a long-term strategic competition that defines the contemporary bilateral relationship and will be the baseline for regional and even global politics for the next 20 years. Through 2008, however, this strategic competition had not evolved into a tension-ridden, Cold War–type competition characterized by regional polarization or arms races. Rather, the competition has coexisted with constructive relations in many areas:

- mutually beneficial economic and cultural ties
- sustained, high-level political, diplomatic, and military dialogues
- East Asian regional stability characterized by nonexclusive economic and political relationships between the great powers and the secondary powers
- cooperation on extraregional affairs, including counterterrorism
- cooperation in multilateral institutions, including in nonproliferation regimes, United Nations peacekeeping activities, and the World Trade Organization
- effective joint management of regional conflicts, including the North Korea and Taiwan issues.

Overall, given the high cost of recent great power competitions, including among the European great powers during the first half of the 20th century and the subsequent U.S.-Soviet Cold War, the combination of substantial cooperation amid strategic competition in current U.S.-China relations must be considered advantageous for U.S. interests, assuming a continued rise of China.

This positive trend in U.S.-China competition reflects, in part, China's preoccupation with long-term economic growth and its emergence as a full-fledged great power, and also with domestic stability and the political survival of the Chinese Communist Party. This preoccupation has contributed to a risk-averse foreign policy, which includes the following policy trends:

- limited conventional military buildup beyond a coastal access denial capability
- patience regarding the unification of Taiwan
- tolerance of maritime territorial challenges by local powers
- persistent efforts to stabilize Sino-Japanese relations.

Multiple trends in U.S. and Chinese policy support these constructive Chinese moves. Continuity in these trends is critical to stability in U.S.-China strategic competition. The primary (interrelated) sources of continuity in Chinese strategic restraint include:

- sustained domestic stability and constrained nationalism
- sustained economic growth
- stable U.S.-China economic relations and sustained U.S. economic prosperity
- sustained U.S. technological superiority and regional strategic commitment
- limited Sino-Soviet strategic cooperation.

Should domestic or international shocks undermine any of these contemporary trends, modernization could fail, alleviating the challenge to the United States of a rising China. Alternatively, such shocks could foster Chinese development of the intention and/or the capability to adopt policies detrimental to U.S. security.

Potential Shocks and Implications

Three likely (interrelated) sources of shocks could impact Chinese foreign policy and affect U.S. interests: domestic political change, external economic change, and external strategic change. The sources and implications of each of these potential shocks are addressed below.

DOMESTIC SOURCES OF SHOCKS AND IMPLICATIONS

As a developing country experiencing rapid economic growth, China has been subject to associated social and political consequences. During the past decade, unemployment, inequality, local and central government corruption, and crime have all increased dramatically. Two political consequences of these negative social and economic trends have been a diminution of performance-based legitimacy for the Chinese Communist Party and a rapid increase in protest demonstrations seeking redress for economic grievances.

Thus far, Chinese Communist Party control over the formation of independent political organizations has kept protest demonstrations small and fragmented. But over the next two decades, with continued economic growth and further proliferation of advanced communications technologies, there will likely be significant weakening of central government ability to monitor social activities, and government controls could become ineffective. This trend would enable the development of large-scale protests and the linking up of local rural movements and distinct social groups in opposition to government policies. Such large-scale and organized demonstrations could assume increased political significance and challenge the stability of the government. This trend would become especially dangerous and be a severe shock to China's one-party system, especially should weakened political authority simultaneously enable the development of urban social movements protesting economic inequality and central government corruption.

Many governments have encountered the shock of economic-driven social and political instability. Usually, they respond in ways that derail economic modernization. The exceptions are the governments that sustain economic growth until social dislocations diminish and political reforms enable alternative channels for dissent. South Korea and Taiwan are notable examples of successful political adjustment to economic change. Perhaps China will be another such exception and maintain economic expansion. But it may not be able to accommodate the sources of instability. To ensure their political survival, Chinese leaders may be compelled to forsake economic reforms to reduce dissent and to consolidate political control over the economy and workers, at the cost of economic growth. Alternatively, heightened instability could lead to a forceful change of government by dissatisfied civilian or military elites, who then could adopt economic and political policies detrimental to sustained growth. Or, absent strong leadership, the combination of widespread popular discontent and weakened central government controls could cause an accelerating breakdown of social and political order, which would also undermine sustained economic growth.

The consequence of a prolonged failure of the Chinese leadership to adequately adjust to the political and social ramifications of economic development would be, at a minimum, reduced economic growth. At the extreme, recession and/or economic stagnation could set in. In either case, assuming slow but steady growth in the U.S. economy, Chinese political and social instability driven by domestic economic change would curtail the rise of the country. This would serve the security interests of the United States. By 2025, China would not yet have caught up to the United States in either the quantitative or qualitative measures of economic and military power. Economic setbacks would reduce the likelihood that it could acquire the resources necessary to challenge the East Asian strategic status quo and contend with the United States for regional dominance. Washington could maintain a beneficial regional status quo at reduced cost.

Social and political instability could encourage the Chinese leadership to rely more on nationalism for legitimacy and survival. Nationalist-based legitimacy could drive the adoption of more contentious foreign and defense policies. Nonetheless, insofar as nationalism could not respond to rural instability without simultaneous use of costly political and economic measures to enforce compliance, a nationalist foreign policy would not enable sustained economic growth. Chinese foreign policy nationalism in the service of a stagnating or declining economic system would pose less of a challenge to the United States than a stable China experiencing 20 years of sustained economic growth. Mao's revolutionary foreign policy would seem benign compared to the security challenges presented by a pragmatic, modernizing, and rising China.

INTERNATIONAL SOURCES OF ECONOMIC SHOCKS

The economic and political foundations of China's rise could come under challenge from economic shocks emanating from the international system. Over the next 20 years, such shocks could arise from developments in the U.S. economy and from disruption in the supply of energy resources.

U.S.-China trade war. Given Washington's concern regarding the implications of the rise of Beijing for U.S. economic and military security, and its domestic politicization of the trade deficit with China (reflecting U.S. sectoral unemployment, stagnant living standards, and partisan politics), it is not certain that the United States will be able to resist imposition of costly protectionist measures, including tariffs and/or quotas. Such trade measures could elicit retaliation. By 2025, it is likely that China will have become a critical market for U.S. exports and a critical part of U.S. economic growth, while its own dependence on the American market will have declined, reflecting the growth of its domestic market. These trends will create a balance in U.S.-China economic interdependence and in negotiating leverage, so the United States will possess considerably reduced advantage to compel Chinese acquiescence to its unilateral protectionism. Such circumstances could provoke a trade war. Moreover, a bilateral trade war could undermine the global economic system in that it could lead to protectionism in Japan and the European Union.

The United States and China, two continental economies with large domestic markets, would be the two countries best positioned to endure a trade war. Nonetheless, the critical strategic issue would be which country would emerge less damaged and better able to compete. Assuming that in 2025 China had maintained political stability and sustained high levels of economic growth, it would probably be less vulnerable than the United States to a disruption of global trade. Because China's domestic market is larger than that of the United States and its economy is growing faster, it might well be better able to absorb the slack in demand than could the U.S. domestic market, so its economy would likely experience relatively higher rates of growth during a trade war. In these circumstances, the net effect of a trade war would be an acceleration of the rise of China, which would be detrimental to U.S. security. Moreover, hostile economic relations would also contribute to escalated tensions over regional and extraregional political and military conflicts, so the relative economic costs of a trade war would affect the entire U.S.-China strategic competition.

U.S. economic instability. If China remains highly dependent on the global market for economic growth and employment stability, American economic mismanagement (increasing budget deficits or a declining dollar) and/or unfavorable demographic trends resulting in stagnation or prolonged economic recession would undermine its economic growth. Moreover, a prolonged and deep U.S. recession would reduce the demand for Chinese products in other large economies that depend on the U.S. market for growth, including Western Europe and Japan. Should China also enter a recession, the resulting dramatic rise in unemployment, combined with reduced leadership legitimacy, could cause social and political instability, exacerbating the negative economic implications of a recession for the rise of China. At the extreme, a prolonged recession could produce significant rural instability, including the growth of banditry and a breakdown of rural markets and the urban economy. In these circumstances, an American recession would have relatively greater impact on China's capabilities than on U.S. capabilities and would increase Washington's relative power while enhancing its security.

There is an alternative scenario emerging from a U.S. recession. Assuming that China's development trajectory follows the pattern of other large economies, in 20 years its dependence on the global market will have declined as its growth is increasingly driven by domestic demand, a trend reflecting the growth of its own economy and a corresponding increase in discretionary spending and domestic consumption. In these circumstances, China could sustain economic growth, albeit at a lower level, despite reduced exports.

In this scenario, an American recession would challenge Chinese political stability by reducing the rate of job production, but, absent other potentially destabilizing shocks to its rise, China might be able to weather the economic consequences of the recession better than the United States. If so, a prolonged U.S. economic recession might accelerate the rise of China by increasing the differential rate of economic growth between the two countries. In addition, loss of confidence in the U.S. economy in China, as well as in other countries, could lead to a sell-off of the dollar, exacerbating America's economic problems. These trends could undermine Washington's ability to offset the growth of Chinese military power through sustained defense spending and regional deployments. These adverse trends could contribute to both bilateral tension and regional instability by encouraging a more confident China to challenge the status quo.

Oil shock. Political instability in a major oil-producing country and/or war in the Middle East or North Africa could produce both a significant global shortage of energy supplies and a dramatic rise in the price of oil. The economic effect would be felt by nearly every country in the world. The strategic issue in U.S.-China relations of an oil shock is the relative cost to economic growth in the two countries. This will be a function of their relative economic dependence on imported oil.

In 20 years, it is likely that an oil shock would disproportionately affect the United States, reflecting its greater dependence on imported oil. Currently, China is one of the most energy-autarchic industrialized countries in the world. Imported oil accounts for approximately 10 percent of its total energy consumption. The recent rise in oil imports primarily reflects the growth in automobile ownership.

Industrial and energy production relies heavily on coal, a resource in which China is self-sufficient. Despite continued growth in oil imports, over the next 20 years China likely will be able to minimize dependence. Its energy plans stress development of hydropower and nuclear power. Its priority will be continued reliance on coal, and in the absence of pluralistic multiparty politics, this should be easily managed. Moreover, given the nascent stage of domestic automobile manufacturing, over the next 20 years China should be able to increase automobile manufacturing while introducing energy-efficient technologies that will reduce the dependence of its automobile sector on imported oil. Finally, China's political system will be able to adjust to decreased supplies and increased prices by price or administrative methods to ration gasoline use.

In contrast, the United States will find it more difficult to adjust to an oil shock. Currently, it is twice as dependent as China on imported oil, which accounts for approximately 20 percent of total U.S. energy consumption (imported natural gas further contributes to dependence). Automobile use accounts for the overwhelming share of dependence on imported oil. Over the next 20 years, it will be difficult for America's mature manufacturing and services industries to introduce new technologies for the manufacture and support of fuel-efficient automobiles. In that period, U.S. dependence on imported oil likely will increase more than Chinese dependence. Moreover, during an oil crisis, electoral politics may undermine American ability to use price or administrative mechanisms to reduce gasoline consumption. Finally, the automobile is a more important part of the U.S. economy than the Chinese economy.

In the absence of other destabilizing shocks to the Chinese economy, the net effect of an oil shock in the year 2025 on U.S.-China relations could be an acceleration of the rise of China by causing disproportionate negative economic consequences for the United States. Similar to the effect of a U.S. recession on the bilateral strategic relationship, an oil shock could undermine America's financial ability to balance the rise of China by augmenting its own capabilities and encourage Chinese confidence and strategic initiative. The result could be greater strategic tension and regional instability.

EXTERNAL SOURCES OF STRATEGIC SHOCKS

Outside sources of strategic shocks are the policies of the United States and Russia. These two countries have the ability to affect each other's and China's domestic and international circumstances.

U.S. strategic isolationism. The United States has periodically engaged in episodes of isolation, with unfortunate consequences for the behavior of other countries. Such was the case following World War I with its ensuing European instability and after the Vietnam War and its resulting Soviet opportunism.

Following a prolonged, low-intensity war associated with contentious domestic debates and an ambiguous outcome, the American people could once again become weary of international activism and high defense spending. Should such weariness be accompanied by downward economic pressures reflecting prior spending on wartime guns and butter, as was the case following the Vietnam War, budget pressures would exacerbate diminished U.S. ability to devote resources for defense spending. Such isolationism and economic instability might well convey counterproductive signals to Chinese leaders, suggesting "overextension" and "decline" and a corresponding "window of opportunity" for expansion, potentially eliciting Chinese activist and revisionist foreign and defense policies that challenge the regional status quo and U.S. security interests.

If Chinese leaders were to take advantage of American isolationism by expanding defense acquisitions and regional deployments, there likely would be a heightened U.S. threat perception and balancing of China's rise. Assuming renewed U.S. economic health and a robust response from Washington, Beijing likely would not be able to pose a critical strategic challenge to American interests. The short-term consequences for U.S.-China relations could be a costly maritime arms race, potentially harmful politicization of bilateral economic relations and bilateral and global diplomacy, and destabilizing polarization of regional alignments.

Russian reemergence as a European power. Change in Russian defense policy and an associated shock to the global strategic status quo would occur should Russia reemerge as a conventionally capable great power. In these circumstances, how Russia would deploy its military capabilities and toward what end would determine how the United States and China would experience the shock of significant Russian power and how it affects U.S.-China competition. Assuming that a recently reemergent Russia would necessarily prioritize its strategic objectives, rather than attempt to contend on multiple fronts simultaneously, Moscow presumably would focus its strategic resources on rolling back the expansion of U.S./North Atlantic Treaty Organization (NATO) power to Russia's western borders. Its European frontiers always have been its strategic priority; the European front is closest to its industrial and population centers and is the region from which Russia is best able to project power. The Russian Far East traditionally has been a lower priority, and national leaders will find it far more difficult to develop strategic power in distant Northeast Asia.

It would not be technologically or financially difficult for Russia to reemerge as a European military power. A well-disciplined and well-funded low-tech army could establish a ground force footprint in Eastern Europe and develop strategic power simply by having "boots on the ground." This approach would reflect a return to the sources of Soviet power in early Cold War Europe from 1945 to 1955, following the devastation of World War II. Such a strategic transformation of the European balance could take place by 2025 or sooner.

Should Russia reemerge as a capable and revisionist European power, the direct effect would be experienced primarily by the United States, with the resulting shock to U.S.-China relations significantly affecting American security. Russian military pressure to change the European status quo, and the implications for the security and alignments of both longstanding and new NATO allies, would require Washington to deploy significant capabilities to Europe to defend its allies and to maintain the current favorable balance of power. Failure to do so could compel much of Europe to accommodate Russian interests. Should such Russian reemergence occur, the United States would have to contend simultaneously with rising Russian power in Europe and equal Chinese ascendency in East Asia. This two-front scenario and the resulting division of U.S. strategic resources would constrain Washington's ability to maintain the current pace of its buildup in East Asia. Assuming that its economy continues to rise (even at a somewhat reduced rate) and its defense budget increases proportionately, China's defense resources available for the East Asian theater would be expanding as U.S. resources were contracting. Moreover, these adverse trends could occur just as China's nearly 50-year modernization effort was producing the financial and technological resources enabling significant expansion of its naval capabilities, particularly those appropriate for the East Asian theater.

The shock to U.S.-China relations would be severe. China could well view Washington's strategic overextension, Moscow's renewed ability to contribute to constraining U.S. global activism, and de facto or even active Sino-Russian cooperation against U.S. power as opportunities to challenge U.S. presence in East Asia and to reconfigure the East Asian security order by increasing its maritime power projection capability and regional military presence, thus compelling local power realignments. In a replay of the early Cold War, U.S. global power would be balanced by the pressure from two other great powers acting in different regions, but in 2025 China would be far more capable than in the 1950s, and the "mature" U.S. economy would be much less dynamic. These strategic circumstances would undermine both regional stability and critical aspects of U.S.-China cooperation—cultural, diplomatic, political, and economic cooperation would all fall victim to intensified U.S.-China competition and heightened threat perception in the United States. Moreover, given the trend in the balance of capabilities, it is uncertain that the United States would peacefully be able to maintain the current regional order.

13

Europe and NATO

Ian O. Lesser

The Region: How Settled? How Wide?

SEVERAL POINTS ARE WORTH noting as context for discussing trends and shocks in Europe. First, the region is more dynamic than it appears. At first glance the Western Europe/North Atlantic Treaty Organization (NATO) region seems relatively settled, with a reasonably predictable trajectory, few opportunities for conflict, and gradual social, economic, and political adjustments—a place of gentle trends and few shocks. Is this realistic? Even in this area of relatively stable societies and settled geopolitics, the next 5 years could see pronounced change, with the potential for significant shocks and substantial discontinuities. Looking out 10, 15, or 20 years or beyond, the cumulative effect of longer term trends, and low-probability but high-consequence events, could produce a very different Europe.

Second, trends and shocks in Europe will matter to the United States. Close economic and strategic ties across the Atlantic make dramatic developments in Europe highly consequential for American interests. In this region in particular, the United States is unlikely to have the option of ignoring adverse events. Developments that might have a marginal effect on American security or prosperity if they occurred elsewhere will be keenly felt in an Atlantic setting.

Third, the region is not settled in terms of its reach or composition. Almost two decades after the end of Cold War divisions in Europe, the definition of *Europe* remains in flux. Driven by successive waves of European Union (EU) and NATO enlargement, longstanding differences between European subregions are eroding as societies converge in political and economic terms. Twenty years ago, Washington had a series of distinctive bilateral relationships around southern Europe. Today, southern Europe is less distinctive within NATO Europe, and the bilateral aspect of transatlantic relations is less pronounced. Where does Europe end? Poland is beginning to raise awkward questions inside the EU. The enlargement process clearly has become more challenging for the EU as Turkey and Ukraine appear on the horizon, and as some recent enlargements in the Balkans remain unconsolidated. Even if full membership for Turkey or Ukraine is at least a decade away, political and security engagement in "wider" Europe will continue to redefine the extent of the European space. Turkey's position in NATO means that the Alliance already confronts a host of essentially extra-European issues on its periphery. Even defined narrowly as "old Europe" and NATO members, some trends and many shocks affecting the continent will emanate from outside the traditional European area.

Most Relevant Trends

A number of global and regional trends are likely to have especially pronounced effects on the European environment. These, in turn, may be accelerated, reinforced, ameliorated, or reversed by shocks within Europe or emanating from elsewhere.

DEMOGRAPHICS: AGING POPULATIONS AND PENSION PRESSURES

European societies are aging and shrinking, although the pace of this trend is likely to moderate over the coming years. Demographic change will create a continuing incentive for economic migration into Western Europe from the south and east. It also will pose a series of adjustment challenges for European societies seeking to fund traditionally high levels of social welfare from a shrinking labor base. This looming pension gap will compel tough political and economic choices, such as whether or not to lower benefits, loosen migration and labor regulations, raise taxes, or face reduced competitiveness. The debate and resulting decisions may vary considerably across the region. Turkey, with its relatively large and young population, will have a very different perspective than France or Italy. Apart from questions of competitiveness and quality of life, the stability and security of the continent may be affected by demographics-driven challenges. Social strife and renewed ideological friction could arise from the failure to reconcile expectations and demographic realities. Economic stress from other national or global sources would make adjustment more difficult and could well spur the rise of radical nationalist or other ideologies.

Aging populations and low birthrates likely will strengthen the existing European resistance to large military establishments and the deployment of draftees beyond Europe and might also reinforce in a more general way the "de-bellicization" of Europe—a resistance to casualties and a distaste for the use of force evident in many European societies since the end of the First World War. Other trends and shocks might work against this, but demographics will be an important driver of this longstanding tendency.

Demand for labor also might encourage a more liberal attitude toward economic migrants from the global south and east, or the development of new guest worker arrangements with North African and other states, perhaps on a European level. This does not mean that new rounds of illegal or even sanctioned migration into Western Europe will be accommodated gracefully. Economies might benefit even as social cohesion and internal stability deteriorate.

MIGRATION AND THE RETURN OF A MULTICULTURAL EUROPE

Migration pressures, both pull (as discussed above) and push, are another significant trend affecting Europe. Without substantial strategic initiatives aimed at economic development across the Mediterranean, in Africa, and elsewhere on the European periphery, Europe is likely to face continued, substantial economic migration, with many potential spikes as a result of natural and manmade stresses. Today, the north-south prosperity divide on Europe's southern border is second only to that on the Korean Peninsula. Migration pressures and challenges for immigration policy are likely to be a durable feature of the European environment for the next few decades. The migration challenge is also likely to be a key test for common EU strategies for interdiction and regional development. If successful, European integration at the policy level, including security and home affairs, may be significantly advanced. If common approaches fail, this could just as easily spur a renationalization of policy in critical areas, with implications for transatlantic partnership.

At a minimum, migration trends will probably make relations with North Africa and the Middle East increasingly central to Europe's external policy and a key facet of European interest in cooperation with Washington. This effect is already observable in the search for new and more effective approaches to security and development in adjacent regions, from the EU's new "neighborhood policy" to the most recent French proposal for a Mediterranean Union. Demographic and migration trends will also shape European attitudes toward further EU enlargement over the coming 10 to 20 years, most notably in relation to Turkey and Ukraine. A critical and very open question is the extent to which political and cultural anxieties will trump economic and strategic interests in enlargement.

Without question, migration trends, if unabated, will contribute to the objective emergence of Europe as a multicultural region, even if societies and politicians resist this idea. Even if all new migration from Europe's largely Muslim periphery is halted—and this is most unlikely—key European states will contend with the challenge of integrating substantial Muslim communities for some time to come.[1] Societies across the continent may adjust with greater or lesser ease to this challenge, but the underlying trend will remain in place. Taking a historical view, this may be described more accurately as a return to a multicultural Europe after some centuries of homogenization within borders and along religious and cultural lines. Again, a multicultural Europe may or may not spell a more stable continent, or a more predictable partner for the United States. Without question, a more diverse set of communities and cleavages within European societies will require a different set of transatlantic policies and interlocutors. European foreign and security policy elites may become more diverse (look at the cabinet of French President Nicolas Sarkozy for an indication of what may become common across Europe within a decade).

GLOBALIZATION, TECHNOLOGY, AND COMPETITIVENESS
Along with the United States and Japan, Europe will face structural challenges to growth and competitiveness stemming from aging populations, but also from the rise of Brazil, Russia, India, and China. Measured over decades, a "wider" Europe is also likely to be a more "even" Europe, with more uniform levels of prosperity from west to east and from north to south. European firms will continue to respond by going global and by outsourcing at many levels. The continued rise of English as a second or near-first language across Europe—a notable trend in its own right—will facilitate the globalization of European economies. As pressures on innovation and competitiveness increase over the next 10 to 15 years and beyond, there will be demands for a new deal in transatlantic economic relations, affecting key sectors from financial regulation to labor mobility, and from science and technology policy to defense-industrial cooperation.

In security terms, NATO, too, will face pressures to "go global" in response to the increasing interdependence of European and wider regional security and the need to engage new partners in Asia and elsewhere. One possible future could see the evolution of NATO as a globalized security alliance, with Europe's common foreign and security policy focused more narrowly on areas within Europe's reach in the Baltic, Balkans, North Africa, and the Levant. A return to strategic confrontation with Russia could reverse this tendency and lead to a renewed focus on European security more narrowly defined.

ENERGY AND ENERGY SECURITY

With few indigenous sources of oil or gas, Europe will be among the regions in the developed world most exposed to longer term energy trends and developments affecting energy geopolitics. Long-term tightening of energy markets would pose substantial challenges for Europe. Alongside migration, energy security will be a priority for EU-wide strategy over the next decade and beyond. Whereas North America will continue to think in terms of oil, Europe's energy security debate will increasingly turn on the question of gas supply and transport. Europe will have strong incentives to reinforce the current trend toward diversification in gas supply and shipping routes, with Russia, Turkey, and North Africa playing central roles. Energy security concerns also could provide incentives for a more active European policy toward the Mediterranean, Black Sea region, Middle East, and Central Asia, possibly independent of American policies.

European opinion will likely remain highly sensitive and relatively interventionist regarding long-term environmental trends, including climate change. These issues will probably figure even more prominently in transatlantic discourse over the next decade or two. Energy security and global warming concerns may combine to encourage the renewed expansion of nuclear power across Europe, increasing the salience of transatlantic cooperation on a range of related questions, from nonproliferation and safeguards policy to the security of nuclear facilities, civil emergency planning, and consequence management.

MULTIPOLARITY, NEW ALIGNMENTS, AND DRIFT

Key areas on the European periphery, from the Black Sea to Africa, north and south, are already distinctly multipolar, with Russia and China playing important economic and political roles alongside the United States and Europe. Within limits, European societies and leaderships are likely to be comfortable with a trend toward multipolarity in which American influence is balanced by a more active European role. The limits of this preference are likely to be defined by the extent and character of Russian revival and international assertiveness. Similarly, as a region composed of status quo actors, Europe, and especially NATO Europe, will have no interest in the emergence of a more plural global order if it implies a more chaotic strategic environment.

Could key European states actively pursue new global alignments outside the transatlantic frame, with India, China, or others, as an explicit response to American power and to give multipolarity a shove? Yes, but this probably would require a breakdown of traditional transatlantic patterns of affinity and interest, perhaps as the product of generational change on both sides of the Atlantic. Here, the United States itself will be a key variable. To the extent that social and political trends in Europe and the United States diverge, perhaps driven by new economic stresses, new patterns of religiosity, the rise of new ideologies, or strongly unilateral or isolationist policies emerging in the United States, key European actors might wish to balance or hedge against American power through other alignments—an unlikely future, but a possibility that cannot be dismissed.

Possible Shocks and their Consequences

These trends, and the overall evolution of Europe as a partner for the United States, could be shaped dramatically by a number of plausible shocks, transforming events that could alter canonical scenarios for the future. Some of these shocks are global in nature, while others are confined more narrowly to the European scene. All would have transatlantic ramifications.

ECONOMIC COLLAPSE

With their high degree of interdependence, diverse international investments, many economic rigidities, and social welfare obligations, European economies are quite exposed to global economic risks. The recent instability in global financial markets points to the possibility of a wider collapse, with global as well as regional consequences. Europeans have long been attuned to the ability of economic stress elsewhere, and especially across the Atlantic, to wreak havoc in their own societies.[2] A crisis in American financial markets would be felt immediately and might be accelerated by developments in Europe. Economic collapse—not just a managed crisis or a slowdown—could radicalize European politics, provoke social unrest, and halt key EU projects, including further enlargement. It might spur even deeper criticism of globalization and American power and cause further turmoil in transatlantic relations. It would also work against a wider role for Europe in international affairs, or new forms of burden-sharing with Washington, even in regions of obvious strategic interest. In the worst case, economic collapse could lead to the fall of the political and strategic order, on the pattern of the interwar years.

MIGRATION DRAMA

Over the last decade, Europe has faced a growing migration challenge with social, economic, and security dimensions. The trend has been troubling but manageable, despite the obvious cost in lives and human welfare, especially at key crossing points from the Canary Islands to the Aegean. Over the next decade, there is some risk that a populous state on the immediate periphery of Europe could experience a complete collapse, producing unmanageable numbers of economic migrants and asylum seekers. Egypt is the most dramatic possible case. The arrival of millions of migrants could produce a humanitarian catastrophe, overwhelm European societies, and provoke a serious xenophobic reaction in key countries. Chaos in societies across the Mediterranean need not produce large-scale refugee flows; the Algerian experience in the 1990s offers an example that defied widespread expectations. So, too, have substantial flows been accommodated with some stress, such as the million people added to the Greek population of some 10 million in the 1990s from Albania and elsewhere. But the risk of shocks from this quarter will be a reality for Europe in the years ahead.

DRAMATIC TERRORISM

Europe has long experience with both home-grown and international terrorism. Recent Muslim extremist terrorism in Europe, while disturbing, has not posed an existential threat to European societies. This could change. Many analysts believe that Western Europe is now more exposed than the United States to new forms of terrorism, including superterrorism using weapons of mass destruction (WMD). The next very large attack—on the scale of 9/11 or larger—could take place in a European city. A nuclear explosion in Europe would be a supreme test of social and political cohesion as well as of transatlantic solidarity (an event of this kind in the United States would pose similar challenges). It would be a "world historic event," in Cold War Soviet parlance. Even attacks well short of this scale could have a dramatic and isolating effect on Europe. In the early decades of Palestinian terrorism, Europe was a favored venue for attacks on airports and other targets. A new wave of Palestinian terrorism could appear on European territory. North Africa has already emerged as a leading source of risk for jihadi terrorism, and this trend could be reinforced in a post-Iraq world. "Retail" terrorism, with a steady stream of acts on European territory (daily or weekly) is entirely possible and would, collectively, constitute a significant shock for Europe. NATO, for its part, would either adapt to this new challenge or become irrelevant.

NEW NUCLEAR EXPOSURES

Beyond the risk of superterrorism, Europe increasingly will be exposed to the spread of nuclear weapons and the proliferation of ballistic missiles of longer range. Indeed, Europe is already more exposed to this problem than North America. A nuclear or nuclear-ready Iran as well as the potential emergence of multiple new nuclear-armed states on Europe's periphery over the next decade could have a transforming effect on European security, NATO requirements and posture, and extended deterrence in a transatlantic context. The actual use of a nuclear weapon near Europe would have a galvanizing global effect. It also is possible to imagine near-term scenarios involving European action alongside the United States to secure nuclear weapons and materials in a chaotic Pakistan or Iran.

NEW IDEOLOGIES

Europe has traditionally been the cockpit of revolutionary and often violent ideologies. It is historically naïve to believe that radical politics and violent geopolitical struggles are entirely a thing of the past, even in this apparently benign setting. Taking a long view, the rise of new ideological struggles could have many triggers, including some of the shocks noted here, and especially economic collapse or violent reactions to migration and cultural insecurity. Some antiglobalization, anticapitalist, or nationalist movements could have the United States as a leading target. Others could have a separatist or anarchist impulse. All would vastly complicate transatlantic and Alliance relations. Xenophobia and resurgent nationalism are the leading contenders for ideological revival on the European scene.

A NEW COLD WAR

Somewhere between a trend and a shock, renewed strategic competition with a more assertive Russia would have deep implications for Europe. Tense relations with Russia would threaten Europe's energy security and could produce more tangible conventional and unconventional threats to European security overall. The Baltic states and Poland especially would be exposed. A new cold war with Moscow could also have focal points quite far to the east and south, around the Black Sea and adjacent areas. It would have the most direct effect on Turkish security and underscore the importance of future EU and NATO policy toward "wider" Europe. At a minimum, a resurgent Russia would return to areas where it has been largely absent for the last 15 years, including the Mediterranean and the Middle East. Key European states would be compelled to debate whether close ties with the United States are an asset or a liability under conditions of renewed threat from the east. The net effect of this slow-moving shock would be to bring hard security issues back to European geopolitics. This scenario would be particularly stressful for American strategy if accompanied by growing strategic competition with China.

A NEW HOT WAR

The Balkans have been the scene of hot wars in a post-communist setting. The next 5 to 20 years could see new conflicts of greater or lesser scale on Europe's periphery. Several locales are possible for such shocks. Some could be highly consequential for the future of the region. First, new insurgencies and irregular wars could arise from unresolved disputes in the Balkans or around the Black Sea. These could interact with renewed east-west tension, as suggested above. A more nationalistic Turkey whose EU candidacy proves hollow, or a return to nationalistic policies in Greece—perhaps against a backdrop of wider economic or political instability within the EU—could prompt a return to the Aegean brinkmanship of earlier decades. Numerous flashpoints are possible for conflict in the Aegean, or even on Cyprus, if the current commitment to regional détente is weakened. A war in the eastern Mediterranean would likely end Turkey's EU aspirations and could provoke a crisis within NATO.

Another improbable but not impossible scenario concerns the Spanish enclaves of Ceuta and Melilla on the coast of Morocco. Under conditions of heightened north-south tension in the Mediterranean, or with different regimes in place in North Africa, the crises of recent years could spill over into actual conflict. This could make southern Europe even more of a front line in tense relations between Islam and the West as well as contribute to the radicalization of Muslim communities in Western Europe.

POSITIVE SHOCKS

Inevitably, the catalog of potential shocks affecting a relatively stable region has a negative flavor, ranging from the merely stressful to the outright disastrous. But some highly positive shocks also are worth considering. A successful Israeli-Palestinian peace agreement, leading to a two-state solution and a comprehensive Arab-Israeli settlement, would have a number of salutary effects on the European environment. Above all, it would defuse a leading source of instability and conflict on Europe's periphery, including spillovers of terrorism and political violence inside Europe. It is entirely possible that a surprise secret agreement on the pattern of Oslo could once again be brokered by Europeans. Unlike Oslo, an accord of this kind, under current or future conditions, might be concluded without any significant U.S. role. That would be a shock on a number of levels.

In a very different setting, it is possible that Europe and the United States will conclude a sweeping new free trade agreement that would set the stage for a reinvigorated strategic relationship. It would also reinforce the place of the

Atlantic as a global center of gravity in economic terms even in the face of a rising India and China. For many important actors outside the diplomatic and security sectors, an agreement of this kind would be a transforming shock.

Conclusions and Policy Implications

Relative to other rapidly changing areas, trends are likely to be gentle and shocks few in the Europe/NATO region. But the effects of either trends or shocks can be large from the perspective of U.S. interests and policy. Taking a longer term view, in particular, Europe could turn out to be an unsettled and insecure partner. The key drivers are likely to be social dynamics within Europe as the continent faces demographic and cultural challenges. Under more stressful conditions, ideological convulsion and conflict could reemerge in disturbing ways.

Europe is exposed to a range of potential shocks capable of accelerating or derailing established patterns of behavior. One prominent challenge is the risk of economic collapse, probably emanating from American markets but having global consequences. This could, in turn, set in motion a range of political and strategic crises with troubling precedents in a European context. Another shock to which the continent is fully exposed would be a dramatic new terrorism, either superterrorism or pervasive conventional terrorism on European soil. These very different shocks are entirely plausible and near-term risks. The other shocks discussed here are less plausible or have important countervailing features but cannot be dismissed by the prudent analyst.

These conclusions suggest some broad-gauge transatlantic policy implications. First, there is a need to think more imaginatively about the range of the possible, even in this most settled of regions and Alliance relationships. Second, it is revealing that many of the trends and shocks to which Europe is exposed are also prominent on this side of the Atlantic, not least of which is the risk of financial meltdown or catastrophic terrorism. The possible responses and hedges are similarly transatlantic and multilateral. In fact, the potential renationalization of strategies and policies is a leading risk implicit in a number of the trends and shocks noted here. For Europe, American behavior turns out to be one of the key variables in the strategic environment, from economic stability to proliferation exposure. Third, existing transatlantic security institutions and strategies are not well suited to addressing the range of trends and possible shocks on the horizon. Even in relation to renewed confrontation with Russia, NATO has moved quite far from its Cold War posture (and rightly so), but has not acquired much capability to deal with new trends and shocks. The result is an inadequate ability to hedge against unfavorable and unforeseen developments.

14

Russia and Eurasia

Steven Pifer

RUSSIA FOR THE PAST 4 YEARS has been on an economic roll fueled by high energy prices. The Kremlin in parallel has pursued an increasingly assertive foreign policy, raising the prospect of a more contentious Russia that will challenge U.S. interests in the former Soviet space, Europe, and elsewhere. The challenges posed by a more assertive Russia will command greater time and attention from U.S. national security planners.

It is not only a resurgent Russia that could test the United States in coming years, however. A frail, unstable Russian state is not in the U.S. interest. Russian weakness raises less obvious, but nevertheless serious, possible challenges. Demographic, societal, and economic trends within Russia have the potential, particularly in combination, to create strategic shocks over the next 10 to 30 years that would have major implications for U.S. national security interests. This chapter examines those trends and potential shocks and outlines implications for U.S. national security.

The strategic shocks that trends within Russia could combine to produce include collapse of the Russian state, expansion to take in more ethnic Russians, revolution (leading to a lurch toward democracy or, more likely, to the right), playing the energy card, and a military/technical surprise. While these shocks each have a very low likelihood, any of them would pose critical implications and challenges for key U.S. security interests. This chapter also looks at possible shocks elsewhere in the former Soviet space: Islamic revolution in a Central Asian state and Georgian-Russian military conflict, with the latter being the most likely shock of those addressed.

Russia Today and a Baseline Scenario

Russia in the 1990s suffered from a disastrously broken economy, chaotic politics, and the collapse of Moscow's once powerful foreign image and influence. The experience made a lasting impression on the Russian populace, which deeply values stability and does not want to risk a repetition of that experience. The country has made a dramatic and relatively rapid resurgence under Vladimir Putin, even if much is due to good fortune: rising prices for natural gas and oil have generated striking economic growth and huge revenue streams into state coffers. Following 8 years of growth averaging almost 7 percent per year, Russia's gross domestic product (GDP) in 2006 reached $733 billion ($1.746 billion in purchasing power parity terms). In November 2007, foreign reserves exceeded $425 billion, and an oil stabilization fund established for use if or when energy prices fall totaled some $150 billion.

Putin ended the political chaos of the Boris Yeltsin years but also reversed the democratic progress of the 1990s and turned the country back toward centralized authoritarianism. While Russians have more individual freedoms than in Soviet times, the Kremlin today holds most real power levers, as political power has increasingly been concentrated in the hands of an elite group with roots in the intelligence services and personal loyalty to Putin. This group controls most economic sectors that relate directly to state power.

By contrast, the Duma has become a rubber-stamp legislative body. The once-independent oligarchs have been cowed, in particular by the imprisonment of Mikhail Khodorkovskiy and dismantlement of his Yukos empire. Regional governors are no longer popularly elected. The major broadcast networks are owned by the state or business entities close to the Kremlin and have modified their editorial lines accordingly. The nongovernmental sector has come under increasing pressure. For all this, Putin remains immensely popular, with approval ratings topping 70 percent. Many Russians wished the constitution to be amended to allow him a third term in 2008.

As the Kremlin has tightened its political grip and the economy has grown, Russia has adopted an increasingly assertive foreign policy, including provocative moves against neighboring countries, notably Georgia; an effort to create a region of special Russian influence in the former Soviet space; less readiness to cooperate with the West on global problems; and strident rhetorical attacks on U.S. foreign policy and motives. Russia remains a nuclear superpower but devotes only modestly increased funding to the military, using its revenues instead to build foreign reserves and the stabilization fund while paying down foreign debt. Russia's conventional military power today is a shadow of what it was in Soviet times.

Putin abided by the constitutional bar on a third consecutive presidential term and endorsed as his successor Dmitry Medvedev, who has spent most of his career working for Putin. Medvedev handily won the election in March 2008 and, upon becoming president in May, appointed Putin prime minister. Most analysts expect considerable continuity in Russian domestic and foreign policy, in large part because Putin and the Kremlin inner circle regard the policy course of the past 5 years as successful. While it is unclear whether and how fast Medvedev will come into his own, Putin will retain significant power and influence in the near term, and "Putinism" in some form will likely continue.

Looking out over the next 10 years, the baseline scenario for Russia includes a political system largely managed by the Kremlin ("sovereign democracy") and a growing economy fueled by high energy prices. Military security will continue to rest on a large nuclear component, while conventional force funding increases will be well below what the Russian budget could afford. Relations with the United States and Europe will remain a mix of cooperation and competition, while Moscow pursues tactical cooperation, but not strategic alliance, with China. To the extent that Russia becomes enmeshed in the global economic system, such as World Trade Organization membership, the Kremlin may find that it has less freedom of maneuver than it would like.

U.S. national security planners must monitor Russia's growing power, which could produce traditional clashes of interests with Washington. Europe may face growing tension with Moscow as well, particularly if the latter follows through on suggestions that it might abandon the Conventional Forces in Europe Treaty, the observance of which it has suspended, and the Intermediate Range Nuclear Forces Treaty. The Russo-Chinese relationship also bears watching. Tighter military and security coordination between the two countries could significantly complicate the pursuit of U.S. interests in areas such as Central Asia, though cooperation between Moscow and Beijing has its limits.

Several trends evident within Russia bear monitoring, because by weakening or destabilizing the country, they could pose serious tests for the United States. One such trend is demographic, the decline of a population that is unhealthy, aging, and increasingly not ethnically Russian. Other trends are more susceptible to change but, if continued, could have major effects. These are societal/governance (growing nationalism encouraged by the state, coupled with xenophobia, ethnic prejudice, and anti-Americanism) and economic (growing economic inequality and heavy reliance on the energy sector).

DEMOGRAPHIC TRENDS: FEWER RUSSIANS, LESS RUSSIAN

Russia faces an alarming demographic picture. The overall population will fall, as will the number of people in the labor force and pool of males available for conscription. The population will be increasingly older and non–ethnic Russian.

Compared to 148.3 million in 1991, Russia's population fell to 141.4 million in 2007, and the U.S. Census Bureau projects further declines to 134.5 million (2017), 126.5 million (2027), and 118.7 million (2037), and eventually to 109.2 million in 2050. These projections are conservative compared to others, which suggest the population could dip below 100 million by 2050. Murray Feshbach has predicted the population in 2050 could fall to between 77 million and 101 million. The population decline reflects both low fertility and a high death rate, with average life expectancy for a Russian male now just 59 years.

Health problems reflecting poor lifestyle choices (diet, alcohol, tobacco), environmental woes, and infectious diseases (HIV/AIDS, tuberculosis), as well as low investment in health infrastructure continue to bedevil the Russian population. Health considerations will impact the quality of the labor force and the conscription pool; currently, over one-third of young men are deemed medically unfit for service.

Concerning a shrinking labor force, U.S. Census Bureau projections suggest the number of Russians of working age will fall from some 87 million today to below 65 million in 2037, and perhaps as low as 51.6 million in 2050. Those workers will have to support a growing elderly population, as the number of Russians older than 60 will increase from 24.7 million in 2007 to 34 million in 2037.

Demographics also have major implications for the Russian military, which conscripts some 350,000 young men per year, a number that the military currently has a hard time meeting. This requirement may have to increase, moreover, as the length of conscript service was reduced from 18 to 12 months in 2008. Efforts to convert to a volunteer/contract force are under way, but conscripts in 2005 accounted for almost 70 percent of manpower, and senior Russian officers express doubt about the prospect of converting to an all-volunteer force. The number of males turning 18 (conscription age) over the next 10 years will fall by half, from about 1.3 million to 680,000 per year.

As Russia's population decreases, it will become increasingly non–ethnic Russian. According to the 2002 Russian census, ethnic Russians were 80 percent of the population, while Tatars, Caucasians, and other Muslim populations were 10–15 percent. The census showed the highest fertility rates in the country were in the north Caucasus (Chechnya, Dagestan, and Ingushetia). Describing one particular extreme, Paul Goble has noted that the average fertility rate for ethnic Russian women living in Moscow was 1.1 compared to rates for Khazan-Tatar and Chechen/Ingush women in Moscow, which average 6 and 10 respectively; he has even suggested Muslims could become the largest ethnic group in Russia within 30 years. While that is unlikely, ethnic Russians will see their relative position as well as their absolute numbers erode.

Changing this demographic trend in any significant way is likely impossible in the near term. The government has announced monetary incentives to increase the fertility rate, but experts doubt these will have much impact. While improving health is one of four national projects announced in 2005 (the other three are education, agriculture, and housing infrastructure), the government has not radically boosted health funding. Even if government policies were seriously pursued and funded, their impact would be long-term; for example, babies born in 2008 will only enter the labor/conscription pool in 2025–2026.

SOCIETAL/GOVERNANCE TRENDS:
NATIONALISM, PREJUDICE, AND XENOPHOBIA

Throughout his presidency, Putin embraced, appealed to, and encouraged traditional Russian nationalism. Restoring Russia's great power status was a constant theme of Kremlin foreign policy under his leadership. "Russia is back" plays well domestically with both the foreign/security policy elite and the broader public.

As portrayed by the Kremlin, Russian sovereignty is under threat from outside. The United States seeks to dominate a unipolar world and weaken Russia, presenting a danger on par with international terrorism. The perception, actively encouraged from on high, that the West took advantage of Russian weakness during the 1990s underpins broader negative attitudes toward the United States and the West in general. One result is growing anti-American sentiment among the public. Other aspects of Putin's nationalism include the whitewashing of Soviet history and the creation of *Nashi*, a patriotic youth group with a strong nationalist ideology. Major national broadcast outlets controlled by the Kremlin, or business interests allied to it, regularly and increasingly promote nationalist and anti-American themes.

Russian nationalism can take on an uglier edge when combined with xenophobia, racism, and prejudice against non–ethnic Russians, sentiments that endure in many segments of Russian society. Although large-scale conflict in Chechnya appears to be over for now and a degree of normalcy is being restored, feelings against the Chechens and other Caucasian ethnic groups continue to run high among many ethnic Russians. Dagestan and Ingushetia remain unstable, with political violence on the rise.

Of particular concern are attitudes among the young. A survey examining the political views of Russian youth conducted in 2007 by Sarah Mendelson and Ted Gerber showed that 63 percent agreed with Putin that the Soviet Union's collapse was the "greatest geopolitical catastrophe" of the 20th century; 62 percent agreed the government should evict immigrants; and 66 percent saw the United States as an enemy or rival (more than any other country).

The trend toward an increasingly assertive nationalism—with a potent mix of prejudice, xenophobia, and anti-Americanism—is far more susceptible to change than the demographic reality confronting Russia. But this robust nationalism constitutes a key element of Putinism and can be expected to remain a factor in Russian society for the foreseeable future. A loose amalgamation of themes, Putinism could evolve in an ultranationalist, radically xenophobic, or even more anti-American direction, perhaps led by the *Nashi* movement, whose ranks are growing by more than 10 percent per year. This trend could, in combination with other trends, contribute to future shocks.

Over the past several years, the Kremlin decisionmaking *apparat* has shown itself to be subject to surprises and not agile in managing unforeseen developments. The result has been ham-handed responses to Ukraine's Orange Revolution and to public opposition to changes in social benefits. This insensitivity could undercut the Kremlin's ability to detect and deal appropriately with ethnic or xenophobic tensions or other internal problems in the future. A bloated, corrupt, and hidebound bureaucracy below the Kremlin is unlikely to be more effective in coping with such challenges.

ECONOMIC TRENDS: GREATER INEQUALITY AND DEPENDENCE ON ENERGY

As Russia's economy has expanded, average incomes and living standards have increased dramatically. By 2006, annual per capita income (in purchasing power parity terms) had reached more than $12,000. But the benefits of economic growth have been uneven. Moscow and St. Petersburg have boomed—indeed, the Moscow region generates about a third of the country's GDP—and many in those cities enjoy living standards comparable to those elsewhere in Europe. There is a growing middle class. However, in rural areas and certain regions (such as the north Caucasus, home to most of Russia's nonsecular Muslims), the economic picture is far more dire, with many living on $100 per month without the benefit of Soviet-era safety nets.

Income inequality is high, and the gap between rich and poor is growing. Should this trend continue, Russia risks the development of a large class of have-nots who will compare their situation to that of their richer compatriots. Older Russians who are less able to take advantage of the new economic opportunities will draw unfavorable comparisons to their own situation in Soviet times. Addressing inequality does not appear to be a priority for the Kremlin. The national projects to improve health, education, agriculture, and housing infrastructure have been neither generously funded nor well managed, producing little real impact to date. The rich/poor gap poses particular risks should the government falter in delivering essential services.

A second economic trend has been the increasing importance of the energy sector, which is the dominant factor in the economy. While energy has long been a major element of the Soviet/Russian economy, it has been the key factor in powering the country's remarkable recovery since the 1998 economic crisis. Russia now is the world's largest producer and exporter of natural gas, and equals Saudi Arabia in production of oil (though Russia has neither the reserves nor the capacity that Saudi Arabia has to expand production). The energy sector accounts for some 20 percent of GDP, more than 60 percent of export earnings, and a significant share of government revenues. Economic rents generated in the energy sector fuel many other parts of the economy.

The Kremlin views its command of oil and gas supplies as offering not only a source of great wealth, but also conferring opportunities to exercise leverage over other countries, though to date Moscow has for political purposes cut energy flows only to former Soviet states. In contrast, Russia has strived to maintain a reputation as a reliable provider of gas to Europe, as those exports represent its largest source of export earnings. Given the gas transport system presently available, Russia has no alternative export market.

This trend has two major negative implications. First, with the economy spurred by the growing energy sector, the Putin administration during its second term attached less urgency to reforming other sectors. After 2003, meaningful reforms were few, and it is too early to tell whether Medvedev will press reforms more aggressively. Second, the heavy reliance on energy leaves the economy vulnerable to price drops. Falling energy prices in the 1980s contributed greatly to the economic strains that helped unravel the Soviet Union. Such price drops appear unlikely in the near future but remain possible, particularly if the West and others were to vigorously pursue energy conservation and nontraditional energy sources out of concern about the impact of global climate change. A serious fall in energy prices would hurt the energy sector, cut government revenues, and impact other industries dependent on economic rents generated in the energy sector.

Despite high world energy prices, Russian gas and oil production hit a plateau in 2005, registering little or no annual increase since then. Getting at and developing new oil and gas fields is difficult and expensive, and Russia does not appear to be making investments in new extraction needed to significantly boost production. The Kremlin has tried to lock up gas exports from Central Asia, particularly Turkmenistan, in part to compensate and to avoid a dilemma in which it would have to choose between meeting export contracts and domestic demand. While the Kremlin plans new gas pipelines to Europe—and talks of a pipeline to Asia—it is not clear how soon Russian gas production will rise to the point where it could fill all pipelines under construction or planned.

Possible Negative Effects

The trends described above could produce a variety of effects within Russia:

- A shrinking labor pool will require more immigrants and guest workers. They most likely would come from Central Asia, China, and the south Caucasus. Such an influx could raise tensions with ethnic Russians.
- An increasingly nationalist and fearful ethnic Russian population could worry that its decline, in absolute numbers and relative to other ethnic groups, will threaten the country's unique Russian identity.
- Political and economic power could be further concentrated in the hands of a select elite increasingly isolated from, and out of touch with, broader societal concerns.
- Tensions in the north Caucasus could reignite, triggering a new insurgency in Chechnya or one of the neighboring areas, perhaps aided by foreign jihadists.
- Declining manpower will deny Moscow the possibility of recreating a large conventional army. This could prompt a search for leapfrogging military technologies.
- A large class of economic have-nots angry at income inequality, or a quasi–middle class frustrated by corruption, infrastructure breakdown, and general government incompetence, could lose patience and launch strikes and other economic or political actions against the regime.
- A substantial fall in global energy prices (perhaps as the West embraces green technologies) could leave the Russian economy dependent on an unreformed industrial sector that is unable to compete in global markets, prompting a major recession.

- Alternatively, energy prices could stay high, and construction of a pipeline system to Asia and/or of liquid natural gas (LNG) export terminals could give Russia the capacity to export more gas than it has available for foreign sale. This might tempt the Kremlin to wield the energy lever against countries outside the former Soviet space.

How these effects develop and interact could produce various shocks, with serious implications for U.S. national security.

SHOCK 1: RUSSIA COLLAPSES

In this scenario, a "perfect storm" combines several trends: ethnic tensions rise sharply as demographics make Russia less populous and increasingly less Russian, exacerbated by a resumption of armed insurgency in the north Caucasus; falling energy prices, a declining work force, and an uncompetitive industrial sector prompt economic recession; frustrations rise over the general decay of medical, transport, and housing infrastructure; and regional authorities become dissatisfied with the center's inability to deal with the problems of the day and push to take greater powers upon themselves. These stresses overwhelm a moribund Kremlin, and Russia, much like the Soviet Union in 1991, simply collapses. Alternatively, Moscow could attempt to hold things together by force.

The likelihood of either the peaceful or violent variant of this scenario is small and can be completely discounted over the next 10 years. But the possibility remains in 2017–2037, as demographic and societal trends deepen. Moreover, other events could trigger a collapse. For example, terrorist acquisition and detonation of a nuclear device in Moscow, while also a very low probability event, would have a devastating impact on the country—and perhaps its ability to remain intact—given the concentration of political and economic power in the capital.

While the likelihood of Russia's collapse is small, the implications for U.S. national security would be immense:

- As Russia collapsed, who and what structures would maintain—or gain—control of Russian nuclear weapons and nuclear material?
- What "state-like" entities would emerge in Russia's place? Presumably a "rump" Russia, centered on Moscow and St. Petersburg would survive, but what would develop in the north Caucasus, Tatarstan, Siberia, and the Russian Far East?

- Would outside powers such as China be pulled in? Would outside powers encourage collapse? (China would naturally be interested in the resources of the Russian Far East, whose population is falling even faster than it is in Russia as a whole.)
- What would be the geopolitical consequences for Central Asia of Russia's fall? How would China move to protect/strengthen its position in the region? Would other peripheral powers such as Turkey, Iran, and India become more heavily involved?

SHOCK 1A: RUSSIA LASHES OUT AS IT GOES DOWN

This scenario builds on shock 1. As Russia faces collapse or is in the process of doing so, the Kremlin employs military force not just to try to maintain control over its borders but also to strike countries it believes are encouraging, or directly aiding and abetting, centrifugal forces within Russia.

This scenario would be likely to the extent that the Kremlin saw (real or imagined) foreign hands contributing to the country's collapse. The implications for U.S. national security interests would be similar to those of shock 1, with a greater probability of interstate military conflict involving countries with close relations with Washington. For example, in the event of outside support for renewed insurgency in the north Caucasus, the Russians would pay particular attention to any assistance coming from or through Georgia and Azerbaijan and might well take action.

SHOCK 2: RUSSIA SEEKS MORE RUSSIANS

This scenario develops as a result of the combination of a robust Russian nationalist mood, strong ethnic prejudice, and growing fear that, with the demographic decline of ethnic Russians in both absolute and relative terms, Russia is on the verge of losing its identity. Moscow attempts to protect and increase its "Russianness" by launching a pan-Russian/Slav movement aimed at incorporating, or forming a union with, neighboring states or territories with large numbers of ethnic Russians or closely related Slavic populations: Belarus, eastern Ukraine, and northern Kazakhstan. The primary tools to achieve this would be political, economic, and covert action, not military force. The prospects for this scenario's success would depend as much, if not more, on the stability, sense of national identity, and economic well-being in the bordering states as it would on Moscow's skill at attracting neighboring populations. Belarus would offer the easiest (though not necessarily easy) target, while drawing in eastern

Ukraine would prove the most problematic and might not be possible under any circumstances.

This scenario is currently of very low likelihood, with a higher probability that Russia will attempt it in 2027–2037 than in 2007–2027, since continuing demographic trends could prompt greater anxiety about loss of national identity. While the implications for U.S. interests in this scenario would be less dire than in the case of shock 1 or shock 1A, it would still pose serious challenges:

- What would be the reaction of North Atlantic Treaty Organization (NATO) allies in Central Europe and the Baltic states to Russian expansion back into Belarus (and possibly Ukraine), even if peaceful? What would they seek from the United States and NATO in response?
- If eastern Ukrainians succumbed to Moscow's enticements and pressures for a union, would western Ukraine seek independence? Given Western efforts to build closer relations with Ukraine, would the United States, Poland, or others be pulled in?
- What would be the consequences of Kazakhstan's breakup for Central Asia, and of a Russian effort to incorporate the energy-rich territory of Kazakhstan in the Caspian Basin?
- What new challenges would a Russia bolstered by northern Kazakhstan energy resources, the industrial bases of Belarus and eastern Ukraine, and the populations of those regions pose to the United States and Europe?
- How would non–ethnic Russian populations within Russia react? Would this trigger efforts to secure greater autonomy or even independence?

SHOCK 3: RUSSIA REVOLTS AND LURCHES TOWARD DEMOCRACY . . .
OR TO THE RIGHT

In this scenario, a large segment of the Russian population, motivated by anger over persistent economic inequality and personal deprivation, and/or by frustration with an ineffective, unresponsive, and unaccountable regime, launches economic and political actions to bring the government down, akin to the "color" revolutions of Georgia and Ukraine. The result could be a more democratic Russia or a more nationalist, ultraright regime.

The likelihood of the democratic variant is very low. "Democracy," given its legacy from the 1990s (associated as it is with economic collapse, chaotic politics, and loss of international position), does not resonate well now in Russia. Moreover, the Kremlin has taken preemptive steps to reduce any risk of a color revolution. It would be unwise, however, to discount completely the prospect of popular revolution in Russia; the 2003, 2004, and 2005 revolutions in Georgia, Ukraine, and Kyrgyzstan respectively caught Western analysts (as well as most within those countries) by surprise.

A more plausible shock would be a revolution that produced a lurch to the right, perhaps led by *Nashi* and other ultranationalists angry at persistent government failure to perform. While of low likelihood in general, this variant is possible in the 2007–2017 period, as well as the 2017–2037 timeframe.

Were the revolution to remain largely nonviolent and produce a government more open to democracy and accountability to the electorate, the implications for the United States could be positive. Russia might begin to develop toward a more normal European state. But a revolution could just as easily yield more negative implications:

- To the extent that the revolution turned violent (with military and security units using force to try to maintain the regime), would there be all-out civil war? If so, what would this mean for issues such as control over nuclear weapons?
- Would outside powers be pulled in, internationalizing the revolution/civil war?
- Would a new government—especially one formed by ultranationalists— be more implacably hostile toward the United States and the West?
- Would a new government prove as ineffective as its predecessor at address- ing Russia's root problems, meaning continuing uncertainty and unpre- dictability about the stability of the Russian state?

SHOCK 4: RUSSIA PLAYS THE ENERGY CARD

In this scenario, the price of gas stays high, and Russia completes a gas pipeline system to export gas to China and/or Nakhodka (from which LNG could be shipped to Japan and a number of Pacific Rim states), along with a link between western and eastern Siberia (building such a link would be costly and would be justifiable only if the Kremlin sought the ability to swing gas from western Siberia to Asian markets). Growth in Russian gas production, however, remains anemic, so Russian export capacity exceeds the amount of gas it has on hand to export. Taking advantage of the absence of a European Union (EU)–wide energy security policy, and with the ability to export gas to Asia or other non-European markets, the Kremlin begins to hint that political considerations will factor into decisions regarding export volumes to individual European countries.

This would be a risky ploy for the Kremlin. A gas cutoff to a large European country would presumably prompt a vigorous European search for alternative sources, such as LNG and pipelines bypassing Russia to bring Central Asian or Iranian gas to Europe. Moscow would only threaten such a move in extremis, in response to what it viewed as a particularly egregious Western action. The ideal situation for Moscow would be to threaten tacitly, but not impose, a cutoff, encouraging the target country to modify policies accordingly. Working in Russia's favor would be the fact that development of alternative gas sources would be a costly and slow process.

Were Moscow to play the energy card adroitly, there would be serious implications for transatlantic relations and U.S. security interests:

- Would European countries be willing to compromise on foreign or security policy issues in favor of Russia, for example, opposing further NATO (or even EU) enlargement?
- To the extent that Moscow played the energy card without triggering a European effort to reduce energy dependence on Russia, how might the Kremlin be tempted to use the energy card in the future?

SHOCK 5: RUSSIA SPRINGS A MILITARY/TECHNICAL SURPRISE

In this scenario, the Russians conclude that they cannot compete with the U.S., NATO, or Chinese militaries in terms of conventional forces, due to the declining number and quality of their manpower pool and their unreadiness to devote the resources to build large numbers of highly advanced conventional weapons systems. The Russians instead focus spending on new technologies to leapfrog current conventional capabilities and/or yield asymmetrical advantages to offset U.S. or other conventional force advantages.

The Russians could fall back on the Soviet experience with chemical or biological weapons or even revive the antisatellite program. Given U.S. dependence on information technology, the Russians might focus more intense efforts on cyberwarfare. The specific implications for U.S. national security would depend on several questions:

- What technology would the Russians develop? How badly would it offset or compromise U.S. conventional advantages?
- How much would the new technology embolden Russia to act more assertively or aggressively on the global scene?

SHOCKS ELSEWHERE IN EURASIA

Shocks elsewhere in Eurasia invariably would involve Russia and could pose major implications for U.S. interests. Shocks could occur in some Eurasian countries, such as Moldova, Belarus, or Armenia, with no major implications for the United States. Two shocks, however, each of low probability but with major implications, would be Islamic revolution in a Central Asian state and a military conflict between Georgia and Russia.

Islamic revolution in a Central Asian state. The autocratic regimes of Central Asia pay close attention to monitoring and confining indigenous and outside Islamic movements, and would undoubtedly preempt a move that would allow an outside Islamic organization to gain significant political influence. But looking out over 10 to 30 years, there is a possibility that poverty, perceptions of wide economic inequality, dissatisfaction with an unresponsive and unaccountable government, and a growing Islamic awakening could create a situation in which a perhaps radical Islamic movement, aided by outside Islamic forces, comes to power in a Central Asian state.

The risk of this scenario is lowest in Kazakhstan. But Islamic revolution in one of the other four Central Asian states would have negative implications for U.S. security, more so were the country to allow international terrorist organizations access, such as for training sites. The implications would be particularly chilling were the country Turkmenistan, which controls substantial energy resources. The one silver lining to this scenario is that Washington would find Moscow eager to cooperate to contain the fallout. Indeed, Islamic revolution in a Central Asian state would almost certainly draw Russia in, including use of its military forces, to maintain the existing regime.

Georgian-Russian military conflict. The breakaway regions of Abkhazia and South Ossetia remain hot-button issues for the Georgian government, which has taken risky moves in the past several years—for example, the unilateral introduction of military forces into the Kodori Gorge. Russia supports the Abkhaz and South Ossetian regimes and has employed various actions, including periodic air incursions, to keep Tbilisi off balance. In this scenario, the Georgian government, as a result of domestic political pressure or miscalculation of the Russian reaction, would use military force—led by battalions trained and equipped by the United States—to regain control of either Abkhazia or South Ossetia. The breakaway regime would resist, and the Russians would likely assist with ground troops and airstrikes against targets in Georgia.

Of the shocks discussed in this chapter, this may be the most likely, certainly in the near term. Given ever-closer U.S.-Georgian relations and Washington's desire to promote a trade/transport corridor through Georgia and Azerbaijan to the Caspian and Central Asia, Georgian-Russian conflict would have serious implications for U.S. regional interests.

Indicators to Watch For

Monitoring Russian demographics and the Russian economy should be relatively straightforward. Following trends in societal attitudes will be more difficult but nevertheless possible. In watching trends within Russia, certain indicators could signal an increased likelihood of one of the strategic shocks described. Some examples include:

- major growth in and an increasing political role for the *Nashi* movement, in combination with a general rise in ultranationalist sentiment
- further concentration of political and economic power in the hands of a select elite that is out of touch with broader Russian society
- increased tensions between ethnic Russians and other nationalities, such as Caucasians, or immigrants and guest workers
- growing expressions of concern by ethnic Russians that their decline as a relative portion of total population is endangering their unique identity and culture
- increased violence or open insurgency in the north Caucasus
- persistent government failure to provide basic services to large segments of the population plus breakdowns in health, transport, housing, or other infrastructure
- stagnation in Russia's nonenergy sectors, leaving the economy little to fall back on in the event of a collapse in energy prices
- construction of a gas pipeline allowing Russia to "swing" western Siberian gas to Asia without commensurate investment to increase gas production
- increasing closure of certain branches of Russian science to collaboration or other contact with Western scientists.

Influencing Trends and Mitigating the Consequences of Shock

The trends that could lead to the strategic shocks described above are internal to Russia, which means that the ability of the United States or other countries to influence them is marginal at best. This is particularly true when even innocuous

U.S. assistance programs are viewed in Russia with suspicion. Nevertheless, the Department of Defense (DOD), the Department of State, and other U.S. agencies should establish a monitoring system to track demographic, societal, and economic trends within Russia and consider actions that might influence those trends, particularly in shaping the attitudes of key segments of Russian society toward the United States.

Examples of such actions include deeper engagement with the Russian military by U.S. and NATO forces. The Pentagon might look for innovative ways to engage; for example, is there any standing U.S.-Russian or NATO-Russian military capability that would give both sides a tool that they do not now have to address certain contingencies? Continued and deeper cooperation with Russian security agencies against international terrorism is also important.

Expanded exchange programs—educational, professional, and military— offer mechanisms to expose more Russians to American society and values. Broadened contacts with the Russian scientific community would also be useful (and might help provide early warning regarding new research directions with military applications). Finally, active public diplomacy targeted at Russia with the goal of blunting anti-Americanism should be considered, although designing such an effort will be tricky.

DOD and other U.S. agencies can also consider steps that would help mitigate the negative implications of a shock. For example, continued work in and funding for Cooperative Threat Reduction programs to secure and eliminate as much nuclear material in Russia as possible (via conversion to low-enriched uranium or plutonium disposition) would reduce the nuclear concern in a collapse scenario. Likewise, a renewed arms control/disarmament dialogue with Moscow to shrink the number of Russian nuclear weapons (which, of course, would require parallel reductions in U.S. systems) could alleviate the nuclear concern.

Intensified engagement with Ukraine to anchor that country more firmly into European and Euro-Atlantic structures corresponds with the broad U.S. vision for a more stable and secure Europe. It also would make sense in terms of preparing for possible Russian shocks. Moreover, a Ukraine that makes the political and economic transition to become a modern European democracy would provide a significant example for Russians thinking about their own future course. Likewise, continued engagement with Georgia to anchor that country more firmly with the West makes sense, though it will also be important to caution Tbilisi to avoid provocative surprises regarding Abkhazia and South Ossetia.

Closer coordination with Europe on a coherent Western policy toward Russia should also be a focus, as the West speaking with a single voice will carry significantly more weight in Moscow than the United States speaking alone. This means reinvigorated consultations within NATO and with the European Union. A particular emphasis for U.S.-EU discussions should be Europe's energy security situation, along with that of the West more generally, and planning for managing the impact of a disruption in oil or gas supply from Russia.

Although U.S. attention to Russia has dropped since the collapse of the Soviet Union, in part due to increased focus on other regions such as the Middle East, Moscow remains a puzzle for U.S. national security planners. They should consider, however, not just the challenge posed by a resurgent and more assertive Russia; Russian weakness and vulnerabilities could emerge in coming years and pose equally daunting tests.

15

South Asia

Michael Krepon

TREND LINES HAVE SHAPED the nuclear past and will shape the nuclear future. But trend lines are usually set by major events, and major events usually have crosscutting effects. The use of atomic weapons to end World War II, the appearance of the hydrogen bomb, close calls like the Cuban missile crisis, and other game-changing events such as the dissolution of the Soviet Union generate countervailing impulses to control the atom and to build bombs.

Alternative nuclear futures exist; some are far better than others. The choice of a nuclear future does not occur in a vacuum or by happenstance. Nor can the future be masterfully engineered by deliberate choice. Game-changing events can waylay the best-made plans. Whether the net effect of such events is negative or positive depends on the nature of the event and how national leaders and their publics react to it. These reactions, in turn, will be shaped not just by the shock of the new, but also by the political context that precedes major headline events. If that context is generally positive, the probability increases that damage can be contained and that the net effect will be positive. If the preceding context is negative, the headline event is likely to accelerate negative trends.

This chapter will look initially at nuclear shocks globally and then at shocks and trends in South Asia specifically. Dreadful acts of terrorism occur in this region, although with less frequency than in the past. Acts of terrorism that can do the most damage occur in periods of deteriorating relations, in the context of high infiltration rates across the Kashmir divide and prior incidences of terrorism. If a headline act of terrorism occurs in the context of a deep crisis or border skirmish, it can generate military mobilizations and an escalatory spiral—especially if that act involves a mushroom cloud or, to a lesser extent, radiological material, or conventional explosives are used that produce large-scale loss of life, or an act of terror occurs at a highly symbolic national monument or religious shrine. If, however, a headline act of terrorism occurs during a period when national leaders are working to improve bilateral relations, are making progress, and are seeking a settlement to the Kashmir dispute, there is a reasonable chance that the leaders will seek to redouble their efforts, or at least insulate the process of reconciliation from those who attempt to reverse it.

Trends can build imperceptibly at first and unmistakably over time. Headline events can accentuate these trends, slow them down, or reverse them. Change will have positive as well as negative elements. Opportunity can flow from misfortune, or opportunity can encourage hubris. Choice matters, especially when confronted by game-changing events. It is easier to predict major events—at least in generic form—than it is to forecast their net consequences. This chapter will focus initially on the major events that could lie ahead, because they are the axes on which the nuclear future may turn. Constructive actions now and in the years ahead—or sins of omission and commission—will shape the trend lines that follow, for good or ill.

This is, of course, a speculative exercise. The difficulty in following George Santayana's famous dictum about being condemned to repeat history is determining which lessons among the large menu of choices bear remembering. Our shared nuclear history will assuredly shape future choices, but as Bernard Brodie, the first great analyst of the nuclear age, once observed, "The phrase 'history proves' usually signals poor logic and worse history." International relations theorist Kenneth N. Waltz agrees: "History tells us only what we want to know."

Unpleasant as well as pleasant surprises happen in life, and it would be quite extraordinary if they did not apply to the bomb as well. Some big events make sense in retrospect but still come as surprises. Continuities can accumulate to the tipping point, where they produce significant discontinuities. Sound analysis and common sense suggest that every act of proliferation has unique aspects, but every new aspect of proliferation also connects in some fashion to some preceding step. The hipbone, in this business, is usually connected to the thighbone. One permutation of the problem can lead to the next, and as this organism grows, it can become more complex, less predictable, and less manageable.

The flip side of this process could also apply: one wise decision or fortunate development can lead to the next, and the scope of the proliferation dangers can progressively contract. Wise decisions that produce fortunate consequences may produce only temporary relief from proliferation problems. But in the nuclear business, buying time can often be considered a victory.

Shocks and trends in South Asia do not happen in a vacuum, especially those related to nuclear issues. Therefore, before looking at South Asia, let us first consider headline events that can shape our global nuclear future. Perhaps the easiest way to tackle this question—and to identify and prioritize preventive measures—is to identify the events that would produce the most harm. Troubling events could generate positive reactions that contain damage and make subsequent troubling events less likely. Alternatively, negative events could trigger more backsliding. A short list of negative, game-changing developments must therefore factor in the potential for even worse downstream consequences. In order of potential damage to nonproliferation norms, rules, and treaties, my list of the nine worst drivers for a negative nuclear future is:

- use of a nuclear weapon in warfare between states
- failure to stop and reverse the Iranian and North Korean nuclear weapons programs
- breakdown and radical change of governance within Pakistan
- further spread of enrichment and reprocessing plants to nations that are hedging their bets and might want to be a "screwdriver's turn" away from the bomb
- failure to lock down and properly safeguard dangerous weapons and nuclear materials that already exist
- acts of nuclear terrorism directed against states by extremist groups
- demise of international inspections and other nuclear monitoring arrangements
- resumption and cascade of nuclear weapons testing
- continued production of highly enriched uranium and plutonium for nuclear weapons.

This list does not presume to be definitive, and good cases can no doubt be made for additions and reordering. Since my primary intent is to address shocks and trends in South Asia, I will not provide analysis to defend all of these choices, but the third negative driver, the breakdown and radical change of governance within Pakistan, demands comment.

Pakistan has been poorly governed for so long—by both military rulers and civilians—that its demise has been predicted repeatedly. The nation's cadres of civil servants and its public education system and social services have progressively degraded. Political leadership positions within Pakistan have become lifetime appointments; few business opportunities offer as much prospect of success as being an elected official. National elections are rarely fair and usually do not produce representative governments. Growing areas within the country have become autonomous from central rule, not only the tribal belt adjacent to Afghanistan, but also parts of Baluchistan and the North-West Frontier Province. Islamic extremism, once a favored tool of the Pakistan military that was used to dislodge the Soviet Union from Afghanistan and to punish India across the Kashmir divide, has turned against the organs of the state. Acts of violence are on the rise within Pakistan and have been directed against former paymasters in the military.

Pakistan's strains have grown appreciably since the 9/11 attacks, when the ruling chief of army staff, Pervez Musharraf, abruptly turned against al Qaeda and repositioned his country as a U.S. ally in the "war on terror." The Pakistan army's links to the Taliban have proved harder to sever. To do so would create rifts within the country's ethnic Pashtun population, which lives astride the border with Afghanistan; to avoid doing so would create a wider rift with the United States. Musharraf did, however, engineer a quieting of the Kashmir divide. Pakistan's military leaders follow the precept that one inflamed border is manageable, while two constitute a severe threat to the state. Consequently, the army seeks to avoid severe crises with India prompted by high rates of infiltration and acts of terror while the Afghanistan border remains explosive. The military leadership also faces growing domestic discontent over its extended stay in power. The army has been trained, equipped, and led to fight India, not to counter extremist groups that engage in domestic violence.

Despite Pakistan's many weaknesses, the country has managed to hold together, and its populace has long been forbearing of misrule. Religious parties have historically received little more than 10 percent of the vote in relatively fair elections. Pakistan remains a rare example of an Islamic state in which the two largest political parties do not define themselves primarily in religious terms. Both parties, however, have suffered from the weaknesses of their leaders, Benazir Bhutto and Nawaz Sharif, who spent most of Musharraf's rule in foreign exile. The Bhutto and Sharif families oversee the only truly national parties within the country. The assassination of Benazir Bhutto raises the possibility that her party will fissure.

Pakistan's multiple weaknesses have long raised concerns that it could suffer a massive upheaval from below, akin to the Iranian political revolution. Iran under the shah was also a secular, progressive, Islamic state until many Iranians and their religious leaders rebelled and engineered a toxic shift in national reorientation. The United States had little ability to monitor and predict a revolution from below because its ties to Iranian society were from the top down. The same holds true for Pakistan; Washington is poorly situated to track bottom-up changes in Pakistani society that could result in a breakdown and radical change of governance within the country. U.S. concerns over the country's future stability have reinforced Washington's support for military rule, which, in turn, has accentuated the very trends that Washington fears most. The progressive destabilization of Pakistan could reach the point of no return, but sufficient capabilities remain within the country to avoid this outcome. The departure of military strongmen who create conditions of great political instability within the country is a necessary step before national equilibrium is restored.

Dominant Trends in South Asia

Dominant trends can be defined as significant drivers in the security calculus on the subcontinent. These trends are not necessarily irreversible, but doing so would be hard.

The first such dominant tend is that Pakistan and India probably will keep viewing economic growth as essential to national well-being, domestic cohesion, and national security. Trade between the two countries presumably will continue to grow. While the perceived primacy of economic growth does not ensure peaceful relations between Pakistan and India, the pursuit of this goal is likely to further ameliorate animosity. Pakistan's future growth is limited in part by constrained trading partnerships with India and states in Central Asia. As long as Pakistan's ties to neighboring India and Afghanistan remain conflicted, these natural trade routes will generate results that are far from optimal. This dominant trend is conducive to improved bilateral relationships on the subcontinent.

Second, in view of the primacy of economics in the national security calculations of Pakistan and India, it is probable that the leadership in both countries will seek to avoid major crises and border skirmishes in the years ahead. Pakistan's interest in nonhostile relations with India is likely to be reinforced by continued difficulties along its border with Afghanistan. The leadership goal of peaceful borders between Pakistan and India could, however, be challenged by significant acts of terrorism perpetrated by extremists with quite different agendas. Nonetheless, there are greater buffers against escalation arising from significant acts of terrorism than in previous years. This dominant trend also points in the direction of improved bilateral relations on the subcontinent. It is hard to envision another standoff like that of the "Twin Peaks" crisis in 2001–2002.[1] This does not, however, exclude lesser cases in which extremist acts trigger retaliatory measures.

A third dominant trend is that Pakistani and Indian leaders will seek to avoid arms racing. Arms racing characterized the U.S.-Soviet competition during the Cold War and resulted in extreme vertical proliferation. With the end of the Cold War and the demise of the Soviet Union, arms races have been replaced by asymmetrical warfare. No nation is interested in replicating the U.S.-Soviet model, which resulted in grotesquely large nuclear stockpiles. Instead, national leaders in Pakistan, India, and China repeatedly have declared their intention to follow the requirements of minimal credible deterrence.

While Pakistan acknowledges the disparity in conventional military capability with India, this disparity also appears to reinforce its inclination to compete with India in nuclear weapons capabilities and delivery systems. India appears intent on having the ability to deliver nuclear weapons from land, sea, and air, as does Pakistan. India appears intent on complementing a diverse family of ballistic missiles with cruise missiles that are capable of delivering nuclear weapons. Pakistan does as well. Thus, the requirements of minimal credible nuclear deterrence in both countries appear to be relative and not absolute.

If this analysis is accurate, Pakistan and India will seek to avoid arms racing, but they will still compete in fielding more capable nuclear weapons and their means of delivery. Thus, if India resumes nuclear testing, Pakistan likely will as well. Countries that acquire more and more nuclear weapons and more sophisticated ways to deliver them typically do not feel more secure as a result. Instead, they feel increased concern over the improved nuclear capabilities of a potential adversary. This dynamic is likely to apply to South Asia.

The nuclear arms competition between Pakistan and India has an additional driver—Chinese reactions to U.S. national security policies that seek "decisive" victory in the event of warfare with China over Taiwan. Beijing has long pursued what, in Cold War terms, has been a lackadaisical strategic modernization program. This relaxed pace is changing. The Bush administration's incorporation of conventional strike capabilities into strategic war plans, the proposed deployment of more than 40 ground-based interceptors in Alaska and California, the revised U.S. Air Force guidance related to space superiority, and other military initiatives have gained Beijing's attention, as they have particular relevance vis-à-vis contingencies related to Taiwan.

The accelerating pace of China's strategic modernization programs will feed into India's calculations for a minimal nuclear deterrent, which in turn will feed into Pakistan's perceived needs. The China-India-Pakistan nuclear triangle is likely to be the primary axis of vertical proliferation over the next 10 years or more. While this competition will fall well short of an arms race—at least in Cold War terms—it will work against nuclear stabilization on the subcontinent.

The fourth dominant trend posited here is that internal security concerns will continue to be paramount for both Pakistan and India. Pakistan's domestic cohesion is being stressed by several separate but mutually reinforcing factors, including the strains generated by prolonged military rule, the resurgence of al Qaeda and the Taliban, and the difficulties generated by being an ally of the Bush administration in its war on terror. Tensions between provinces and Islamabad have been acute under military rule. Competing demands over resources, particularly water, are likely to exacerbate these tensions in the future. Pakistan's leaders also must work toward ameliorating sectarian and communal friction.

India, too, must focus on internal security concerns in the northeast, which are growing, and in Kashmir, which appear to be waning. Violence against the state perpetrated by the Muslim minority also must preoccupy India's leadership. It is a rare conjunction when internal security concerns are greater than external security concerns in both Pakistan and India. This trend could be conducive to improved relations between New Delhi and Islamabad unless Pakistan's military and intelligence leaders seek to revive militancy in Kashmir.

A fifth dominant trend is that the United States will seek to maintain strong ties with both governments. This has been a rare occurrence in the diplomatic history of independent India and Pakistan. For most of the Cold War, American diplomacy toward the subcontinent was an either/or proposition: when U.S. ties with Pakistan were strong, they were troubled with India, and vice versa. The Bush administration has made a concerted effort to improve ties with both countries, and the tragic events of September 11, 2001, have resulted in better, but by no means uncomplicated, relations with both governments.

U.S. ties with India have never been stronger. While overly optimistic views are likely to lead to disappointment, the upswing in bilateral relations can be expected to continue, bolstered by increased economic ties and trade, as well as the increasingly active role in U.S. politics of the Indian-American community.

The United States also has an important stake in Pakistan's future. If Pakistan transitions to a progressive, moderate Islamic state, it will become a model for other nations and will contain Islamic extremism, which has become a permanent element of national life. Given Islamabad's importance, Washington will continue to seek improved ties, despite lingering issues of contention.

Nonetheless, the legacy of the past and the mutual mistrust will not go away. Pakistan's prior support for the Taliban, its ties to extremist groups that have been active in Kashmir and Afghanistan, and its export of nuclear weapon–making equipment and designs to Iran, North Korea, and elsewhere continue to shadow bilateral relations. The other side of the coin is that many Pakistanis remember the imposition of sanctions over their nuclear program shortly after their country helped the United States succeed in prompting the Soviet withdrawal from Afghanistan. There is a widespread view that the United States can be counted on to advance its own interests but not to be a reliable supporter of Pakistan.

Even with this recent history, Washington and Islamabad have managed to keep bilateral relations on a mostly even keel. The biggest stumbling block for the relationship at present is the resurgence of al Qaeda and the Taliban, which have established sanctuaries on Pakistani soil along the Afghan border, from which cross-border military operations are carried out. Extremist groups within the country are not confined to border regions, however. They can carry out acts of violence in all of Pakistan's cities. Washington understands that the Federally Administered Tribal Areas along the Afghan border have always had considerable autonomy and resent efforts by the government of Pakistan to exercise direct control. Nonetheless, Washington cannot accept this as a reason to allow sanctuaries and training camps that carry out attacks against U.S. and North Atlantic Treaty Organization (NATO) forces and undermine the government of Afghanistan.

Both Islamabad and Washington understand that this issue carries the possibility of another break in relations, which could have severely negative consequences for Pakistan's national security and domestic politics, regional stability, and U.S. national security interests. Both capitals can, therefore, be expected to try to prevent these outcomes. Another sharp break in U.S.-Pakistan ties likely would remove an important shock absorber in the subcontinent.

Influencing Factors

Influencing factors are those that could reinforce both positive and negative trend lines on the subcontinent but that are unlikely to sharply accentuate or reverse them. The India-U.S. nuclear cooperation agreement, China's test of an antisatellite weapon, India's testing and pursuit of theater missile defenses, and India's and Pakistan's military modernization programs can all be defined as influencing factors. Leadership changes in both New Delhi and Islamabad also could become important influencing factors.

The India-U.S. nuclear cooperation agreement is a significant initiative that is likely to have negative repercussions for global nonproliferation norms, but it is unlikely to markedly impact the nuclear balance on the subcontinent. Even assuming that all of the national and international hurdles are surmounted to proceed with this agreement, the construction of nuclear facilities is a lengthy and expensive process. It is far from clear at this writing whether domestic sensitivities concerning the proposed agreement would allow the Indian government to proceed. It is also unclear, after the 1984 industrial accident at a Union Carbide facility in Bhopal, that the Indian parliament would approve legislation to limit liability to foreign companies in the event of a nuclear accident. This may not prevent Russia and France from building nuclear power stations in India, but it would likely foreclose U.S. investment in this energy sector.

If existing hurdles could be overcome, Indian and U.S. approvals of the nuclear cooperation agreement would further bolster India's standing as an exceptional nation and heighten Pakistan's sense of grievance. Even so, if past remains prologue, Indian governmental entities are likely to proceed with civil nuclear power generation at a measured pace, given the entrenched bureaucratic and political hurdles associated with building nuclear power plants. If this projection is accurate, significant energy dividends resulting from the nuclear agreement are unlikely to materialize over the next decade or more—including the growth of civil nuclear infrastructure that could be redirected to India's military nuclear programs. The most likely nuclear accord would not lead to a convergence of Indian and U.S. strategic objectives. With or without the nuclear deal, New Delhi would seek to improve ties with both Beijing and Washington. And with or without the nuclear deal, New Delhi would seek to cover growing energy needs, including dealing with Iran.

China's successful test of an antisatellite weapon in January 2007, like the India-U.S. nuclear cooperation agreement, is a significant development. It does not, however, fundamentally change security calculations on the subcontinent or elsewhere. Satellites are inherently vulnerable and extremely difficult to defend. Any nation that possesses medium-range missiles and nuclear weapons has the means to do great harm to satellites in low Earth orbit. In this context, India, Pakistan, and China all have rudimentary, indiscriminate means of harming satellites. Some spacefaring nations also possess the means of destroying or disabling satellites by using hit-to-kill technologies—as China and the United States have demonstrated—or by using lasers and jammers. China has invested substantially in these capabilities.

China's demonstrated antisatellite capabilities could be used against India as well as the United States. It therefore would not be surprising if India's military space sector is also investigating such capabilities. Pakistan relies less on satellites than India, but neither country's military capabilities appear to be heavily dependent on satellites for warfighting. The same can be said regarding China. Over time, all three countries are likely to become more dependent on satellites, but this timeline is likely to be extended. Moreover, dominant trends suggest that the likelihood of warfare between Pakistan and India or between India and China is low and decreasing. And if the dominant trends were reversed and war were to occur, it would likely be focused on the ground, not in space.

It can be expected that the Chinese antisatellite test might somewhat accelerate Indian research and development programs related to space warfare applications. It is probable that hedging strategies will be further developed in Pakistan as well. But it is even more likely that other security concerns will continue to dominate Pakistani and Indian military plans and programs.

Pakistan's military plans also must take into account India's interest in theater ballistic missile defense programs, as well as the possibility that New Delhi might invest considerable resources to acquire and field such defenses. India's demonstrated interest in such capabilities has been greater than the interest it has shown in space warfare capabilities. Nonetheless, Pakistani military planners appear to have a well-founded appreciation of the technical difficulties associated with deploying effective missile defenses. Indian officials also are likely to be keenly aware of the opportunity costs of investing in missile defenses that may be ineffective compared to, say, investments in improved offensive military capabilities of proven effectiveness. If, despite these calculations, India chooses to invest in ballistic missile defenses, Pakistan can decide to increase its investments in both ballistic and cruise missiles.

Thus, while Pakistan is likely to view India's interest in missile defenses warily, the primary concern in Rawalpindi, headquarters of Pakistan's army, may relate to New Delhi's acquisition of multipurpose military technologies rather than the deployment of effective missile defenses. The acquisition of such technologies would further extend India's conventional military advantages over the next decade but would not fundamentally change dominant trends or the continuation of mutual vulnerability to nuclear attack.

India and Pakistan will modernize and expand their conventional military capabilities over the next decade through domestic and foreign procurement. These programs are most likely to accentuate the growing disparity between the power projection capabilities of India and Pakistan, but not fundamentally change dominant trends, which include more normal bilateral relations, increased trade, and a mutual unwillingness to turn back the clock to intense crises, brinkmanship, or another limited war. India's conventional advantages over Pakistan relate to domestic infrastructure, purchasing power, and a larger set of military suppliers. Over the next decade, New Delhi can be expected to make its procurement decisions increasingly with an eye toward China rather than Pakistan.

Pakistan cannot match India's conventional capabilities, but it appears intent on keeping pace with respect to nuclear modernization over the next decade or more. Islamabad has invested heavily in this competition and might well view its nuclear stockpile, fissile material production capacity, and delivery vehicles as compensation for the growing conventional imbalance. Both countries, as well as China, are likely to test and acquire more effective ballistic and cruise missiles. Over the next decade, all three countries are likely to obtain improved means of delivering nuclear weapons from seabased platforms. The possibility of resuming nuclear weapons testing cannot be ruled out, but leaders in all three countries would prefer that their nation not be the first to break the global moratorium. Modestly paced nuclear force modernization programs should not fundamentally alter the subcontinent's strategic environment.

The last potential influencing factor relates to the possibility of leadership changes that disrupt positive trends or accentuate negative trends. Changing leadership in both countries has slowed efforts at normalization and could do so again. Successive coalition governments in New Delhi have spanned the political spectrum, but these governments have pursued similar national security policies. India's contentious domestic politics can, however, seek to accentuate differences, as is now the case with respect to the Bharatiya Janata Party's opposition to the civil nuclear cooperation agreement it previously sought. The likely conclusion from this record is that changes in Indian governance and the vigorous domestic political challenges that sitting governments face are likely to slow but not greatly alter dominant trends.

While potential changes in governance in Pakistan offer a wider range of choices, there is little reason to believe, as is expressed in some quarters, that Pakistan could experience a significant shift in which religious extremists gain the levers of power. Nothing in Pakistan's history lends credence to this scenario. If the two major political parties, which do not define themselves primarily in religious terms, are allowed to compete freely in national elections and to mobilize their respective political bases, this scenario becomes even more remote. Nonetheless, political destabilization within Pakistan would surely slow positive regional trends.

There is considerable speculation at present about how the departure of General Pervez Musharraf might affect Pakistan's domestic and regional policies. This eventuality is not included along with the other potential shocks, wild cards, or game changers discussed below. First, as noted above, President Musharraf's loss of power would be a precondition for stabilization. Second, his successor as army chief, Ashfaq Kiyani, and the corps commanders around him have been handpicked by Musharraf and reflect his views on issues related to Islamic extremism, the Taliban, and relations with India, China, and the United States. The corporate interests of the army are not subject to radical swings, nor are they likely to be shifted dramatically by a change at the top.

Shocks, Wild Cards, and Game Changers

Shocks, wild cards, and game changers are developments that could greatly impact political, national, and regional security on the subcontinent. These developments could significantly accentuate or shift the dominant trends already identified.

The biggest shock would be a radical change in governance in Pakistan. One contributing factor could be U.S. military operations within the country to combat the resurgence of the Taliban and al Qaeda as well as their continued use of Pakistani territory to carry out attacks on U.S. and NATO forces operating across the border in Afghanistan. The resurgence of the Taliban, the widely presumed location of Taliban and al Qaeda leaders on Pakistani soil, and unrest in Pakistan's tribal belt along the Afghan border pose major challenges for U.S.-Pakistan ties and the Islamabad government. If the executive and/or legislative branches in the United States conclude that Pakistan is unwilling or unable to control the Taliban and al Qaeda, bilateral ties will face rough sledding. Pressures would likely build on U.S. military and political leaders to undertake cross-border actions against perceived sanctuaries for the Taliban and al Qaeda leadership, which could have extremely negative impacts on relations between Washington and Islamabad and for Pakistan's domestic politics.

A second shock would be an incident of nuclear terrorism on the subcontinent. Concerns about nuclear terrorism are well founded in this region; there are extremist groups operating in both India and Pakistan that could have the means as well as the motive to acquire radiological and perhaps even fissile materials.

Fears of nuclear terrorism could eclipse concerns over the India-Pakistan nuclear balance over the next decade.

Warfighting scenarios involving total mobilization along the two traditional fighting corridors, as well as the deliberate escalation of a conventional conflict across the nuclear threshold, do not appear likely for the foreseeable future, although these scenarios cannot entirely be ruled out. New crises could still unfold, and the use of nuclear weapons, whether by accident, a breakdown of command and control, or inadvertence, cannot be dismissed by relying on an academic theory such as the stability-instability paradox. One possible driver of unwanted crises and escalation could be an act of nuclear terrorism in either India or Pakistan that is attributed to extremists who have received foreign support. An act of nuclear terrorism could be particularly hard to contain if it occurs in the context of ongoing deterioration of Pakistan-India relations.

The use of a radiological dispersal device or "dirty bomb" is more plausible than the detonation of a nuclear weapon that has been stolen or constructed out of highly enriched uranium. In both India and Pakistan, as elsewhere, materials that could be used to make dirty bombs are widely available and poorly guarded in the civil sector. These devices would not cause great loss of life, but they could provoke widespread public anxiety and economic disruption.

A third shock, wild card, or game changer on the subcontinent could be a crisis between the United States and Iran in which Washington uses military force against Tehran, perhaps to delay its nuclear programs or in retaliation for Iranian-backed attacks against U.S. interests or military forces in the region. In these scenarios, Washington would expect diplomatic support from Islamabad and New Delhi. If support were not forthcoming in one or both cases, the U.S. executive and/or legislative branches might reevaluate ongoing bilateral cooperation efforts, particularly with respect to military assistance and, in the case of India, civil nuclear cooperation.

A clash between the United States and Iran likely would be problematic for both U.S.-Pakistan and U.S.-India relations. Domestic backlash against the United States could be expected in both countries. Pakistani authorities also might face the prospect of increased sectarian violence and domestic unrest. Leaders in both countries would find it difficult to improve ties with Washington. Instead, backsliding could occur.

A fourth potential shock, wild card, and game changer would be a U.S.-China clash over Taiwan. Another Taiwan crisis also could become a test of U.S. ties with both Islamabad and New Delhi. India seeks improved ties with Beijing as well as Washington and would seek to avoid antagonizing either capital. Pakistan also would be placed in a tough spot in the event of a possible clash between its two most important patrons. Depending on how a U.S.-China confrontation over Taiwan were to play out, Pakistan and India could choose different sides. In that event, U.S. ties with India could improve even more, while ties with Pakistan could deteriorate further.

Not all shocks, wild cards, and game-changing developments are negative. A Pakistan-India agreement on the key elements for settling the Kashmir dispute would be a significant accomplishment, even if negotiations on implementing details take considerable time. Agreement on the key elements of a Kashmir settlement would likely generate extremist acts as well as provide insulation against a downturn in bilateral Pakistan-India ties. It would facilitate economic growth and cross-border and regional trade, providing one basis for greater domestic tranquility in both countries, and a counter to the negative wild cards described above.

Policy Consequences

What policy consequences that flow from this analysis would apply more narrowly to the Pentagon, and what should the Pentagon do as a result? First, it should strive to improve military-to-military ties with both Pakistan and India. Clearly, this will be more challenging with Pakistan, but solid ties with both countries will help prevent unintended escalation arising from the triggering events discussed above.

Second, two standard instruments for improved military-to-military ties are bilateral training exercises and bilateral arms sales. What kinds of training exercises and arms sales deserve prioritization? Some major U.S. arms sales with India could, ironically, become a casualty of the civil nuclear cooperation agreement; others are likely to proceed. It is unavoidable that conventional arms sales to India will reinforce Pakistani reasoning for more nuclear weapons programs to compensate for conventional imbalances. This reasoning can be accentuated by engaging in arms sales, such as missile defense programs, that have a more direct bearing on presumed nuclear requirements. The more indirect the connection between U.S. arms sales to India and Pakistan's nuclear requirements, the better. The more direct the connection between U.S. arms transfers and monitoring the Kashmir divide, the better.

Third, the Pakistan army's raison d'être since its inception has been to defend against the Indian army. A relatively small fraction of Pakistan's armed forces are trained and equipped to deal with internal security and counterterrorism operations. The primary focus of the Pentagon's arms sales and training programs for Pakistan should accordingly be explicitly oriented toward those requirements. This approach is obviously needed and has the added benefit of providing the best chance of sustaining a domestic political consensus in the United States for continued military ties to Pakistan.

Similarly, the Pentagon should seek, over time, to engage in trilateral counterterrorism military exercises with India and Pakistan. In addition, DOD leadership should seek to accelerate and broaden cooperative threat reduction programs that fall under its purview with India and Pakistan. Finally, despite time constraints, high-level Pentagon visitors should make it a point to request meetings with a range of political and military leaders when they visit Pakistan.

16

Latin America

Edward Schumacher-Matos

FOR MOST OF LATIN AMERICA, the next 20 years should be a period of stability and increased prosperity. Economic, demographic, governance, and cultural trends are all in the region's favor. That said, pockets of instability could present shocks and a security challenge for the United States. These potential shocks include political implosions in Cuba and Venezuela, nativist backlashes against immigration in the United States, local guerrilla insurgencies, and one or more failed or narco states. How Latin Americans react will be the key determinant of whether the overall trends stay positive or shocks emerge. Still, U.S. responses will have critical impact, especially on whether the challenges convert into shocks. Domestic political and immigration trends in the United States also add complications.

In a more subtle trend, Washington may not be able to count on what often has been automatic Latin American support for its positions on strategic or critical global issues as new actors, especially China, enter the region.

Major Relevant Trends

THE DEMOGRAPHIC WINDOW OF OPPORTUNITY

The single most important trend for the next 20 years will be the region's passing through a demographic sweet spot. Demographically, Latin America is where East Asia was in 1960. Most of the population is at or near replacement birthrates of roughly two children per family. Mortality rates in most countries long ago dropped to levels near that of the United States, a reflection of improvements in health care and nutrition. The population, which hit the 500 million mark in 1995, is expected to stabilize in 2040 at 660 million. The growth today is due primarily to the large number of women still of childbearing age, and not their fertility rates. More importantly, Latin America's is a young population, with an average age approaching 27, compared to 32 in East Asia and 37 in developed countries. Therein lies the tale.

More than just reflecting vigor, that age average is significant because 26 is considered a magic launching pad for development. The historical experience within the populations in East Asia and in developed countries is that beginning at the average age of 26 until 39, national productivity takes off, savings grow, education improves, wages increase, women enter the work force, and crime drops. Other factors are at play, but the demographic issues take on particular weight as fertility, child dependency, and mortality curves overlap and work their way through the national population. It is not that education magically grows, for instance, but rather that the reduced number of children usually means more spending per child. The greater proportional number of workers over 26 usually means more tax contributions and work productivity and less drain on social expenses.

There is one major caveat: much depends on national development policy, and especially openness to trade. East Asia, which was behind Latin America in most development measures into the 1960s, brilliantly exploited its demographic window. Most countries in Latin America are in a good position, having opened their economies and undertaken structural reforms over the past 20 years. Shortcomings in their legal systems, corruption, weak tax systems, and bureaucratic inefficiencies remain hurdles, but the macroeconomics in most countries is sound.

All countries, of course, are not equal. Venezuela and Cuba are following different development models. Meanwhile, the region's poorest countries, including some in Central America as well as Bolivia, are demographic exceptions. They continue to have high fertility, low literacy, and significantly younger populations. Fertility rates in Guatemala, Honduras, Nicaragua, Bolivia, and Haiti are still around five children. In contrast to Argentina, Uruguay, and Chile, for example, the poorer countries also suffer problems of cultural and national identity, often because of large indigenous populations.

The intersection of two other related trends—urbanization and global warming—further hits the poorer countries disproportionately. Latin America today is 70 percent urban on average, the great internal migration from the countryside to cities and towns having taken place over the last 40 years. The poor countries, however, remain mostly rural and only now are undergoing the dislocation caused by urbanization. At the same time, warming climate is leading to more and larger hurricanes. The poorer countries of Central America and the

Caribbean lie in their paths, and in those countries it is the newly concentrated populations, many on the coast and living in poorly constructed and sited shanties, that are most exposed.

The human and economic costs from these natural disasters will likely continue to escalate. Until countries such as Nicaragua, Honduras, and Guatemala are able to get control of their development and internal migration, they will probably present an ever-larger challenge to the United States for emergency humanitarian and military assistance.

Sitting in the middle of this demographic panorama is Mexico, the country most important to the United States. The average age of Mexicans is 25, still slightly short of the launch point of 26 but rapidly closing in on it. Inside Mexico, the poorer rural regions in the south have the highest fertility rates, but southern villages are emptying as farmers migrate to cities, duty-free factory towns, and the United States.

For the United States, Latin demographic trends foretell a reduction in immigration pressure that may have begun in 2007 and will become more pronounced with each passing year. As opportunities improve at home, fewer Latin Americans presumably will want to move to the United States. These demographic trends will also contribute to political and economic stability, including a possible reduction in crime and political violence. Other factors, however, may mitigate the impact.

ECONOMICS AND IDEOLOGY

A Latin American move to the left in recent years, despite the popular hype, has been confined and may have reached its limits. The election of left-of-center presidents in Brazil, Argentina, Chile, Bolivia, Ecuador, and Nicaragua raised concerns of a leftist, anti-American bloc led by Fidel Castro and Hugo Chavez. That has not happened, and nothing today indicates that it will.

Castro is on his deathbed. He formally stepped down in February as president of the council of state, turning over the reins of government to his more pragmatic and less regionally ambitious brother, Raúl. Cuban influence in most of the region has long been negligible anyway. Castro has some sentimental popularity as an historic figure, but whatever influence that gives Cuba will go with him to the grave. Chavez has pretensions of succeeding Castro regionally, but he is more court jester than crown. Chavez is entertained around the region for his oil largesse and his laughs, but he is hardly followed. President Evo Morales in Bolivia, an indigenous former coca grower, and President Daniel Ortega, of Sandinista fame, are the nearest acolytes, but so far they are proving to be more practical than ideological. Both at different times have reached out to the United States. The other left-leaning presidents, led by Brazil's Luiz Inacio Lula de Silva, are even more pragmatic. The free market reforms and privatizations under the so-called Washington Consensus (an unfortunate name, for the U.S. Government had nothing to do with it) of the last 15 years have been derided as neoliberal failures but left more or less intact.

The main impact of the move to the left has been a greater emphasis on social programs, but the Washington Consensus called for these so-called second-generation reforms. Only the communist government in Cuba and the increasingly socialist one in Venezuela openly oppose the United States. It is Venezuela, however, that suffers the most serious internal ideological tensions. Bolivia, Ecuador, and Mexico lack ideological consensus to lesser degrees.

In Mexico, Felipe Calderón, a centrist, barely won the presidency in an election in 2006 against the fiery, left-leaning mayor of Mexico City, Andrés Manuel Lopez Obrador. Still, Mexico has had leftist presidents before, and Obrador's victory likely would have been only a minor nuisance for the United States. Mexicans may rue being far from God and close to the United States, but almost all understand that the country has a symbiotic relationship with its northern neighbor that must be tended. A campaign by the losing leftists to challenge the legitimacy of the current government, moreover, has slowly lost steam, and Calderón has proven to be far more politically adept than his predecessor, Vicente Fox. He has been able to compromise with, or co-opt, segments of the opposition. There is welcome legislative movement to government in Mexico City. More fundamentally, the country's democracy, stunted by single-party rule up until the election of Fox in 2000, is maturing well.

Trade is the major international issue in the hemisphere, and that will likely continue. At a global level, Brazil is a central leader opposing U.S. and European agricultural subsidies and blocking the Doha Round of trade talks. At a hemispheric level, the movement for a Free Trade Area of the Americas that began in Latin America and was taken up as a crusading cause by Presidents George H.W. Bush and Bill Clinton has become the chronicle of a death foretold. Misgivings abound on all sides. U.S. policy has switched to favoring bilaterals. The template is agreements signed in recent years with Chile and with various Central American countries. But the original such accord, the North American Free Trade Agreement, remains controversial in both the United States and Mexico, and each country in Latin America has a sizeable bloc opposing free trade with the United States, at least on the commercial, labor, and environmental terms demanded by powerful interest groups in Washington. The bilateral strategy continued to advance, bringing Peru into the fold in late 2007. But opposition in Congress to pending treaties with Colombia and Panama is leaving many bruised feelings in the South.

Every Latin American president today, regardless of political leaning, is a nationalist first. Not even Colombia's Alvaro Uribe, the president most closely identified with the United States, supports U.S. intervention in Iraq, the isolation of Chavez, or such internationally unpopular policies as the U.S. stance on the Kyoto Treaty. Calderón and others also have been quick to criticize American immigration policy. Chavez and Castro aside, the pro- or anti-American moniker placed on Latin American governments is largely meaningless.

One reason for the ideological stability is that the center left in Latin America does not want to repeat the disastrous statist economic policies of the 1960s and 1970s, which led to hyperinflation and bankrupted much of the region. Economic growth has been around 5 percent in recent years, which pales in comparison to Asia but is good nonetheless. The specter of inflation, which hurts the poor disproportionately, has been largely vanquished. Interest rates are increasingly accessible. Government debt is manageable in most countries, many of which run surpluses. While corruption tainted some past privatizations, and other free market reforms were never fully implemented, most governments are now loath to unwind what they have accomplished.

That said, the gap between rich and poor has widened, especially in Brazil, where it is the widest in the world. Some of that gap is due to a continuing oligopoly, but more of it (perhaps most of it) is due to the premium paid for information-age skills held mostly by the university-educated class. Every government in the region has been trying to address the gap, mostly through education programs, though the quality is mixed, and early childhood education barely exists. The hope is that the new demographic window of opportunity will stimulate improvement.

The primary economic weakness in Latin America is that growth is externally driven. It has been fueled by low international interest rates, high commodity prices, and remittances. Only 6 months ago, economic analysts were crowing that the soaring stock markets in the region were proof that Latin America was no longer financially dependent on the United States. That optimism crashed in about a day and a half in summer 2008 as U.S. markets dove in response to the subprime mortgage crisis. The Latin markets dropped even more, out of realization that rising interest rates in the United States mean larger rate rises in Latin America and less international investment capital. The markets recovered somewhat but remain unstable.

With only a few exceptions, Latin America has not been able to industrialize the way Asia did, leaving it more vulnerable to international shocks and trends. The booms in India and China have contributed to high prices for Latin American commodities such as food, minerals, and oil. That high demand will likely continue for some years, but the boom-and-bust cycles of commodity markets will surely exact a price sooner or later. Some countries, such as Chile and Colombia, are partly protected by stabilization funds, while others are not.

Current economic and demographic trends are reasons to be optimistic that the region will continue to grow at a solid pace. But for the region to truly break the shackles of its underdevelopment and move alongside Asia as an emerging global power, it must build domestic savings, investments, and consumption. It also must grow some 8–10 percent a year. The favorable demographics are estimated by some economists to be worth up to 1.5 percent in extra economic growth, but there is little to suggest today that Latin America will be as aggressive as Asia has been.

Even Brazil, grouped with Russia, India, and China as one of the so-called BRIC countries with rapidly developing economies, will likely remain what it always has been: the country of the future. Brazil will grow in influence as an international and regional political actor, perhaps even joining a rejiggered United Nations Security Council or its equivalent. But the country's global influence will come more from its diplomatic savvy and its representation of Latin America than from its own economic muscle. Brazil's exports will consist mostly of agricultural and other commodities and some heavy industrial products, such as airplanes and steel. But they will not include fruits of the technological revolution that will be the essence of economic power in the future. A technological exception is in biofuels, where Brazil is indeed a leader, but that, too, is a commodity.

Military influence emanating from the region, meanwhile, is out of the question. Brazil and Argentina shut down their nuclear weapons research years ago, in a show of political maturity.

From a U.S. perspective, all this is not bad. While it denies the United States and the world a larger economic partner, it also simplifies the world with one less contender for leadership.

MIGRATION TO THE UNITED STATES

Latin American immigration into the United States will continue to grow at a fast rate. Combined with birthrate trends among Hispanic women already in the country, that immigration will lead to a continued browning of America.

The rate of migration, legal and illegal, peaked in 2006 and has declined since, due in some measure to heightened border enforcement. But the absolute number of Hispanics entering the country still remains historically high. The nation's 43 million Hispanics are projected to grow from 14 percent of the population today to more than 22 percent by 2025. Hispanics are projected to be a quarter of the population by 2050. Already one in four teens is Hispanic.

This trend has raised divisive issues at home and concerns among European allies abroad. At home, the issue is whether this great Hispanization of America might affect its culture, identity, and even governance. The argument is that the Latin American migrants, especially the two-thirds who are Mexicans, do not share the country's founding Protestant values and will not assimilate and acculturate. The proximity of Mexico, the pervasiveness of Spanish, and the sheer size of the Hispanic immigration flow make this migration different from previous ones. It is an argument made most cogently by Samuel Huntington but taken up more rabidly by conservative talk radio and a populist, nativist backlash to the immigration. Much of the focus is on the 13 million immigrants here illegally and on the pressure put on some local school and hospital budgets to service the new arrivals. Racism among some of the nativists adds a potentially violent undercurrent.

European allies are more concerned by the foreign policy implications. Will the demographic trend result in a U.S. foreign policy that raises Latin America in priority and lowers Europe and Asia? President George W. Bush, a Texan with Hispanic affinity, underlined that fear by giving Mexico pride of place in his early months in office.

The concerns at home and abroad are misplaced. Repeated studies show that while first-generation Latin immigrants retain their close ties to home and speak Spanish, their children are thoroughly American. The school systems and the media are the great integrators, as they were for past immigration waves. Second- and third-generation Hispanics speak limited Spanish and read and write less. Their patriotism, on the other hand, is high, as reflected in military enlistment rates and participation in community organizations. The sizeable Hispanic caucus in the Congress, which includes two Senators, focuses on domestic policy, including immigration, but has shown little interest in North-South issues. The exception is Cuba, Cuban exiles, and Cuban-American legislators, though new generations of Cuban-Americans are more flexible than their predecessors.

The great Hispanic minority is already having a major impact on popular culture, from food to sports to music, but is unlikely to affect the values and identity that hold the country together and define it. After all, Spain, which was the first colonizer of what is now the United States, is a fully Western country and has left a strong mark on traditions in many parts of the United States. The new arrivals from Latin America follow mostly in Spanish footsteps.

Indeed, the real concern is the opposite: the country would be adversely affected by the loss of first-generation Hispanic immigrants, including those here illegally. The Nation's economic growth rate has been historically high and its unemployment rate historically low during the immigration surge of the last two decades, suggesting if not a causal link, at least the absence of a negative impact. It also suggests that jobs are not being taken from natives, though there has been some effect on the level of wages at the low end. Due to low fertility rates among non-Hispanic whites, the growth in the labor force going forward will be stagnant without immigration, creating a major economic bottleneck. Even those here illegally, moreover, are helping shore up Social Security by their contributions, while the future value of residential real estate, the primary asset of middle-class Americans, depends on the immigrant surge. As the baby boom generation moves into retirement, the supply of houses going on the market will otherwise far outstrip demand.

There conceivably is a tipping point at which unchecked immigration growth can turn adverse for the Nation's economy, culture, identity, and governance. And clearly the unprecedented level of illegal immigration suggests a need for better regulation and controls. The Bush administration's proposed immigration package balanced those concerns with the country's economic requirements. The bill was buried in the fury of the anti-immigrant backlash. One assumes that sooner or later, reason will prevail.

Chinese Influence in Latin America

Chinese influence in Latin America has grown at a remarkable clip. What began as science, sports, and minor military exchanges in the 1980s has developed into a major trade and investment partnership. The trend presents challenges for the United States as China forages the world in search of oil, foodstuffs, and other natural resources to fuel its economic engine.

Chinese trade with Latin America is about one-tenth that of the United States, but that figure is misleading. Mexico and the small nations of Central America are closely integrated with the U.S. economy and skew the regional numbers. Chinese economic influence is felt most in South America. Exports from Argentina, Brazil, and Chile to China soared from insignificant amounts in 1990 to 10–12 percent today, or roughly equal to what those three Southern Cone countries export to the United States. Between 2000 and 2003, Brazil's exports to China grew five times, Argentina's nearly four times, Chile's more than two times, and even Mexico's ten times off a small base. One result has been record trade surpluses in many Latin American countries.

Since 2001, a Chinese president or communist party chairman has visited almost every South American country and Mexico, and South American presidents have traveled to Beijing in return. Trade is now evolving rapidly into capital investment. In 2004, President Hu Jintao signed 39 bilateral agreements in Latin America and announced $100 billion in investments over the next 10 years, most of it in railroads, ports, and other infrastructure, as well as in oil exploration and extraction, mining, and steel production.

For Latin America, China offers welcome diversification of markets. The downside is that it is also a competitor for manufactured goods, both domestically and internationally. Average Chinese wages are one-fourth of Latin America's, undercutting in particular much of Mexico and Central America's export advantage to the United States.

The prime challenge looking forward for the United States would seem to be more than merely commercial. The region provides some 30 percent of all U.S. oil imports. Venezuela alone fluctuates between the fourth and fifth largest supplier. But "resource nationalism" is popping up in the region. Ecuador and Bolivia have moved to nationalize foreign oil and gas companies, and all the oil exporters are looking for ways to reduce their dependence on the United States. Venezuela has signed an agreement with Colombia to build a pipeline to the Pacific with the express purpose of diverting some of its U.S. sales to China. Competition for resources could become a security concern.

The Chinese military is not absent. It has direct military-to-military relations with many Latin American countries and is collaborating with Brazil on rocket and satellite technology. Since 1999, China has replaced Russia in using Cuba as a communications and electronic espionage base.

More subtly, China also presents itself as an alternative development model. That model focuses on reducing poverty at the expense of democracy, and forsakes international economic institutions such as the International Monetary Fund and their imposition of formulas that are more free market than China's. The Chinese example has resonance in Cuba, Venezuela, and the more backward Andean countries, such as Bolivia and Ecuador. There is, of course, nothing unique about the model. The United States supported similar authoritarian formulas in some East Asian countries in earlier decades. But to the extent there is a favored American model today, it is one of democracy, human rights, open markets, and respect for First World concerns such as ecology and labor rights. Translated pragmatically, Chinese money, unlike American, comes with no strings attached. That is an attraction.

China's influence in the region will only grow, given its need for natural resources. That said, Beijing will not be a security threat to Washington for some time. More than anything, the Latin Americans are looking for trade diversification, which is normal. China is now the third largest trade partner of the United States, but its political and military influence in the region is negligible. Latin America is culturally Western. Most of its political and economic elite have studied in the United States and have close personal North-South ties. The biggest danger may be overreaction by the United States to a perceived threat that is more idea than reality.

DRUGS, GUERRILLA VIOLENCE, AND INDIGENOUS GROUPS

This might seem an unusual grouping, but the link between drug trafficking and guerrilla violence has become symbiotic. Much of the violence, meanwhile, takes place in indigenous areas, where separate political sensitivities might boil over to become of concern to the hemisphere.

The "war on drugs" is an unfortunate policy title, for it raises unrealistic expectations and frustrations between the United States and Latin America. So long as the U.S. market for illegal Latin American drugs such as cocaine and heroin exists, the supply will continue. There is no reason to believe that either will wane in the foreseeable future. The impact of drug traffic on the United States, however, is negligible compared to its impact in Latin America, which has suffered the brunt of the violence, including the murder of political leaders and many innocent civilians. The direct challenge to governance in Latin America by drug traffickers peaked with the suppression of the Medellin cartel in Colombia in the 1990s. But the traffickers remain a strong and fluid presence that will continue to exploit weak governments in the region. Even in Brazil, for example, drug gangs have brazenly attacked city halls and police posts in cities such as Rio de Janeiro. An ongoing war between drug gangs has increased tensions along the U.S.-Mexican border.

In Colombia over the last decade, the trafficking has taken a more insidious turn. Bogota faces the region's only major guerrilla insurgency, involving mostly the leftist Revolutionary Armed Forces of Colombia (*Fuerzas Armadas Revolucionarias de Colombia,* or FARC), which numbers some 15,000. Under President Uribe, the FARC has been beaten back mostly to isolated mountain jungles, but it maintains a capacity to strike anywhere in the country. Having survived 40 years, it is unlikely to disappear over the next decade. One reason is that it now lives off the lucrative drug trade. A complication is that the right-wing paramilitary groups that grew up 20 years ago to combat the guerrillas in areas where the military was weak also live off the drug trade. The government has managed to demobilize many of the paramilitaries, but it is proving difficult to sever their drug ties. Through Plan Colombia, the United States has been instrumental in helping the military regain ascendancy in the fighting, but the only real hope for the FARC to disappear over the next 20 years is for its leaders to tire of jungle life. Rural development programs, a genuine electoral democracy, and strong economic growth in recent years deny the guerrillas some of their reason for being, but problems of poverty remain. More importantly, however, ideological inertia and drug profits are too much for the guerrillas to abandon easily.

Indigenous groups are not directly involved at the violent end of the traffic, or with the FARC. But they have historically grown much of the coca leaf crop throughout the Andean region, first for their own consumption, then for the traffickers. More importantly, they are emerging as a resentful political force in heavily indigenous countries such as Ecuador, Bolivia, Peru, Mexico, and Guatemala. In Bolivia, the war on drugs is seen as an affront to local indigenous culture and helped spur Morales to electoral victory (even though many of the growers in Bolivia and Colombia are in fact ambitious town dwellers moving to the countryside to cash in on a lucrative crop). Bolivia in early 2008 was in the midst of drawing and instituting a new constitution, and the most explosive issue was the quandary that has divided the country since its beginning: the different cultures and economic interests of the more Hispanic lowlands and the more indigenous mountains. In Ecuador, where rioting by indigenous groups has overthrown several governments in recent years, and in Peru and Colombia, the issues often involve mining in indigenous areas or government social policies. In Chiapas, indigenous resentment dating back to colonial land grabs erupted in rebellion. It was no coincidence that Oaxaca was the center of a long, violent standoff between the government and leftist protestors in 2007. Oaxaca is also the unofficial capital of Mexico's indigenous culture. Tiny terrorist groups that continue to blow up pipelines and other targets in Mexico often invoke indigenous themes in their tracts, as did the telegenic Subcomandante Marcos in Chiapas. Many of these "revolutionary" leaders are not indigenous themselves, but the bigger point is that it is all part of a brewing indigenous backlash throughout the region that threatens cultural cohesion, national identity, and governance. From a U.S. point of view, what deserves watching is whether that backlash might lead to generalized violence, a link to drug trafficking, or the failure of an Andean state.

Shocks
CUBA
Cuba will undergo a transition, probably to a democratic, noncommunist government, following the death of Castro. He has held together the "revolution" through force and personality and by exploiting resentment against the United States over such issues as the shortsighted American embargo. But Cuba in the end is part of a Western cultural tradition and, with the end of the Cold War, there is no international environment to nourish Cuba on a continued separate path in the hemisphere. Chavez is hardly an inspiration for nationalistic Cubans.

The democratic transition will not be immediate but will likely take place over the 5 to 10 years following Castro's death, which may be imminent. Certainly his brother or any other conceivable replacement is highly unlikely to make any major changes while Fidel is alive. There is little popular pressure inside Cuba for immediate change. Cubans are not particularly happy under Castro, but they fear instability and the considerable repressive apparatus still in place. Most of the dissidents, moreover, are in Miami, where they have made new lives. Still, the forces seem to be in place for an unraveling, probably not unlike what happened in the Soviet Union or communist Eastern Europe. The potential for a shock amid so much flux is obvious, complicated not only by internal actors in Cuba, but also by the Cuban-American community in the United States.

Anything that smacks of a power grab by the United States in Cuba, even intervention on behalf of exiles hoping to regain lost properties, will be sure to set off a wave of anti-American protests and possible violence in Cuba and throughout Latin America. It would also reinforce the regional left led by Chavez. The motivation will not be nostalgia for Castro or communism, but solidarity behind what will be seen as Latin American independence from historical U.S. bullying in the hemisphere.

On the other hand, if Cuba disintegrates into anarchy, the United States will feel a responsibility to intervene. The smart way, following the Haitian example, will be through multilateral institutions such as the Organization of American States or United Nations. The American populace, which in polls has never supported the embargo, and the government will have to control the exile community—no easy task given the exiles' passions and skills in manipulating Congress.

VENEZUELA

A positive shock is that the Chavez government likely will implode, perhaps in the next 10 years, although it could last as many as 20. Chavez follows in the tradition of many populist *caudillos*, almost all of whom were impaled on their economic policies. Chavez's own policies are economically unsustainable. Buoyed by high oil income, he has been able to buy off the masses and even segments of the business community. But he is running large budget deficits and has put the country's cash cow, Petróleos de Venezuela, S.A., the state oil company, in the hands of political cronies. The company's famed professionalism through the ups and downs of previous governments has been lost. Corruption under Chavez has generally ballooned, though that is hardly peculiar to his government. Venezuela, cursed by oil, has for the past century been plagued by some of the most corrupt and ineffective governments in the hemisphere.

Chavez has skillfully created an "illiberal democracy" in which he has used the vote and the constitution to build an authoritarian state. The narrow defeat in late 2007 of an ambitious smorgasbord of constitutional changes that would have further solidified his power and allowed his reelection for life slowed and may have stopped the slide toward dictatorship. Still, he has used his considerable power to reinstitute the failed Latin American big government policies of the 1960s.

Oil wealth can paper over the cracks for only so long. Whether the end will come by military coup is hard to predict. Chavez has been careful to promote his friends in the military and, with Cuban aid, to create parallel paramilitary structures. But however the collapse of Chavez comes, Venezuela has sufficiently strong social and political institutions to survive Chavez and is unlikely to become a failed state. The United States need not be involved more than tangentially. Latin America has seen many collapses and coups. This will be just one more.

The recommended policy for the United States is to ignore Chavez instead of getting in public disputes with him or with Castro. Both are brilliant manipulators of public opinion.

NARCO OR FAILED STATE

We have been living off and on with a failed state in Haiti for years. As in Haiti, a failed state likely would imply military involvement by the United States or by other countries in the region to restore order. No other failed states are imminent. But planning would be prudent.

The same is true for a narco state. The U.S. solution for the emergence of a narco state in Panama was to invade. Earlier diplomatic intervention to control Manuel Noriega, then-president of Panama and a drug trafficker, could have avoided that small war. In Colombia, although Ernesto Samper did not create a narco state, the U.S. answer to his receiving campaign contributions from traffickers was to cut off aid. It was a disastrous policy, creating a vacuum that allowed both traffickers and guerrillas to grow considerably. No narco state is imminent. But again, planning would be prudent.

MIGRATION SURGE INTO THE UNITED STATES AND
POLITICAL BACKLASH

Chaos in Venezuela or Cuba, natural disasters in Central America, global recession, or a failed Andean state are all events that could lead to a surge in migration, legal or illegal, to the United States. Yet the angry nativist movement in the United States is already on the political warpath over current immigration. What might a surge bring?

A shock is unlikely to come from the immigration itself. Improved border and employment controls likely will block inordinate numbers of new immigrants from arriving. The country probably has the capacity to absorb the rest. More problematic is the populist backlash. The wall and fences going up on the Mexican border are already seen in Latin America as a slap in the face. The mass witch hunts and deportations demanded by the nativists, if adopted, would create a reverse backlash in Latin America, including among America's friends. It could easily shock our Latin American neighbors into a solid anti-American stance that could damage the security interests of the United States vis-à-vis oil imports, international alliance politics, and economic and political competition with China. How your people are handled in other countries is taken personally at home. American history itself is filled with examples.

Inside the United States, meanwhile, mass deportations would be tantamount to shooting ourselves in the foot. The economy would be strapped by labor shortages. Both economic growth and competitiveness would be undercut. Taken to an extreme, national hysteria against immigration could be a genuine shock, changing the historical direction of the country and its place in the world.

Policy Recommendations

In addition to the specific recommendations mentioned above, a general one not mentioned stands out glaringly. The United States must reengage the region with a positive, inspiring agenda.

Latin American policy today has no direction. It is dominated by negatives. The right has forced American policies into one set of negatives. Anti-Castro, anti-Chavez, anti-immigrant, anti-drug, anti-Kyoto, anti–anything that smells of social generosity or moving to the left are part of that set. Meanwhile, human rights, ecological, union, and farming groups have hijacked trade negotiations, imposing another set of negative conditions and restrictions. The U.S. response to the one genuine security issue in the hemisphere—the guerrilla challenge in Colombia—is conditioned by human rights negatives, despite overwhelming public opposition to the guerrillas and demands for more military action by the government. It is not that some of these negatives are not worthy. Being for labor rights or against the Castro dictatorship, for example, are laudable goals. The problem is that the negatives, whether worthy or not, have too often been turned by their respective lobbies into single-issue obsessions—some self-righteous, others stingy and crabby—and have taken over policy. Lost is any sense of an overarching positive vision of our national interest in the region and what we offer in the best interest for Latin Americans. Lost also is a sense of mature perspective, and of leadership to reach consensus. Instead of inspiring, we seem more to be bullying, which naturally creates resentments, no matter the policy or cause in question.

A visionary policy should have as its aim a stable, prosperous, democratic hemisphere. Some of the components would include doing the following:

- accelerate free trade agreements, approve the pending Colombia agreement, and loosen patently unfair and hypocritical American agricultural and steel subsidies
- continue military support under Plan Colombia against the insurgents there

- for development aid, minimize the blunt instrument of performance requirements, such as counternarcotics measures that have little to do with the real world
- institute immigration cooperation, including temporary worker programs
- provide favorable treatment for biofuel imports and technical cooperation, especially to insure food needs
- renew emphasis on antipoverty programs.

A visionary policy would also include an element of public diplomacy that shows a respect for our neighbors by listening to them, while projecting our vision for the hemisphere and its peoples. Such a visionary policy would also be more effective in winning support from Latin America for many of those individual policy goals important to us, in the hemisphere and in the world.

Part III: Conclusions

17

Challenges for National Security Organizations and Leadership Development: Trends and Shocks in Complex Adaptive Systems

Transformation Chairs Network[1]

THIS CHAPTER IS DIVIDED into three sections. The first includes examples from the rest of the book to highlight issues that national security organizations and their leaders will have to face. Some of these are not often considered by national security professionals today. The second section outlines characteristics of the national security organizations that will be needed to meet these complex emerging challenges and describes the leadership capabilities needed to promote organizational adaptability. The final section focuses on ways to develop leaders for these organizations and how Department of Defense (DOD) educational institutions can contribute.

Issues for Leaders to Consider

The forces described in these chapters will affect the future national security environment deeply. Many impose increasing, and seemingly inexorable, rates of change. Linkages among the trends introduce poorly understood second- and third-order effects and amplify the complexity of these consequences. We will use five examples to illustrate some features of the emerging national security environment to help demonstrate how to develop institutional responses and educate future leaders:

- The velocity of change in information technology (IT) could lead to more than a 100,000 percent increase in processing power per unit of cost over the next 15 years. In addition to IT, concurrent revolutions are under way in biotechnology, robotics, nanotechnology, the search for alternatives to hydrocarbons, and socio-cognitive science. Progress in biotechnology is breaking down the boundaries between living and nonliving systems.[2]

Besides their technical outcomes, the collective developments in "info-bio-robo-nano-hydro-cogno" also will have profound effects on the social, ethical, legal, and political structures of many different societies in many different ways.

- The youth bulges in developing countries will exacerbate tensions in "disorderly spaces," such as Thomas Barnett's "gap" areas, even as the aging populations of our traditional allies may make them less dependable partners for security contingencies, especially expeditionary ones.[3]

- Globally empowered individuals and small groups increasingly are able to collaborate, compete, and even fight while widely dispersed. Improvised explosive devices, cyber tools, and perhaps biological weapons will allow them to inflict more and more damage. Moreover, many of these players can use the Internet, cell phones, and other information-age tools to organize and operate more rapidly than most governments.

- Nation-states no longer have a monopoly on the wealth created within their borders, the ideas generated by their citizens, or even the use of force. The number of nonstate actors is growing, and they can not only influence the culture, opinions, and governance of millions but also inflict dispropor-tionate damage on populations and on the brittle, critical infrastructures of modern societies.

- Environmental, energy, resource, demographic, and health issues are interlinked and will become much more important in global and domestic affairs. Across these areas, collaboration, competition, and conflict will intermingle on many levels, often without clear demarcation;[4] witness the emerging food crisis.

The trends outlined in these chapters suggest developments that are pro-ducing the conditions for a "military revolution," a phenomenon that occurs when key aspects of society change, as in the industrial or information revolutions, thereby changing the environment in which the military operates and forcing the armed forces to make fundamental adjustments. The military will need radically new thinking to address not only less predictable and less stable futures, but also societies whose constructs, values, and reward structures will be shift-ing rapidly.

Changes in thinking are under way. From the beginning, advocates of network-centric operations (NCO)[5] understood that effective implementation would require cultural change and that factors such as doctrine, organization, training, material, leadership and education, personnel, and facilities would have to evolve together for NCO to succeed. In late 2005, DOD Directive 3000.05 on stability, security, transition, and reconstruction noted that such operations were as important as major combat operations—an enormous change. This was soon followed by National Security Presidential Directive 44, which addressed the management of interagency efforts and established the Coordinator for Reconstruction and Stabilization in the State Department. The range of DOD concerns was expanded through the "asymmetric, catastrophic and disruptive" threat categories introduced in the 2006 Quadrennial Defense Review.[6] More recently, the Maritime Strategy has said that "preventing wars is as important as winning wars." The Army's new operations manual (Field Manual 3-0) "recognizes that current conflicts defy solutions by military means alone."[7]

This thinking must now extend beyond the traditional boundaries of defense to encompass the full range of national security concerns, recognizing that many new categories need to be integrated. How the public-private elements of national power are integrated, and vulnerabilities mitigated, will be key issues for future decisionmakers. In the aggregate, the national security structure for this environment will need:

- an early warning system to spot problems at the national level. A group of "forecasters/spotters" should be assigned within the government to look ahead and make judgments as to where the next crises (not necessarily wars) are coming from.
- agile organizations able to anticipate, prepare for, and respond effectively to crises. The government needs to minimize bureaucratic obstacles.
- enlightened leadership. Leaders must be willing to listen and make good judgments about what they hear. As a prerequisite, the leadership selection process needs to produce and promote such people.
- a broad spectrum of capabilities and people. The U.S. Government will need to harness the wide range of talents and capabilities existing within the government, and leverage those in the private sector, to respond to the types of crises identified in these pages. This will extend well beyond the types of interagency collaboration proposed for stability operations.
- an education base. The Nation must begin to develop the educational base to support these capabilities, especially in those attracted to military or civilian government service.

Ongoing research suggests ways to shape the development of these components. Concepts from complexity theory, such as nonlinear dynamics and multiscale systems, apply to many problems. A common theme in this research is that new components emerge from the convergence of trends, leading to "discontinuous, nonlinear, macro-level changes in the environment," often triggered by "micro-level events."[8] These nonlinear, discontinuous events challenge institutions and leaders, but can be addressed through organization design, leadership, education, and training.

Organizational Characteristics and Leadership Capabilities for Adaptability

Future national security organizations will need to be agile and effective over the wide range of complex interactions and high rates of change described throughout this book. But today's organizational designs and cultures do not support, much less nurture, the mindsets and skills needed to achieve the rates of learning and innovation required to adapt effectively. As one group of observers noted:

> Organizational issues are as critical as technology issues. The innovative thinking we apply to our organizational and collaborative designs is as important as our actual innovations in science and technology. The central tenets of this innovation are how we form questions; how we organize; how we execute; and how we understand and cope with our limits.[9]

The group went on to say:

> Our core academic and government institutions have fundamentally rigid structures: they are non-responsive, non-flexible, and non-adaptive, and they exist outside of the marketplace. Enabling them to collaborate, innovate, and take risks entails making significant changes in their design.[10]

This section outlines the broad characteristics of organizations that might be able to meet these challenges and the leadership capabilities required for adaptability.

EARLY WARNING

The complexity of the emerging environment, the velocity of change, and the "macro effects from micro inputs" phenomena will complicate the already difficult task of avoiding surprise. Moreover, the drivers of such change often will not be the traditional targets of intelligence and warning staffs, and the speed of emergence will tax the ability of traditional government mechanisms to anticipate, or even react.[11]

An analysis of trends and shocks can help decisionmakers prepare, and it can perhaps encourage steps to increase national resilience. But taking timely action will require new instruments. Two, in particular, are worth considering:

- Effective, collaborative linkages between the public and private sectors will need to be established. The complexity of the problems and their nontraditional drivers will exceed the ability of the government alone to address them. A small group of senior advisors, drawn from inside and out of government, should be available to review emergent issues to look for divergences from trends that could lead to near-term shocks. This will not be an easy problem—the failure of both government and industry to establish effective information sharing and analysis centers (ISACs) over more than a decade shows how hard public–private sector information exchange can be, but effective, integrated action will not be possible without it.

- Scientific change will be such an important driver of the emerging environment that the President will need a widely experienced, technically skilled set of advisors as a core part of the administration. Science and technology–related early warning and science policy development cannot be pigeonholed as merely the province of technical specialists. Science is teeing up messy issues that will affect the life, liberty, and pursuit of happiness of the American people, such as synthetic biology, directed evolution, and neural prostheses. But there is no forum in the United States today to conduct a sustained, reasoned, in-depth debate over the legal, social, moral, and ethical implications of these questions. Whether political leaders like it or not, these issues will impact people's lives, often with unintended consequences. Even though many individuals may not be interested, the people as a whole deserve a means for the national leadership to understand their potential impact and act on them in a timely manner.

AGILE AND EFFECTIVE ORGANIZATIONS

Agile, robust, and effective organizations will need to draw on the "requisite variety"[12] of capabilities at the individual, team, organization, and societal levels to respond in a timely way to challenges and adapt more quickly than our adversaries.

Such organizations need a culture that encourages five main traits:

- a sustained commitment to organization-wide learning, including both broad education and focused training
- an open-minded and inquiring mindset among its leaders
- management practices that focus attention on key issues, then align and converge resources with minimal use of detailed, top-down direction
- collaborative approaches that seek out connections and determine patterns, while emphasizing the importance of cultural understanding
- an ability to leverage technology, anticipate its opportunities and challenges, and understand potential social, political, and economic interactions.

Moving toward this organizational model will not be easy. Leadership of such organizations will be challenging. Fortunately, research on leadership is helping to define which mindsets, capabilities, and behaviors support sustainable, competitive social systems, including organizations and societies. These capabilities are generally scalable or fractal—the structure and dynamics of the capabilities are the same, irrespective of the size or level of an effort (in other words, they apply to individuals, teams, organizations, and societies).

Theoretical and empirical work, plus operational experience, in applying complexity theories (sometimes known as "emergent perspective") have contributed to a deeper understanding of social systems.[13] *Social systems* can be defined as dynamic networks of multiple individual agents (individuals, organizations, or societies) that constantly respond and adapt to one another's actions in competitive and collaborative ways. These systems show a capacity for self-organization. Importantly, the outcomes are rarely predictable; the causal relationships are nonlinear, and control tends to be highly decentralized. In the military sphere, the underlying concepts of network-centric operations were developed with an understanding of complex adaptive systems.[14]

Results from the Trends and Shocks project reinforce the view of social systems as complex entities where collaboration, competition, and conflict often coexist. In this context, one definition of transformation is "accelerated adaptation." To achieve this, both learning and developing the capacity to learn are of strategic importance in sustaining our national competitive position globally.

CHARACTERISTICS OF LEADERS
An extensive body of literature addresses desirable leadership capabilities, mindsets, and behaviors for the above environment. Such characteristics include:

- *sufficient cognitive agility* to reconcile multiple and diverse mental frameworks[15]
- *sufficient cognitive complexity* to respond and adapt to diverse and changing environmental and internal stimuli. From the perspective of complexity, individuals, teams, organizations, and societies must include enough variety in their cognitive frameworks to be able to adapt to a range of circumstances. A subset of this capability is a high degree of self-awareness, including emotional awareness, enabling the entity (whether an individual, organization, or society) to identify the assumptions being brought to particular settings and understand the limits of their application.[16]
- a *worldview consistent with complexity*—for example, embracing uncertainty and change as opportunity, learning from diverse points of view, and tolerating differences
- enhanced *capabilities for mutual feedback and power-sharing*[17]
- an *ability to recognize emergent patterns* in both social and physical systems[18]
- an *ability to harness collective intelligence* by working in an inclusive, collaborative way to grow communities of trust, including the ability to encourage conversations, enhance connections to share information, and support mutual sense-making[19]
- an *understanding of sense-making and learning processes* and how they contribute to an organization's capability for innovation and adaptation, and ultimately for timely action at the individual, team, organizational, and societal level.[20]

From these insights, it is clear that effective leaders, at many levels of an organization, must understand the implications of sense-making and learning so they can support organizational cultures and processes that enhance innovation and adaptation. However, these are demanding skill sets. Developing them will need hard, sustained work.

DEVELOPING THE ABILITY TO HARNESS RESOURCES

The government's ability to harness resources is constrained by stovepipes within and between departments and agencies. Information-sharing is hard enough; differing personnel and financial processes compound the difficulties. The longstanding failure of the ISACs to promote effective information exchange between industry and government was noted earlier. Moreover, efforts by government agencies to outsource more and more functions have had decidedly mixed results.

Governments certainly can mobilize the Nation's public and private resources when it articulates clear goals and follows through (defeat the Axis, build the interstate highway system, put a man on the moon). But there are even more examples of heroic objectives that have not been achieved (war on poverty, "whip inflation now," war on drugs). The preceding discussion suggests that uncoordinated approaches by lone government agencies are not likely to succeed in the future.

In this vein, Secretary of Defense Robert Gates' November 2007 speech on the need to put more emphasis on diplomatic and foreign assistance aspects of U.S. foreign policy[21] was encouraging. However, the types of crises identified in the Trends and Shocks project will need coordination well beyond the types of interagency collaboration proposed for stability operations. The partnerships needed to harness resources effectively will involve all three branches of the Federal Government, as well as the active participation of the private sector.

THE IMPORTANCE OF SOCIAL AND COGNITIVE RESEARCH

To improve DOD's ability to collaborate and meet the challenges of information-age structures,[22] some researchers have challenged the department to explore organizational and leadership behaviors and models beyond traditional, centralized, hierarchical command and control (C^2). In this context, the 2007 article "Agility, Focus and Convergence"[23] is a seminal paper. It bridges the gap between military C^2 and the more nuanced approaches needed with civil-military partners in complex contingencies, such as disaster relief and stabilization operations. The growing body of research in the cognitive and social domains deserves more attention in military discussions on C^2, NCO, and complex contingencies.[24] To carry the challenge to military cultures further, researchers outside DOD argue that leadership is a process, not a phenomenon lodged in a role or in a specific individual.

In sum, wide-ranging research offers insights into leadership traits and organizational characteristics that can improve execution in both military operations and enterprise management. As noted above, these concepts apply far beyond DOD.

Leadership Development and the Roles of Educational Institutions

This section describes the challenges of developing leaders with the above characteristics and explains how DOD educational institutions can help prepare future leaders for complex environments.

DIFFICULTIES IN CHANGING ACADEMIC CURRICULA

The interacting trends outlined in the first section need to be taught in DOD academic institutions. But experience shows that it is hard to get even straightforward changes into professional military education (PME) curricula. For example, given the significant impact that communications and computing trends are having on the conduct of military operations, one would expect DOD educational institutions, particularly intermediate and senior war colleges, to be in the vanguard in ensuring that their students develop an in-depth understanding of the impact of information on military operations. In some cases, this has happened. For example, some elective courses have incorporated cutting-edge aspects of cyberspace operations and new definitions of transformation that extend beyond high-end warfare to include stabilization and reconstruction, homeland defense, allied and coalition relationships, and whole-of-government solutions. But core curricula typically have not embraced such changes. Some of the challenges faced by instructors at the Air University in introducing courses on IT trends and their implications are described as an example below. Faculty at other schools report similar experiences.[25]

In December 2005, the United States Air Force added cyberspace as a domain of operations to its mission statement, "fly and fight in air, space and cyberspace." The Air Force leadership directed that the Service embrace cyberspace as a warfighting domain of operations on par with air, land, sea, and space. Key to success is embracing a *cultural change,* such that every Airman understands the cyberspace domain and how the United States uses it to project national power and deliver sovereign options. Clearly, this cultural change must be reflected throughout training and education processes, and Air Force programs must consider cultural factors as they introduce capabilities.

However, despite this emphasis by senior Service leadership, the Air War College included just two instructional periods on cyberspace in academic year 2006. This will increase to approximately three instruction periods (one in each term) in academic year 2009, but only after the personal intervention of senior leadership. Fear of the unknown and curricula inflexibility have been key impediments. For example, much still needs to be clarified about cyberspace and cyberpower. Such doctrine as exists is incomplete and insufficient to serve as the basis for lesson materials. Also, if cyberspace is to be elevated, what is to be removed from or changed in existing educational programs?

The Officer Professional Military Education Policy (OPMEP) plays an important role in such decisions.[26] Curriculum development at PME institutions is a zero-sum game. Adding a lecture on the impact of technology on warfare usually means that an existing lecture would have to be removed. When the OPMEP required education on "how technological change affects the art and science of war" from 1996 to 2004, instructors at the Air War College were able to provide enhanced exposure to technology trends and their implications. But in August 2004, the OPMEP was revised, and the language was changed to incorporate education on technology only to the extent required to gain an "understanding of the role of technology in joint experimentation." The result was that all discussion of the impacts of new technologies on the art and science of warfare was deleted from the curriculum in some schools.

Between OPMEP revisions, topics of interest to DOD senior leaders can be designated as special areas of emphasis, but these often have little impact on curriculum development.[27] Within the Air Force, faculty at the Air Force Institute of Technology and cyberspace subject matter experts synthesized a list of five competencies for understanding and applying cyberspace and cyberpower concepts:[28] nature and characteristics of the domain; cyberspace capabilities and functions; integration of cyberspace effects with kinetic effects; employment of cyberspace capabilities; and law, policy, and ethics. A common theme is that cyberspace awareness alone is not enough—we must grow warriors who understand how cyberspace operations integrate with conventional kinetic operations.

A useful suggestion offered by Air Commodore Martin Doel of the Royal Air Force is to explore *horizontally integrating the impact of technology on warfare into the curriculum*. For example, military history courses could examine how various militaries responded to the high rates of change in aircraft propulsion technology by making investments in carrier aviation. Both horizontal and vertical curricula changes may be needed to give leaders the skills and knowledge to understand the complex sets of issues related to trends and shocks. Also in this vein, discussions of Clausewitz's concepts of fog and friction could include the impact of information and communications technology on fog and friction. To carry this even further, one observer recently described the convergence of the physical and cyber worlds by saying: "Virtualization is the continuation of war (and politics) by other means."[29] This is a profound observation, reflecting the growing importance of virtual reality in business, entertainment, training, and even diplomacy. Perhaps a bit premature at present, it will become more accurate as virtual worlds and gaming technology affect more and more aspects of human endeavor.

WAYS AHEAD

The trends presented in these pages describe an emerging environment that calls for much more organizational and planning adaptability than has been needed up to now. One respected observer has postulated that today's challenges must involve the whole of government, while conflicts of the future will involve the whole of society.[30] These challenges demand an instructional scope beyond just DOD educational institutions, and reinforce the importance of exposing students and faculty to new ways of thinking.

Within DOD, the cross-cutting nature of the challenges recommends more integrated and cooperative approaches among DOD educational institutions.[31] The process could start in three areas: leadership perspectives, collaborative communities, and best educational practices.

Recommendation 1: There should be greater collaboration among DOD educational institutions on defining and teaching the leadership perspectives and skills needed throughout national security organizations to achieve adaptability in the face of emerging national security challenges.

More leadership adaptability at all levels is essential. General Charles Krulak, then-Commandant of the Marine Corps, recognized this a decade ago with his concepts of the "strategic corporal" and the "three-block war."[32] Today, some environments require even more fundamental changes in thinking. Consider the following scenario: A combination of pandemic influenza and demographics is overwhelming the health care system in parts of the world and triggering mass migrations, leading to crises of governance in some areas and collapses of the economy in others. Concurrently, a cyberattack targets the power grid in a major developed country, cutting off electricity to many hospitals and threatening the integrity of the medical records system. Power interruptions at key national security installations threaten the ability to execute operational plans, while interruptions in fuel delivery put transportation systems at risk.

From an educational perspective, students need to be able to think through the organizational capabilities, leadership, and advanced planning skills needed to deal with such a situation. How do the required leadership competencies and organizational structures differ in order to meet the different challenges noted above? How much do the existing "core" leadership curricula need to be modified? If, as Amory Lovins has postulated, "real security" means "freedom from fear of privation and freedom from fear of attack," how can it be achieved? Are our students being prepared to address these kinds of questions?

Whatever knowledge is imparted while in school, effective leadership in the future will depend on continuous learning. Behaving in strategically effective ways in ill-defined, rapidly changing contexts requires that individuals, teams, organizations, and even networks of organizations be able to learn adaptively. Increasingly, strategy (and, by implication, its development, communication, implementation, and refinement) needs to be thought of as an ongoing learning process throughout the organization rather than as a document (the "strategic plan"). What senior leaders know will become less important than their ability to create conditions in which continuous and pertinent information-sharing and learning throughout the organization are prized and practiced.[33]

Recommendation 2: DOD educational institutions should create collaborative communities across their respective schools to share expertise and address issues of general relevance and importance.

Collaborative communities, working across school and Service boundaries, could be models of how to develop more adaptable organizations as well as sources of continuing insights about how to work across institutional stovepipes. Each collaborative community could focus on a different content area, such as cyberspace or leadership development. Whatever substance they produced, such networks would develop team identities and capabilities that could enhance future cooperative projects. The Transformation Chairs' network, sponsored by the Office of the Secretary of Defense and with representatives at educational institutions across DOD, is one such community. To date, this network has contributed to the analysis of issues such as cyberspace-related education, organizational development, leadership education, transformational concepts, and the Trends and Shocks project.

Students should be involved in these collaborative communities, drawing on their expertise and recent experiences. In addition, research and experimentation should be given more emphasis in the PME curricula. Faculty members can benefit from augmenting teaching with research, and students need to experiment with new concepts in addition to simply writing about what they read.

Recommendation 3: By collaborating across the network of DOD educational institutions, more consistent approaches can be developed to help schools do well at their respective missions and share best practices for continuing improvement.

This process should focus on measures of success. These include outcome assessments, such as the knowledge and skills a school wants students to have at graduation, how it will assess its effectiveness in achieving those outcomes, and how it will use such assessment data. This is consistent with nationwide practices. An educational institution's very accreditation may depend on the ability of its outcome assessment to show that the impacts it is having on its students are consistent with desired results.

Such outcomes are considered to be the relatively specific aspects of what people mean when they extol the benefits of "a good general education." This extends beyond particular course content to include fundamental intellectual and/or interpersonal skills such as effective writing, critical thinking, and teamwork. A school needs to provide relatively independent evidence, beyond just grades and transcripts, to show that students really are achieving the outcomes the institution considers most important, given its heritage, mission, and students.

As a test case, the Vice Chairman's recent initiative to enhance the readiness of graduates from all levels of PME to function effectively in an increasingly network-centric environment[34] can be used to drive curriculum change through outcome-oriented questions. This goes beyond just adding courses on cyber-space. A key part of the implicit outcomes assessment is the need to ask, "What do you want your students to learn?" rather than the more common, "What shall I teach?"

In this context, cyberspace should be thought of not just as a content area that only "cyberspace experts" should teach, but rather as something that affects virtually every subject taught in a school. This is consistent with Air Commodore Doel's suggestion about horizontal and vertical integration. For example, cyberspace familiarity might be developed among students much as "writing across the curriculum" is taught at some colleges. At such schools, the responsibility of developing effective student writing is assigned not just to the English department, but rather becomes part of the job description of every instructor in every department. There would certainly be growing pains to get to a steady state where that approach has been internalized by most instructors, but the benefits would be considerable. Among them are the student's ability to connect cyberspace insights to a wide range of disciplines and possibilities, and the related benefit of the student's greater likelihood of being more open-minded and willing to embrace the importance of cyberspace. Eventually, similar processes will be needed to assess the impact of emergent subjects such as biotechnology and nanotechnology.

The trends outlined in this book are making the world more complex. They will interact with and adapt to each other, and to society's responses, in ways that will challenge the ability of existing bureaucracies to function effectively. Collaboration, competition, and conflict will frequently overlap. Some now expand familiar diplomatic, information, military, and economic domains into a broader construct called MIDLIFE (military, information, diplomatic, legal, intelligence, financial, and economic), demanding more competencies. The scale and pace of scientific change will affect not just technologists, but also society and culture as a whole. Collectively, these changes will force a military revolution on the Armed Forces. The country's national security institutions must anticipate these changes and be able to adapt to meet them. In turn, DOD educational institutions must lean forward to prepare future leaders for the impending challenges. Collaborative approaches offer opportunities. *Effective, continuous learning is of strategic, national importance.*

18
Summarizing the Trends and Shocks

Neyla Arnas

Conflict

CONFLICTS ARE OFTEN considered the result of tensions between diverse forces. These trends in conflict can be explained by three points: the nature of the conflict, the reasons behind the conflict, and the way the conflict is conducted. The causes of today's conflicts are a mix of political, economic, social, psychological, and environmental elements, usually in some combination. Neo-medievalism, psychological factors, resources, and individual need drive conflict forward.

Modern conflicts typically will not be fought with advanced conventional weapons: the combatants are not always trained soldiers; they may be unskilled fighters with unsophisticated weapons. The technology of conflict will not remain static. Predicting how technological advances will fluctuate is difficult as technology is often subject to governmental jurisdiction, and such interference slows mission progress. A major attack on a military adversary is but one method of waging conflict. Infrastructures, economic and social symbols, and civilians have all become targets. Modern conflict is less and less about defeating the enemy in the physical arena, and more about prevailing in the cognitive domain.

Many contemporary conflicts are advanced by the exploitation of underground activities, which provide income and resources for illicit operations as well as operational support. Combatants operate out of remote or inaccessible locations. The legal instruments defining the laws of armed conflict are not observed.

A number of shocks can make the trends in conflict more disturbing. These shocks would be global in nature and could include:

- the use of a chemical, biological, radiological, or nuclear (CBRN) weapon
- the collapse of a major regional ally
- a major conflict over water

- community conflicts in Europe erupting from demographic and social tensions
- a domestic CBRN terrorism campaign
- U.S. withdrawal from global politics, creating widespread instability and conflict.

Global Demographics

All global population growth will occur in the poorest developing countries while the populations of many developing countries decline. The greatest impact from this shock will be felt in 20 years. It is now certain that the population of traditional U.S. allies—for example, the countries of Western Europe as well as Japan, South Korea, and others—will see significant aging, depletion of their labor force, and a decrease in population size. This can be expected to affect their ability to maintain a sufficient level of defense commitments. The consequences of this shock are being felt at present but are likely to intensify over the next 20 years.

Related to the aging trend described above is the need for labor force replenishment through immigration in many Western European countries. Beyond a simple need for workers, this deficiency applies equally for an improved ratio of workers to retirees on public pensions. While the impact of this shock is being felt currently, the need for immigrants can be expected to grow substantially over the next 20 years.

In addition, it now appears that population growth in sub-Saharan Africa may be greater than previously thought. This is primarily due to slower declines in birthrates than projected and, to a lesser extent, lower levels of HIV than previously estimated. The combination of poverty, population growth, and subnational conflicts is likely to be a dangerous one. The consequences of this shock will be most acute in approximately 20 years.

Economics and Energy

The United States, Western Europe, and Japan will remain the dominant economic powers, but their advantage will narrow as China, India, and possibly Russia continue to grow rapidly. Continued growth in the smaller economies, especially in Southeast Asia, in combination with changes in the financial architecture and the distribution of international reserves, will reshape the nature and outcomes of future shocks and likely reduce U.S. influence in countries that previously might have been open to partnership in efforts to contain China and Russia.

Continued growth in energy demand, slow progress on technology, and constraints on access to resources will mean sustained uncertainty in energy markets. Also, the concentration of energy resources and of demand growth in a limited number of countries will mean a new energy architecture, probably dominated by bilateral deals and alliances, many of which may not involve the Western countries that created the current architecture.

Potential economic shocks include:

* a major readjustment in China's trade with the United States and the European Union
* continuing, but as yet incomplete, transition to a new financial architecture
* pursuit of countries' immediate interests over policies favoring free trade and free flows of capital.

Environment and Energy

Water scarcity is a negative trend that threatens not only human life, but also sources of food. Emphasis, however, should be placed on specific regional contexts, where human activities change the demographics of natural resources. The greatest water-related threats are rapid changes in flow and rapid declines in quality, not scarcity.

A chemical spill not only would deprive a population of water security and access to clean water but also would illustrate how governments react to controlling information in times of disaster. This issue, therefore, has political potential as well. Unilateral dam-building poses a threat as it can create destabilizing dynamics in flow volume and timing in water control. A positive trend is the technological breakthrough in desalination that can provide a measure of conflict deterrence. Research shows evidence for cooperation rather than conflict over water between states, contrary to the intuitively appealing but evidence-weak "water wars" hypothesis.

Potential forest-related shocks are the trends in rapid deforestation, which represent a possible ingredient in the destabilization of key strategic states such as Indonesia. A change in the landscape due to deforestation has significant impact on those people who are highly dependent on forests for their livelihoods.

Energy and the race for natural resources will dominate the years ahead. The growing economies of India and especially China are increasingly bringing the United States into competition for access to resources, during which proxy conflicts may develop. Developed countries may provide financial and security aid to forces in resource-rich countries with the expectation of easier access to natural resources. The widespread fragility of the oil-producing nations in sub-Saharan Africa as well as the Middle East poses a threat to energy supply that could become a critical shock.

Climate change will likely impact security. Although shocks due to climate change might not occur for another two decades, impacts of climate change manifest themselves in the form of human migration, grievances, and loss of livelihoods. The establishment of U.S. Africa Command presents opportunities for the U.S. military to work with military and civilian partners to address negative environmental trends and advance security goals through environmental engagement.

If the U.S. security community wants to help mitigate the impacts of these trends and potential shocks, it must find direct and indirect means to support greater civilian efforts to address the environmental and energy trends that are bound up with related economic, social, and political challenges. The United States must also adjust its definition of long-term security planning to accommodate the still longer timeframes associated with environmental and energy trends.

Health Care

The cost of U.S. health care has risen dramatically and may soon reach a breaking point. Much of the U.S. medical infrastructure, regulations, and mindset is inefficient, decaying, and becoming obsolete. Public health is underfunded, and its interaction with clinical medicine is changing. Health care manpower needs are increasingly misappropriated or unmet. The culture and education of health care are changing. Future medical professionals must be properly trained in order to deal with this trend.

International trends include growing numbers of elderly patients straining medical systems and consuming resources and increasing amounts of international travel and movement of people across borders. Beneficial and malevolent technological advances are flourishing internationally and domestically even as microbial drug resistance is increasing and new antibiotic and vaccine development is floundering.

Societies are experiencing increased crowding, industrialization, and urbanization, stressing their health care systems. Clean water for drinking and sanitation is becoming scarcer. Wars and regional conflicts are increasingly straining militaries, peacekeeping forces, and health care systems.

Interest in infectious disease, chronic disease, and global surveillance of disease is changing. Health care, and particularly infectious disease containment in the developing world, is being overwhelmed by a broken system of governance, corruption, and marginal economies.

Potential shocks include:

- a disaster such as pandemic influenza that could overwhelm the surge capacity of the medical system
- rapid economic or other change that would disrupt medical care with or without a defined external disaster
- a large-scale cyber, electrical grid, or other directed technological attack, which could prove crippling on every level
- assault against the medical infrastructure—such as attacks on hospitals, clinics, essential suppliers, first responders, and doctors—that could severely disrupt the system
- a large-scale disruption in trust of the medical establishment caused by fear.

Nanotechnology

The United States currently appears to be ahead in research and development (R&D) on nanoscale materials and applications. The ability to stay ahead in this fast-moving interdisciplinary field is entirely dependent on the supply of creative and technically educated R&D talent. Cross referencing the known demographic trends in the United States and the world with respect to the production of scientists and engineers indicates that the United States may lose its preeminent position unless it can rapidly grow or import sufficient talent to keep up with demand.

Other populous countries such as India and China could, over the next 20 years, outstrip the science and engineering talent base of the United States. If the assumption is that the distribution of genius is roughly equal in different populations in the world, India and China will each have approximately a four-to-one advantage. They may not be as efficient in developing their human resources, but the demographic and educational trends are relatively clear—and are often taboo to discuss openly.

The United States may not keep up with the rest of the world in tackling molecular manufacturing. The factors include discounting the possibility that molecular manufacturing could be developed within the next 25 years (of linear progress), concerns about accidental or deliberate abuse, and religious scruples about intervening with death and the natural scheme of things.

Nanoscale technology is now being pursued worldwide and is showing no signs of slowing down. Technology S curves, such as Moore's law, predict a reduction by half in semiconductor device feature size every 18 months (conversely, packing density doubles). This trend will continue on an accelerating exponential curve, fueled in part by the compounding of "know how" knowledge that Ray Kurzweil[1] calls the Law of Accelerating Returns. Capabilities growing on an exponential curve actually accelerate due to the positive feedback effect of increasing knowledge. The outcomes of this trend in knowledge-driven technologies are counterintuitive. The effect in new knowledge-based technological fields will likely become "obvious" after the facts and examples accumulate and the compression factor becomes more extreme. Any attempt by experts in the field to assess the timing of molecular manufacturing without taking these factors into account is doomed to be too conservative and could squander the competitive opportunity.

Cyberspace

Given the growing significance of cyberspace and the possibilities for dis-continuous change, the Department of Defense (DOD) must push for more mature national mechanisms to determine strategy and set policy. The challenge is to synchronize economic, military, diplomatic, and informational activity in cyberspace to achieve synergy with national values and goals, particularly the ability to pursue free trade in global markets and freedom of political choice. DOD will need to play a leading role in these efforts.

The impact of different national approaches on the ability to manage strategic conflict in cyberspace is not clear. A loosely controlled, diverse but robust network infrastructure may fare better than a centrally managed infrastructure with mandated barriers and defense but retaining a limited capacity for rapid adaptation in the face of new threats. We must develop the methods and intellectual capital to analyze and resolve such issues.

A key concern will be how to manage cyber security risks posed by the increasingly global production, operation, and ownership of key information technology (IT) and communications that underpin the ability of the U.S. military, other government, and critical infrastructure operations. Establishing such capabilities will require dedicated programs employing significant financial resources and intellectual capital over the long term as part of strategies to mitigate risk at all levels from weapons programs to national cyber infrastructure evolution.

To be able to adapt to shocks to the system, DOD must ensure it has a highly capable cadre at all levels—tactical, operational, and strategic. These personnel must be capable of analyzing the ever-changing opportunities and risks present in the environment, operating and protecting the large enterprises and infrastructures that sustain cyberspace, and performing specific tasks ranging from developing new modes of sharing information to providing actors with the capacity for disruptive attack.

For the U.S. military, the challenge is nurturing a strong cadre of cyber experts similar to the naval, air, and space leaders and operators who have enabled its success in other realms. At the core, the issue is one of vision and will to pull limited resources away from traditional military missions and invest them in the core capabilities that will enable pursuing ever-more important objectives through operating and controlling the cyber environment.

Life Sciences

How does the ecology underlying the annual evolution of the influenza virus relate to farming practices in rural China? Chinese leadership is in a difficult position, as it must choose between being responsible for the origin of the next flu pandemic with potential economic consequences, or proactively creating rural societal disruption to promote global health, possibly losing political power or stability in the process.

There is a growing trend toward diffuse networked threats. In general, these threats include traditional terrorists and contemporary computer hackers. Within the realm of the life sciences, advancements in biotechnology and global communications allow strangers with common interests to collaborate on bioengineering projects. This will enable traditional terrorists to more easily create and use advanced biological materials as weapons. More worrisome, however, is a distinct scenario: amateur biohackers conducting benign research could contribute to criminals or terrorists obtaining sophisticated biological agents that are potential threats. This could occur through hijacking or copycatting research, or through disaffected biohackers taking on a criminal mission after developing an ideology related to scientific research.

Another trend is that of civilian and military human performance enhancement via interactions of the body with both biological and inert technologies. A potential shock here—perhaps foreshadowed by the contemporary political and scientific debate over stem cell research—is that a myriad of ethical concerns may delay U.S. advancement in this area. Moreover, potential enemies may not similarly restrict themselves. This situation may result in an emergent power using the life sciences as an asymmetric force multiplier. More importantly, it may cause us to alter our values and bioethics as a society to meet such a threat.

We explore the long view of advances in biotechnology, including genetics, genomics, proteomics, and advanced technology—such as DNA sequencing, gene "chips," and advanced information-sharing—all of which make the biological research possible. In the long view, applying new biotech to old problems will most likely result in a bio-based economy (rather than a petro-based one) in which most everyday objects will be manufactured from renewable biological resources. Potential shocks to this trend are the reversal of urbanization trends due to regional biorefineries located primarily in rural areas, and hot or cold conflicts over access to renewable biological resources arising between gene-rich/technology-poor countries along the equator versus the gene-poor/technology-rich countries of the more developed world.

Culture and Identity in the Middle East

Underestimating the need to understand how religious, tribal, and ethnic identities shape and constrain understandings of authority—and how U.S. actions in the Middle East and elsewhere have inadvertently exacerbated ethnic and sectarian conflict—is already sharply containing the U.S. ability to act effectively on the world stage. Far from receding in significance, sectarian, ethnic, tribal, and religious identities are reemerging as identities for which people die. In the Horn of Africa, the lands bordering the Sahara, Iraq, Afghanistan, Pakistan, Lebanon, Palestine, and the Balkans, such divisions profoundly affect areas of concern to U.S. interests. Between economic crises, population movements caused by inadequate water and other resources, and additional shocks, such conflicts are likely to increase in the next 5 to 10 years.

Globalization—once thought to lead to a homogenization of culture and politics—instead is leading to a strengthening of culturally and religiously based "ties that bind." It is likely to increase the ability of ethnic and sectarian groups to act locally and globally. In the case of the U.S.-led invasion of Iraq in 2003, the post-invasion disarray provided a shock that dismantled the remains of the Iraqi state and forced Iraqis to rely on ties of sect, tribe, clan, ethnic group, and local community in an effort to make their sociopolitical landscape more predictable.

Developing an ability to recognize the changing shapes of organizational effectiveness and loyalties of religious groups, tribes, ethnicities, sects, and religious groups is a skill that DOD needs to operate in Iraq, Afghanistan, and other parts of the world. Effective defense planning must recognize the complementary institutional settings for foreign language training and foreign area–based research. Only some of this training can be optimally done within government settings. The other part requires renewed investment in public and private universities to sustain strong training in critical languages and international area studies. Building such expertise is far less expensive than building new weapons systems but takes years to achieve.

Africa

Likely trends in Africa over the next 20 years can be tracked along two axes. Along the first, labeled "poor Africa," key trends would include widespread and seemingly intractable poverty, the prevalence of infectious diseases, accelerating environmental degradation and resource depletion, and weak and ineffective governance. Some of the main effects produced by these trends over the next two decades are likely to be rapid and chaotic urbanization, increased human migration and capital flight, and a continuing risk of civil strife and interstate conflict. Any requirement of U.S. developmental, humanitarian, and/or military intervention in Africa would come as a result of shocks along the "poor Africa" axis.

Along the second axis, paradoxically labeled "rich Africa," the key trend is increased investment in and exploitation of Africa's rich resource base. Because of its oil and mineral wealth, Africa will elicit much greater commercial attention in the future, and from a larger number of international suitors. However, it is unclear that tomorrow's African governments will succeed where thus far most have failed—in transforming this wealth into sustainable development.

As predictable trends further develop and generate intersecting effects over the next two decades, shocks that might require a U.S. response include the following:

- a heightened risk of diseases spreading from Africa
- unmanageable levels of illegal migration
- a cutoff of oil exports to the United States
- the capture of a sovereign state by criminal or terrorist groups or other forces hostile to the United States.

China

China is America's most important great power competitor, and the U.S.-China relationship is the most important great power relationship in the 21st century.

The nature of the relationship determines not only American security but also the strategic stability of East Asia and the global economy.

The combination of substantial cooperation amid strategic competition in current U.S.-China relations must be considered advantageous for Washington's interests, assuming a continued rise of Beijing. This positive trend in the bilateral competition reflects, in part, China's preoccupation with long-term economic growth and its emergence as a full-fledged great power, and with domestic political stability and the political survival of the Chinese Communist Party. This preoccupation has contributed to a risk-averse foreign policy. Continuity in these trends is critical to stability in U.S.-China strategic competition. The following are the primary (interrelated) sources of continuity in Chinese strategic restraint:

- sustained domestic stability and constrained nationalism
- continued economic growth
- stable U.S.-China economic relations and sustained U.S. economic prosperity
- sustained U.S. technological superiority and regional strategic commitment
- limited Sino-Soviet strategic cooperation.

Should domestic or international shocks undermine any of these contemporary trends, modernization could fail, alleviating the challenge to the United States of a rising China. Alternatively, such shocks could foster Chinese development of the intention and/or the capability to adopt policies detrimental to U.S. security.

Western Europe and NATO

Relative to other rapidly changing areas, in the Europe/North Atlantic Treaty Organization (NATO) region, trends are likely to be gentle and shocks few. But the effects could be very large from the perspective of U.S. interests and policy. Taking a longer term view, Europe, in particular, could turn out to be a very insecure partner. The key drivers are likely to be social dynamics within Europe as the continent faces demographic and cultural challenges. Under more stressful conditions, ideological convulsion and conflict could reemerge in Europe in disturbing ways.

Demographic change will create a continuing incentive for economic migration into Western Europe from the south and east. It will also pose a series of adjustment challenges for European societies seeking to fund traditionally high levels of social welfare from a shrinking labor base.

Without substantial strategic initiatives aimed at economic development across the Mediterranean, in Africa, and elsewhere on the European periphery, Europe is likely to face continued and substantial economic migration, with many potential spikes as a result of natural and manmade stresses.

As pressures on innovation and competitiveness increase, there will be demands for a new deal in transatlantic economic relations, affecting key sectors from financial regulation to labor mobility, from science and technology policy to defense-industrial cooperation. NATO, too, will face pressures to "go global" in response to the increasing interdependence of European and wider regional security, and the need to engage new partners in Asia and elsewhere.

With few indigenous sources of oil or gas, Europe will be among the most exposed regions in the developed world to longer term energy trends and developments affecting energy geopolitics. Long-term tightening of energy markets would pose substantial challenges.

Within limits, European societies and leaderships are likely to be comfortable, with a trend toward multipolarity in which American influence is balanced by a more active European role. Also, key European states will actively pursue new global alignments with India, China, or others outside the transatlantic frame as an explicit response to American power and a way to give multipolarity a shove.

With highly interdependent economies, diverse international investments, many economic rigidities, and heavy social welfare obligations, European economies are especially exposed to global economic risks. The migration trend has been troubling but manageable, despite the obvious cost in lives and human welfare. Over the next decade, there is risk that a populous state on the immediate periphery of Europe could experience a complete collapse, producing unmanageable numbers of economic migrants and asylum seekers.

Many analysts believe that Western Europe is now more vulnerable than the United States to new forms of terrorism, including super-terrorism using weapons of mass destruction. Beyond the risk of super-terrorism, Europe will be increasingly exposed to the spread of nuclear weapons and the proliferation of ballistic missiles of longer range.

The rise of new ideological struggles could have many triggers, including some of the shocks noted here, and especially economic collapse or violent reactions to migration and cultural insecurity. Tense relations with Russia would threaten Europe's energy security and could produce more tangible conventional and unconventional threats to its military security. The Balkans have been the scene of hot wars in a post-communist setting. The next 5 to 20 years could well see new conflicts of greater or lesser scale on Europe's periphery.

Russia and Eurasia

Russia for the past 4 years has been on an economic roll, fueled by high energy prices. The Kremlin in parallel has pursued an increasingly assertive foreign policy, raising the prospect of a more contentious Russia that will challenge U.S. interests in the former Soviet space, Europe, and elsewhere. The dangers posed by a more assertive Russia will command greater time and attention from U.S. national security planners.

It is not only a resurgent Russia that could pose serious tests for the United States in coming years, however. A frail, unstable Russian state is not in the U.S. interest. Russian weakness raises less obvious, but nevertheless serious, possible challenges. Demographic, societal, and economic trends within Russia have the potential, particularly in combination, to create strategic shocks over the next 10 to 30 years that would have major implications for U.S. national security interests.

Dominant trends include demographic changes that lead to fewer Russians and less Russian influence; increasing nationalism, prejudice, and xenophobia; and greater inequality and dependence on energy. These trends could interact to produce strategic shocks that include:

- collapse of the Russian state
- launching of a pan-Russian/Slav movement aimed at incorporating neighboring states or territories with large numbers of ethnic Russians or closely related Slavic populations
- a "color" revolution resulting in a more democratic Russia or a more nationalist, ultra-right regime
- playing the energy card, hinting that political considerations will factor into decisions regarding export volumes to individual European countries
- launch of military/technical surprise in the form of new technologies to leapfrog current conventional capabilities and/or yield asymmetrical advantages to offset U.S. or other conventional force advantages.

While these shocks each have a very low to low likelihood, any of them would pose critical implications for key U.S. security interests.

South Asia

In order of potential damage to nonproliferation norms, rules, and treaties, the author lists the nine worst drivers for a negative nuclear future. These include the next use of a nuclear weapon in warfare between states; failure to stop and reverse the Iranian and North Korean nuclear weapons programs; the breakdown and radical change of governance within Pakistan; the further spread of enrichment and reprocessing plants to nations that are hedging their bets and might want to be a "screwdriver's turn" away from the bomb; and failure to lock down and properly safeguard dangerous weapons and nuclear materials that already exist.

Additional drivers are acts of nuclear terrorism directed against states by extremist groups; the demise of international inspections and other nuclear monitoring arrangements; a resumption and cascade of nuclear weapons testing; and continued production of highly enriched uranium and plutonium for nuclear weapons.

Several dominant trends bear watching. Pakistan and India will continue to view economic growth as essential to national well-being, domestic cohesion, and national security. The leadership in both countries will seek to avoid major crises and border skirmishes in the years ahead. Pakistani and Indian leaders will shy away from arms racing. Internal security concerns will continue to be paramount for both countries. Washington will seek to maintain strong ties with both New Delhi and Islamabad.

Shocks, wild cards, and game changers are developments that could greatly impact political, national, and regional security on the subcontinent. The following developments could significantly accentuate or shift the dominant trends identified above:

- radical change in governance in Pakistan
- an incident of nuclear terrorism on the subcontinent
- a crisis between the United States and Iran
- a U.S.-China clash over Taiwan
- a Pakistan-India agreement on the key elements for settling the Kashmir dispute.

Latin America

For most of Latin America, the next 20 years should be a period of stability and increased prosperity. Economic, demographic, governance, and cultural trends are all in the region's favor. However, pockets of instability could present shocks and a security challenge for the United States. How the Latin Americans react will be the key determinant in whether the overall trends stay positive or shocks emerge. Still, U.S. responses will have critical impact, especially on whether the challenges convert into shocks. Domestic political and immigration trends in the United States also add complications. In a more subtle trend, the United States may not be able to count on what often has been automatic Latin American support for Washington's positions on strategic or critical global issues, as new actors, especially China, enter the region.

The single most important trend for the next 20 years will be the region's passing through a demographic sweet spot. Most of the Latin population is at or near replacement birthrates of roughly two children per family. Mortality rates in most countries long ago dropped to levels near that of the United States, a reflection of improvements in health care and nutrition. These demographic trends will contribute to political and economic stability, including a possible reduction in crime and political violence.

A Latin American move to the ideological left in recent years, despite the popular hype, has been limited and may have reached its limits. Every Latin American president today, of whatever political leaning, is a nationalist first. One reason for this ideological stability is that the center left in Latin America does not want to repeat the disastrous statist economic policies of the 1960s and 1970s. Economic growth has been around 5 percent in recent years. The primary economic weakness in Latin America is that the growth is externally driven. It has been fueled by low international interest rates, high commodity prices, and remittances.

Potential shocks include political changes in Cuba and Venezuela. Cuba will undergo a transition, probably to a democratic, noncommunist government, following the death of Castro. In Venezuela, the Chavez government will likely implode, perhaps in the next 10 years, though it could last as many as 20.

Another shock could be a migration surge into the United States and an accompanying political backlash. Chaos in Venezuela or Cuba, natural disasters in Central America, global recession, or a failed Andean state are all events that could lead to a surge in migration, legal or illegal. The angry nativist movement in the United States is already on the political warpath over current immigration. A shock is unlikely to come from the immigration itself. More problematic is the populist backlash. Policy recommendations include:

- accelerate free trade agreements, approve the pending Colombia agreement, and loosen patently unfair and hypocritical American agricultural and steel subsidies
- continue military support under Plan Colombia against the insurgents there

- for development aid, minimize the blunt instrument of performance requirements, such as counternarcotic measures, that have little to do with the real world
- institute immigration cooperation, including temporary worker programs
- provide favorable treatment for biofuel imports and technical cooperation, especially to ensure food needs
- renew emphasis on antipoverty programs.

Trends and Shocks in Complex Adaptive Systems

The forces described in these chapters will greatly affect the future national security environment. Many impose increasing rates of change. Linkages among the trends introduce poorly understood second- and third-order effects and amplify the complexity of these consequences. Highlights of issues national security organizations and their leaders will have to face include:

- velocity in change in IT
- youth bulges in developing countries creating tensions in "disorderly spaces"
- globally empowered individuals and small groups who are increasingly able to collaborate, compete, and even fight while widely dispersed
- nation-states that no longer have a monopoly on the wealth created within their borders, the ideas generated by their citizens, or even the use of force
- environmental, energy, resource, demographic, and health issues that are interlinked and will become much more important in global and domestic affairs.

The national security structure for this environment will need an early warning system to spot problems at the national level; agile organizations able to anticipate, prepare, and respond effectively; enlightened leadership; and a broad spectrum of capabilities and people with a strong education base.

19

Postscript: "Swans Happen"

Robert E. Armstrong

THE WORKSHOP ON TRENDS AND SHOCKS that is summarized and expanded on in this edited volume was certainly a valuable exercise for the Department of Defense (DOD). This agency of the U.S. Federal Government puts more effort into planning, preparing, and training than any organization in the world. However, despite best efforts, predicting the future is very difficult. Indeed, it may be that predicting the most important and influential events is nearly impossible, as I outline below.

We do not live in a static world. Raised in the Nation's golden years, baby boomers who might be termed "Garden of Eden preservationists" often use the 1960s as a benchmark and subsequently try to maintain the status quo. But while that period may be a good benchmark for them, it is not so for the Earth and its evolving life forms.

Shocks large and small occur periodically on Earth whether we like it or not. In a region of Russia known as the Siberian Traps, a volcanic event lasting a million years coincided with the Permian-Triassic extinction (about 251 million years ago), resulting in the eradication of 96 percent of marine species and 75 percent of terrestrial species. In a more tangible example, about 70,000 years ago, the most powerful volcanic eruption that we have evidence of appears to have reduced the proto-human population to roughly 1,000 breeding pairs, creating a bottleneck that accelerated the demise of all humanoid species except *Homo Neanderthalis* and *Homo sapiens*.

Assessment of risk involves predictions about rare future events. Natural biological events that can be measured—height, weight, number of flowers on a plant, number of birds in a tree—are scalable and fit a "normal" distribution, commonly known as a bell curve. The properties of such curves are well understood, making them relatively easy to utilize. However, a mistake that is often made is the assumption that manmade events such as social behavior, financial markets, and album sales, are also scalable and similarly fit a normal distribution. Hence, risk models of these events and data are often created using an underlying bell curve and its associated properties like means and standard deviations—which do not apply.

In common parlance we often think of the bell curve as "normal," but it simply does not describe many important things that we observe; nevertheless, statistical measures of risk and uncertainty are often based on this very bell curve—and are fundamentally flawed. This is because framing measurements and data in the bell curve fallacy requires ignoring the possibility of large discontinuities that are too important to be called mere outliers and violate the assumptions of the curve itself.

So while the bell curve works well for some measurements (it is absolutely impossible to observe a person who is 1 mile tall or who weighs 25 tons), for variables important to national security, such extremes in scale cannot necessarily be ruled out. This applies to not only national security but also other areas, including financial market returns, gross income per year, and number of deaths due to natural disaster. In point of fact, most manmade variables are non-Gaussian, non–normally distributed. And these are therefore highly prone to hugely consequential outliers.

Traditionally, analysts (as do regular people) focus on the ordinary first and exceptions later. But an equally if not more valid strategy is to focus on the interesting and most consequential outliers, since the ordinary holds little meaning in the realm of predicting important, influential events. Which company is the most important, most consequential, and most outlying—an average search engine with few visitors or Google? The average author or J.K. Rowling? The average working family or Bill Gates? Which have had the most influence on human society?

We might conclude that DOD should be trying to understand, predict, and model outliers—the random jumps—rather than the average—the mean. But the tools we have developed for modeling risk and uncertainty and predicting the future are by and large based on "normal" distributions for "average" existing data.

Hence, in the case of human-caused "unknown unknowns," we often do not have a good idea of the risk involved. One recent example is the concern during the past year or so with mortgage-backed securities, in which mortgage principles and interest from individual people—with individual degrees of risk of default on their loans—are divided up and packaged in complicated ways into bonds and other securities, and then sold as investment products. Employees at Bear Stearns and other banks did not properly assess the risks involved with such securities. In general, this crisis has had a large, reverberating effect on the U.S. economy, with other global effects, and it could have been worse; it still may become so.

In the life sciences group at the Center for Technology and National Security Policy, we often invoke biological metaphors to explain military issues, and the Black Swan applies to the present discussion. This metaphor is a framework within which to understand uncertainty, randomness, and risk, and a colored lens through which to view this serious topic.

A *black swan*, as defined by the author and by Nassim Nicholas Taleb, is a hard-to-predict, rare event with a large impact. In other words, these are surprising, highly consequential events that the military would term *unknown unknowns*. The nickname stems from the notion that people thought all swans were white until explorers discovered Australia in the 17th century and were shocked to see black swans for the first time. Black swans, as we define them for our purposes, are typified by events that occur outside the realm of normal expectations. Volcanic events and meteor strikes qualify; perhaps 9/11 does as well.

Here is another example that clarifies the idea. On the first thousand days of its lifespan, a turkey is fed wonderfully by its owner. On day 1,001, it is slaughtered for Thanksgiving. The slaughtering was certainly a black swan for the turkey. Note that whether or not a black swan occurs depends on one's perspective; day 1,001 did not contain a black swan for the owner, only the turkey. The same could be said for the terrorists behind 9/11 and the people of New York.

Related to the black swan concept is Taleb's so-called narrative fallacy, which is the notion of linking causes to effects post hoc, despite the fact that observed events preceding a black swan do not necessarily lead to the event, and hence one could not have predicted its occurrence. For example, some tensions between countries lead to great wars and others do not; why? In another arena, why was Google such a big success, while Alta Vista (a long-forgotten competing search engine) was not? While we can devise post hoc explanations, at the time no one logically predicted the enormous success of Google. Did some people predict it would be a successful company? Yes. Did anyone predict it becoming an all-consuming behemoth? Not really. Has Google changed the world in a hugely significant manner? Of course.

We as humans are good at predicting and understanding in what Taleb calls simple domains, or what we might term simple systems. Complex, adaptive systems like the global economy, regional ecosystems, and international diplomatic relations are much harder to understand. A data-collecting observer might easily predict the outcome of a fistfight, but it is difficult to predict the outcome of a large-scale war, whatever our "sophisticated" tools.

Relatedly, one of Taleb's central arguments is that within these complex systems, most historically consequential events come from the realm of the unexpected, yet we rationalize these events after the fact—because that is our nature. Paraphrasing him, humans overestimate the value of rational explanations of past data and underestimate the prevalence of unexplainable randomness in everyday life.

So, given that black swans are so difficult to predict, what is to be done? Are exercises like Trends and Shocks worth the effort? The answer to the second question is *yes* because, despite the fact that these exercises might be poor at predicting black swans with any certainty, they may allow us to prepare for "gray swans," which are near-black swans that are rare but somewhat predictable.

With regard to the former, I am suggesting a proactive rather than reactive approach—a long-term approach to "investment" in predicting the future, if you will. One might call this the "let it ride" strategy. This is not to say we should take an isolationist approach, but at the same time we should not fully rely on modeling and prediction of things that are inherently difficult if not nearly impossible to model and predict.

One can conduct the following thought experiment: Of the intelligence predictions from the last 25 years, how many proved to be correct? And conversely, how many major events (dissolution of the Soviet empire, fall of the Berlin Wall, Iraq invading Kuwait, the 1987 stock market crash "Black Monday," 9/11, and Iran's nuclear weapons program) were correctly predicted? How many were rationalized after the fact?

Such events can be classified as black swans. If they are not predictable, therefore, what should we do to prepare for such history-altering events? We must envision and develop a novel, robust strategy to hedge against possible major blows that cannot be predicted with any certainty.

Appendix
Summary of Possible Shocks

Neyla Arnas

Conflict

- Collapse of a major regional ally
- Use of a chemical, biological, radiological, or nuclear (CBRN) weapon
- Major conflict over water in the Middle East
- Community conflicts in Europe
- Domestic CBRN terrorism campaign
- U.S. withdrawal from global politics

Demographics

- Population explosion in poverty-stricken regions of sub-Saharan Africa
- Lower figures of HIV prevalence in Africa
- Collapse of the birth rate in industrialized countries
- Increased immigration to the United States from the south

Economics and Energy

- Major readjustment in China's trade with the United States and European Union
- Continuing, but as yet incomplete, transition to a new financial architecture
- Countries' pursuit of immediate interests over policies favoring free trade and free flows of capital

Environment and Energy

- Water-related shock due to changes in flow and decline in quality

- Forest-related shock prompting conservation-driven "humanitarian" interventions
- Proxy conflicts in the competition for natural resources
- Shocks related to climate change—human migration, grievances, and loss of livelihoods

Health Care

- Pandemic influenza overwhelms surge capacity of medical system
- Major disruption of global supply chain affects hospitals
- Cyber, electrical grid, or other directed technological attack inhibits functioning of medical system
- Dedicating resources to a "Manhattan"-like project leads to alternatives to carbon-based fuels, changing vaccine-production techniques and magnitude to develop an avian flu vaccine, or reshaping U.S. health care
- Disruption of medical infrastructure through attacks on hospitals, clinics, essential suppliers, first responders, and doctors

Nanotechnology

- Surprising exploitation of early nanoscience in military innovation by other countries
- Inexpensive green manufacturing of massive quantities of material goods for developing world
- Molecular manufacturing of conventional and/or radical military technology
- Nanotechnology arms race resulting in inexpensive production of fundamentally new military technology
- Nanotechnology-enabled opening of space frontier
- Nanotechnology-enabled intelligence explosion

Cyberspace

- Military capacity to leverage cyberspace for network-centric warfare is degraded as the commercial backbone grows more slowly
- First successful, large-scale prosecution of cyber war in a political conflict
- Modes of cyber conflict beyond the battlefield expand dramatically from manipulation of digits to the disruption of electromagnetic means of transmission

- Governments strive to exert control over cyberspace networks and systems within their borders, creating state-driven "walled gardens"
- Stagnation of progress in Internet technical evolution

Life Sciences

- China's farming practices and bird flu result in deadly influenza epidemic in Asia. Alternatively, the Chinese government adopts a counterculture strategy, anticipates a pandemic and its wide-ranging effects, and alters traditional farming practices, disrupting centuries-old cultural traditions, displacing people, and forcing them into new lifestyles and careers
- Decentralized biohacker networks empower a range of actors, overturning the conventional notion about weapons of mass destruction of "intent drives capability," resulting in an atmosphere in which "capability drives intent"
- Ethics of military transhumanism—countries that are potential enemies of the United States with fledgling programs in biotechnology, computer science, or nanotechnology pursue transhumanism as a military strategy, and within the framework of a U.S. aversion to it, provide an asymmetric force multiplier in a cold or hot war
- Petro to agro: the coming age of biology—creation of biorefineries in rural areas results in jobs, slowing migration to urban areas, impacting culture, economics, and demographics in areas with significant bioresources. Conflicts arise between the gene-rich/technology-poor countries along the equator and the gene-poor/technology-rich countries of the more developed world

Culture/Middle East

- Sectarian, ethnic, tribal, and religious identities are reemerging as identities for which people die
- Shared cultural understandings—of trust, obligation, loyalty, family, faith, and hierarchy—have no sharply drawn territorial, ethnic, or religious boundaries. They are contested and emerging concepts. Policies based on assumptions that shared cultural understandings of tribes are "fixed" and static are bound to fail
- Globalization leads to strengthening of culturally and religiously based "ties that bind" rather than to homogenization of culture and politics, increasing the ability of ethnic and sectarian groups to act locally and globally

Africa

- Heightened risk of diseases spreading from Africa
- Unmanageable levels of illegal migration from Africa adversely affecting Europe
- Cutoff of African oil exports to the United States due to factors unrelated to local governments
- Capture of a sovereign state by criminal or terrorist groups or other forces hostile to the United States

China

- Chinese domestic political change: antigovernment protests challenge regime stability; Chinese leaders forsake economic reforms to reduce dissent and to consolidate political control over the economy and workers at the cost of economic growth; social and political instability encourage the Chinese leadership to rely more on nationalism for legitimacy and survival
- External economic change: a U.S.-China trade war, U.S. economic instability, and/or an oil shock challenges China's economic and political foundation
- External strategic change: U.S. strategic isolationism, Russian reemergence as a European power

Western Europe

- Economic collapse linked to highly interdependent economies, diverse international investments, many economic rigidities, and social welfare obligations
- Migration from a populous state (undergoing collapse) on the immediate periphery of Europe
- Dramatic terrorism using weapons of mass destruction
- New nuclear exposures: spread of nuclear weapons and the proliferation of ballistic missiles of longer range
- Rise of new ideological struggles trigger economic collapse or violent reactions to migration and cultural insecurity
- New cold war: tense relations with Russia threaten Europe's energy security and produce more tangible conventional and unconventional threats to European security

- New hot war a la Balkans on Europe's periphery
- Successful Israeli-Palestinian peace agreement, secretly brokered by the Europeans without significant U.S. involvement
- Conclusion of a sweeping new free trade agreement between the United States and Europe reinforces the Atlantic as a global center of gravity in economic terms, even in the face of a rising India and China

Russia and Eurasia

- Collapse of the Russian state
- Launching of a pan-Russian/Slav movement aimed at incorporating neighboring states or territories with large numbers of ethnic Russians or closely related Slavic populations
- A "color" revolution resulting in a more democratic Russia or a more nationalist, ultraright regime
- Playing the energy card, hinting that political considerations will factor into decisions regarding export volumes to individual European countries
- Launch of military/technical surprise in the form of new technologies to leapfrog current conventional capabilities and/or yield asymmetrical advantages to offset U.S. or other conventional force advantages
- Islamic revolution in a Central Asian state
- Georgian-Russian military conflict

South Asia

- Radical change in governance in Pakistan precipitated by U.S. cross-border operations
- Incident of nuclear terrorism on the subcontinent that provokes widespread public anxiety and economic disruption
- Crisis between the United States and Iran that affects both U.S.-Pakistan and U.S.-India relations
- U.S.-China clash over Taiwan that results in improved U.S. ties with India and degraded U.S. ties with Pakistan
- Pakistan-India agreement on the key elements for settling the Kashmir dispute

Latin America

- Political changes in Cuba and Venezuela that lead to democratic governments
- Migration surge into the United States perpetuated by chaos in Venezuela or Cuba, natural disasters in Central America, global recession, or failed Andean state causes populist backlash in United States
- One or more failed or narco states necessitates military involvement by the United States or by other countries in the region to restore order

Notes

Introduction

1. Hans Binnendijk, presentation at Institute for National Strategic Studies conference, "Strategic Re-Assessment: From Long-Range Planning to Future Strategy and Forces," National Defense University, June 4, 2008.
2. Roberta Wohlstetter, *Pearl Harbor: Warning and Decision* (Stanford: Stanford University Press, 1962).
3. *The National Defense Strategy of the United States of America* (Washington, DC: Department of Defense, June 2008), 4.
4. Ibid.
5. Ibid., 5.
6. The Transformation Chairs Network included: John Garstka, John Geis, Ted Hailes, Rich Hughes, Sandra Martinez, and Lin Wells. Dr. Dave Alberts of the DOD Command and Control Research Program; Brigadier General Yih San Tan, Future Systems Architect, Singapore Armed Forces; Air Commodore Martin Doel, Royal Air Force; and Professor Daniel Kuehl, National Defense University, also offered valuable comments.
7. Nassim Nicholas Taleb, *The Black Swan: The Impact of the Highly Improbable* (New York: Random House, 2007).
8. National Defense Strategy, 4.

Chapter 2

1. Baron Antoine-Henri de Jomini, *Summary of the Art of War*, translated by G.H. Mendell and W.P. Craighill (Philadelphia: Lippincott, 1892), 49.
2. Donald Kagan, "History Is Full of Surprises," *Survival* (Summer 1999), 142.
3. National Research Council, *Globalization, Biosecurity, and the Future of the Life Sciences* (Washington, DC: National Academies Press, 2006), 59. The mid-1990s scientific experiment to recover the virus responsible for the 1918 Spanish flu provides an important example of the kind of scientific research that could lead to offensive capability. The research team that did the recovery had recently developed a technique to analyze DNA in old, preserved tissues. Looking for a new application, they decided on the Spanish flu. It appears that "this work was not triggered by a search for flu treatments or the search for a new biowarfare agent, but by a rather simple motivation: [the] team could just do it." According to the team leader, "The 1918 flu was by far and away the most interesting thing we could think of." In short, the work went ahead because the team was curious, the issue was interesting, and they could do it.

299

4. Ronald F. Lehman II and Eileen Vergino, "Unclear and Present Danger: Understanding and Responding to WMD Latency," presentation to the 2005–2006 CGSR Futures Roundtable, Center for Global Security Research, Lawrence Livermore National Laboratory, January 19–20, 2006.

5. This is what Syria has done vis-à-vis Israel. Damascus has responded to Israel's nuclear arsenal by developing at least chemical weapons and possibly biological weapons. Syria probably recognizes that its chemical weapons do not truly offset Israel's nuclear capabilities, but they do provide some countervailing capability that Israeli decisionmakers must take into account in any confrontation. In a deteriorating security environment, other countries faced with a sense of urgency to act and limited resources might emulate this "Syrian option."

6. Phil Williams, "Who Controls the Night? Disorderly Spaces and Global Security," Ecologies of Disorder [Internet Blog] Global Futures Forum, October 17, 2006, accessed at <wwwlglobalfuturesforum.org/BlogComments.php?blogld=179&publd=288&mon=&yr>.

7. J. Joseph Hewitt, Jonathan Wilkenfeld, and Ted Robert Gurr, *Peace and Conflict 2008: Executive Summary* (College Park, MD: Center for Development and Conflict Studies, University of Maryland, 2008), 1.

8. Lawrence Freedman, "The Changing Forms of Military Conflict," *Survival* (Winter 1998/1999).

9. Dan Smith, "The World at War," Center for Defense Information, 1999, available at <www.cdi.org/issues/world_at_War/wwar99.htm>.

10. Philip Cerny, "The New Security Dilemma Revisited: Neomedievalism and the Limits of Hegemony," paper presented at the annual meeting of the International Studies Association, Le Centre Sheraton Hotel, Montreal, Quebec, March 17, 2004, available at <www.allacademic.com/one/prol/prol01/index.php?cmd=Download+Document&key=unpublished_manuscript&file_index=2&pop_up=true&no_click_key=true&attachment_style=attachment&PHPSESSID=dcf9266e65b2e6c6d967fabd2704e2f8>.

11. Michael Mazarr, "Extremism, Terror, and the Future of Conflict," *Policy Review* (March 2006), available at <www.hoover.org/publications/policreview/4897841.html>.

12. "Simple craft improvements" are those that enhance the effectiveness of relatively less advanced systems available to insurgents and other nonstate adversaries such as increasing the reach of shoulder-fired heat-seeking missiles by a few thousand feet. Robert Scales, *Fighting on the Edges: The Nature of War in 2020*, prepared for the Global Trends 2020 Project of the National Intelligence Council, 6.

13. Michael Ignatieff, *Virtual War: Kosovo and Beyond* (New York: Macmillan, 2001), 192.

14. Quoted in Fawaz Gerges, "Al-Qa'ida turns jihad into war by media," *The Independent,* October 24, 2005, available at <www.independent.co.uk/news/media/alqaida-turns-jihad-into-war-by-media-512289.html>.

15. Jean-Marc Rickli, *The Impact of Globalization on the Changing Nature of War*, GCSP Policy Brief no. 24, Geneva Center for Security Policy, February 2007, 6.

16. Williams.

Chapter 3

1. The total fertility rate is the average number of children a woman would have if the rate of childbearing of a particular year remained constant.

2. Demographic and Health Surveys are available at <www.measuredhs.com>.

3. The United Nations definition of Western Asia plus Iran (which is classified as being in South Central Asia) is used here.

Chapter 4
1. Department of Energy (DOE)/Energy Information Administration (EIA), *Annual Energy Outlook, 2007,* DOE/EIA–0383 (Washington, DC: Energy Information Administration, February 2007).
2. The EIA Annual Energy Outlook includes forecasts for population and for purchasing power parity (PPP) gross domestic product (GDP), an alternative to the more familiar foreign exchange rate based approach to international comparisons for GDP. PPP GDP attempts to evaluate economies, not on the basis of the relative values of their currencies as determined in international markets, but on the basis of what things cost in relation to their cost in the United States.
3. A third question concerns accuracy and comparability of Chinese economic statistics. This question has been around for years. It surfaced again in an article by Lester Thurow, "A Chinese Century? Maybe It's the Next One," *The New York Times,* August 19, 2007, available at <www.nytimes.com/2007/08/19/business/yourmoney/19view. html?_r=1&oref=slogin&pagewanted=print>. The question is valid in that, while the statistics reported by the government are generally helpful in understanding what is happening, no one should assume that any particular rate of growth in China is strictly comparable to the same rate of growth in any of the OECD countries. For what it is worth, official growth rates usually tend to be overstated when growth is slow and understated when growth is fast.
4. As a part of a market entry study in 1996–1998, the author discussed the outlook for China with some 75 economists and political scientists in the United States, China, Hong Kong, and Japan. The expert who articulated this point most clearly was Dr. Albert Keidel, then associated with Rock Creek Research and now with the Carnegie Institute for International Peace.
5. An economy growing at an 11 or 12 percent annual rate is almost impossible to understand simply by reading about it. The only way to appreciate it is by seeing what is happening on the ground at different points in time. In the case of China, this often comes down to construction, where new buildings—in my experience, gas stations—appear in the middle of nowhere one year, and a year later are in the middle of a bustling, fully developed, urban area.
6. Favorable demographics—a situation in which the number of people of working age grows more rapidly than the total population—is often positive for economic growth. But these favorable demographics are neither necessary nor sufficient. For growth to occur, there must be opportunities for productive employment, and, if these do not materialize, the favorable demographics can quickly pose problems as too many people chase too few jobs. See, for example, David E. Bloom and Jeffrey G. Williamson, "Demographic Transitions and Economic Miracles in Emerging Asia," *The World Bank Economic Review* 12, no. 3 (September 1998), 419–455.
7. China has had its share of Western economic advisors, including Nobel laureates, over the years. Key decisions on reform, especially as related to the introduction of market principles when these were most needed, have a lot in common with Western economic approaches, but the decisions on when and where to introduce them appear to have been largely domestic, political, and, in the end, pragmatic.
8. There are several reasons for this, including the increasing concentration of oil and gas reserves and spare production capacity in a shrinking number of exporting

countries, the revenue requirements of those countries, and the prospects for continued strong growth in demand in China and India, countries that were not yet major consumers during previous oil shocks.

9. See, for example, Robin West, as quoted in Sheila McNulty, "Nationalism and state ownership seen as main threats to oil supply," *Financial Times*, May 10, 2007.

10. See, for example, Jeffrey D. Sachs, "The IMF and the Asian Flu," *The American Prospect* 9, no. 37 (March 1998).

11. See, for example, Ronald McKinnon and Gunther Schnabl, "China: A Stabilizing Influence in East Asia? The Problem of Conflicted Virtue," *Stanford Economics Working Paper No. 03007,* May 26, 2003, available at <http://papers.ssrn.com/sol3/papers.cfm?abstract_id=753385>.

12. International Monetary Fund, *International Financial Statistics,* Washington, DC.

13. See, for example, Thomas L. Friedman, *The World is Flat: The Globalized World in the Twenty-first Century* (New York: Penguin, 2006).

14. The most recent is the Foreign Investment and National Security Act of 2007, which increases government oversight of deals involving foreign acquisition of U.S. companies and assets.

15. See for example, U.S. DOE EIA, "Country Analysis Briefs: South Korea," 2006.

16. Given the problems with measuring GDP, whether based on foreign exchange rates or PPP, a case could probably be made for using energy demand as a measure of aggregate economic activity or energy demand per capita as a measure of economic welfare.

17. See, for example, International Energy Agency, *Energy Statistics of OECD Countries and Energy Statistics of Non-OECD* Countries, 2007.

18. An earlier version of this analysis was presented in an article by Jason Z. Yin and David F. Gates, "Automobile and Fuel Industries," in Shang-Jin Wei, Guangzhong James Wen, and Huizhong Zhou, *The Globalization of the Chinese Economy* (Northampton, MA: Edward Elgar, 2002), 82–99.

19. Robin West quoted in Sheila McNulty, "Nationalism and state ownership seen as main threats to oil supply," *Financial Times*, May 10, 2007.

20. See, for example, John Calabrese, "Saudi Arabia and China extend ties beyond oil," *China Brief* 5, no. 20 (September 22, 2005).

Chapter 5

1. The author wishes to thank Karin Bencala, Meaghan Parker, Sean Peoples, Sonia Schmanski, and Rachel Weisshaar for research and editorial contributions, and Neyla Arnas, Arthur Bradshaw, and Kent Butts for comments on drafts.

2. Millennium Ecosystem Assessment, *Ecosystems and Human Well-being: Synthesis* (Washington, DC: Island Press, 2005); Intergovernmental Panel on Climate Change, *Climate Change 2007: Synthesis Report,* 2007; United Nations Environment Program (UNEP), *Global Environment Outlook 4* (Nairobi: UNEP, 2007).

3. B. Worm et al., "Impacts of biodiversity loss on ocean ecosystem services," *Science* 314 (2006), 787–790.

4. The June 2007 UNEP's Post-Conflict and Disaster Management Branch environmental assessment of Sudan highlights key environmental challenges. There has been a 50–200 kilometer southward shift of the boundary between desert and semi-desert since the 1930s. Rainfall in northern Darfur has dropped more than 30 percent over 50 years. Climate change and crop models forecast a drop of 20–70 percent in food production capacity in parts of the Sahel Belt by 2030. UNEP, *Sudan*

Post-Conflict Environmental Assessment (Nairobi: UNEP, 2007), available at <www. unep.org/sudan>.

5. See Colin H. Kahl, *States, Scarcity, and Civil Strife in the Developing World* (Princeton: Princeton University Press, 2006).

6. Karin R. Bencala and Geoffrey D. Dabelko, "Water Wars: Obscuring Opportunities," *Journal of International Affairs* 61, no. 2 (Spring/Summer 2008).

7. For formal criteria for "basins at risk" of conflict and a list of qualifying basins, see Aaron T. Wolf, Shira B. Yoffe, and Mark Giordano, "International Waters: Identifying Basins at Risk," *Water Policy* 5, no. 1 (2003), 29–60.

8. The rapid pace of change in water availability raises the question of "whether the future will look like the past" in terms of whether institutions will continue to be able to adapt to water scarcity and avoid formal war between states. See also Aaron T. Wolf et al., "Managing Water Conflict and Cooperation," *State of the World 2005: Redefining Global Security* (New York: Norton, 2005), 80–95.

9. Jane I. Dawson, *Eco-Nationalism: Anti-Nuclear Activism and National Identity in Russia, Lithuania, and Ukraine* (Durham: Duke University Press, 2006).

10. Estimate of the Chinese State Environmental Protection Agency. See the numerous writings of Murray Scot Tanner for detailed analysis and estimates of Chinese protests.

11. Interviews (September 2007) with Dr. Jennifer Turner of the Woodrow Wilson International Center for Scholars' China Environment Forum formed the basis of this scenario. See Turner's "A Closing Window? The Risks of China's Growing Environmental Woes," paper prepared for Carnegie Endowment for International Peace Seminar on "Anticipating Discontinuous Change in China," Washington, DC, September 6, 2007. See also Elizabeth C. Economy, "The Great Leap Backward?" *Foreign Affairs* (September-October 2007).

12. International Rivers Network, available at <www.irn.org/programs/china/>.

13. Milton Osborne, *River at Risk: The Mekong and the Water Politics of China and Southeast Asia* (Double Bay, New South Wales, Australia: Longueville Media, 2004), available at <www.lowyinstitute.org/Publication.asp?pid=160>.

14. X.X. Lu and R.Y. Siew, "Water discharge and sediment flux changes over the past decades in the lower Mekong River: possible impacts of the Chinese dams," *Hydrology and Earth System Sciences* 10 (2006), 181–195.

15. Osborne, 2.

16. Louis Lebel, Po Garden, and Masao Imamura, "The politics of scale, position, and place in the governance of water resources in the Mekong region," *Ecology and Society* 10, no. 2 (2005), 18, available at <www.ecologyandsociety.org/vol10/iss2/art18/>.

17. Osborne, 39.

18. In the late 1990s, the U.S. Foreign Service Institute conducted a multi-day simulation exercise gaming a similar scenario.

19. Philip and Jensen Hirsh and Kurt Morck, *National Interests and Transboundary Water Governance in the Mekong* (May 2006), xv, available at <www.mekong.es.usyd. edu.au/projects/mekwatgov_mainreport.pdf>.

20. Another factor militating against a shock is the diversity of interests *within* downstream countries. Thai engineering firms are helping build Chinese dams, and Thailand and Vietnam are purchasing Chinese hydro power.

21. Wolf et al.

22. UNEP, *Rapid Response Assessment: The Last Stand of the Orangutan*, 2007, available at <www.grida.no/_documents/orangutan/full_orangutanreport.pdf>.

23. "Many millions of forest-dwelling or forest-dependent people also rely on Indonesia's forests for their livelihoods. Many of these communities live by traditional 'portfolio' economic strategies that combine shifting cultivation of rice and other food crops with fishing, hunting, harvesting and selling of timber, and gathering non-timber forest products such as rattan, honey, and resins for use and sale. The cultivation of coffee, rubber, and other tree crops is also an important source of income." Global Forest Watch, available at <www.globalforestwatch.org/English/indonesia/over view.htm>.

24. Mongabay-Borneo, available at <www.mongabay.com/borneo.html>.

25. Thomaz Guedes da Costa, "Brazil's SIVAM: As It Monitors the Amazon, Will It Fulfill Its Human Security Promise?" *Environmental Change and Security Project Report* 7 (2001), 51–58.

26. See Tony Allan of the School of African and Oriental Studies at the University of London on food trade as trade in "virtual water," available at <www.waterfootprint. org/Reports/Allan_1998.pdf>. For example, 1,000 liters of water are needed to produce 1 kilogram of wheat and 15,000 liters are needed for 1 kilogram of beef.

27. Department of Energy/Energy Information Administration (DOE/EIA), "Crude oil imports versus U.S. production, 1920–2005," 2006, available at <http://photos. mongabay.com/06/0809_crude-oil.jpg>.

28. Kenneth Omeje, "Oil Conflict and Accumulation Politics in Nigeria," *Environmental Change and Security Program Report* 12 (2006–2007).

29. Paul Wee, *Responding to Crisis in Nigeria* (Washington, DC: United States Institute of Peace, 2006), available at <www.usip.org/pubs/usipeace_briefings/2006/0426_ nigeria.html>.

30. U.S. Department of State, "Background Note: Nigeria," 2007, available at <www. state.gov/r/pa/ei/bgn/2836.htm>.

31. DOE/EIA, "Crude Oil and Total Petroleum Imports Top 15 Countries," 2007, available at <www.eia.doe.gov/pub/oil_gas/petroleum/data_publications/company_ level_imports/current/import.html>.

32. See <www.pbs.org/wnet/wideangle/shows/saudi/map.html>.

33. OSD Policy Planning provided data and analysis of climate change and energy trends to form the foundation for this discussion. For three scenarios with ascending severity, see Kurt M. Campbell et al., *The Age of Consequences: The Foreign Policy and Security Policy Implications of Global Climate Change* (Washington, DC: Center for Strategic and International Studies, 2007). For European perspectives, see Nick Mabey, *Delivering Climate Security: International Security Responses to a Climate Changed World,* Whitehall Papers (London: Royal United Services Institute for Defence and Security Studies, April 2008), available at <www.rusi.org/publication/ whitehall/ref:I480E2C638B3BC/>. See also German Advisory Council on Global Change, *World in Transition—Climate Change as a Security Risk,* June 2007, available at <www.wbgu.de/wbgu_jg2007_engl.html>.

34. Nils Petter Gleditsch, Idean Salehyan, and Ragnhild Nordås, "Climate Change and Conflict: The Migration Link," International Peace Academy Policy Paper, May 2007, available at <www.ipacademy.org/asset/file/169/CWC_Working_Paper_Climate_ Change.pdf>.

35. The 2000 political protest sparked by water privatization and price hikes in Cochabamba, Bolivia, may provide a model for environmental protests serving as a trigger to protests over a larger set of issues and forcing a change in government.

36. See National Science Foundation–funded research of Marc Levy, Charles Vorosmarty, and Nils Petter Gleditsch, available at <www.wilsoncenter.org/index.

cfm?topic_id=1413&categoryid=A84F71E7-65BF-E7DC-4E3D65C4974A971A& fuseaction=topics.events_item_topics&event_id=219458>; Anthony Nyong, "Climate-Related Conflicts in West Africa," *Environmental Change and Security Program Report* 12 (2006–2007), available at <www.wilsoncenter.org/topics/pubs/ Nyong12.pdf>; and Jon Barnett and W. Neil Adger, "Climate Change, Human Security and Violent Conflict," *Political Geography* 26, no. 6 (2007), 639–655.

37. *The National Security Strategy of the United States of America* (Washington, DC: The White House, March 2006), available at <www.whitehouse.gov/nsc/nss/2006/>.

38. Military Advisory Board, *National Security and the Threat of Climate Change* (Washington, DC: CNA Corporation, 2007).

39. For more on the U.S. African Command Transition Team, see <www.eucom.mil/ africom/index.asp>.

40. See the activities of the UN Environment Program's Post-Conflict and Disaster Management Branch at <http://postconflict.unep.ch/>.

41. Faculty and staff such as Dr. Kent Butts and Colonel Arthur Bradshaw, USA (Ret.), at the Center for Strategic Leadership at the U.S. Army War College have nearly two decades of experience working environmental engagement through all of the combatant commands.

42. See Major Shannon Beebe, USA, Department of the Army, on environmental security and USAFRICOM at <http://newsecuritybeat.blogspot.com/2007/07/guest-contributor-shannon-beebe-on.html>. See also discussions of environmental roles for USAFRICOM facilitated by the Army Environmental Policy Institute and the U.S. Army War College.

43. See <www.securityandclimate.cna.org> for the report, press coverage, congressional testimony, and list of Military Advisory Board members.

44. In 1979, Egyptian President Anwar Sadat said that "the only matter that could take Egypt to war again is water," referring to plans for dams in Ethiopia. Boutros Boutros Ghali echoed this statement as Egypt's Minister of State for Foreign Affairs when he predicted in 1985 that "the next war in the Middle East will be fought over water, not politics."

45. See the Nile Basin Initiative Web site at <www.nilebasin.org/>. See also Patricia Kameri-Mbote, "Water, Conflict, and Cooperation: Lessons from the Nile River Basin," *Navigating Peace*, no. 4 (2007).

Chapter 6

1. Institute of Medicine, Committee on Quality of Health Care in America, *Crossing the Quality Chasm: A New Health System for the 21st Century* (Washington, DC: National Academy Press, 2001).

Chapter 7

1. Committee to Review the National Nanotechnology Initiative National Materials Advisory Board, *A Matter of Size: Triennial Review of the National Nanotechnology Initiative* (Washington, DC: National Academies Press, 2006), 108, available at <www.nap.edu/catalog.php?record_id=11752#toc>.

2. Ray Kurzweil, "The Law of Accelerating Returns," 2003, available at <www.kurz weilai.net/articles/art0134.html?printable=1>.

3. Richard E. Smalley, "Of Chemistry, Love and Nanobots," *Scientific American* 285, no. 3 (2001), 76–77; George M. Whitesides, "The Once and Future Nanomachine," *Scientific American* 285, no. 3 (2001), 78–83.

4. K. Eric Drexler et al., "On Physics, Fundamentals, and Nanorobots: A Rebuttal to Smalley's Assertion That Self-Replicating Mechanical Nanorobots Are Simply Not Possible," *Foresight Update,* no. 46 (2001), 6–7, available at <www.imm.org/SciAmDebate2/smalley.html>; K. Eric Drexler et al., "Many Future Nanomachines: A Rebuttal to Whiteside's Assertion That Mechanical Molecular Assemblers Are Not Workable and Not a Concern," *Foresight Update,* no. 46 (2001), 8–17, available at <www.imm.org/SciAmDebate2/whitesides.html>.

5. Neil Jacobstein et al., "Foresight Guidelines for Responsible Nanotechnology Development," Draft Version 6 (April 2006), available at <www.foresight.org/guidelines/current.html>.

6. Foresight Institute et al., "Productive Nanosystems: A Technology Roadmap, 2007," available at <www.foresight.org/roadmaps/Nanotech_Roadmap_2007_main.pdf>.

7. Foresight Institute et al., "Proceedings of the Roadmap Working Group, 2007," available at <www.foresight.org/roadmaps/Nanotech_Roadmap_2007_WG_Proc.pdf>.

8. Ralph Merkle, "Convergent Assembly," *Nanotechnology* 8, no. 1 (March 1997), 18–22.

9. Ralph Merkle, "Molecular Building Blocks and Development Strategies for Molecular Nanotechnology," *Nanotechnology* 11, no. 2 (2000), 89–99.

10. Jürgen Altmann and Mark A. Gubrud, "Risks from Military Uses of Nanotechnology: The Need for Technology Assessment and Preventive Control," in *Nanotechnology: Revolutionary Opportunities and Societal Implications,* ed. Mihail C. Roco and Renzo Tomellini (Luxembourg: European Communities, 2002), available at <www.ep3.ruhr-uni-bochum.de/bvp/riskmilnt_lecce.html>.

11. Ray Kurzweil, *The Singularity Is Near* (New York: Viking Press, 2005).

Chapter 8

1. A deeper analysis of the characterization of cyberspace is presented in my book, *Strategic Warfare in Cyberspace* (Cambridge, MA: MIT Press, 2001), 11–12.

2. Key early works addressing information warfare and the possibilities for conflicts based on network attacks include Alvin and Heidi Toffler, *War and Anti-War: Survival at the Dawn of the 21ˢᵗ Century* (Boston: Little, Brown and Company, 1993); John Arquilla and David Ronfeldt, "Cyberwar is Coming!" *Comparative Strategy* 12, no. 3 (Spring 1993), 141–165; and Winn Schwartau, *Information Warfare* (New York: Thunder Mouth Press, 1994).

3. Department of Defense, *National Military Strategy for Cyberspace Operations* (Washington, DC: Chairman of the Joint Chiefs of Staff, 2006).

4. See <www.internetworldstats.com/stats.htm>.

5. Gabriel Weimann, "www.terror.net: How Modern Terrorism Uses the Internet," U.S. Institute of Peace Special Report no. 116, March 2004, available at <www.usip.org/pubs/specialreports/sr116.html>.

6. Steve Coll and Susan B. Glasser, "Terrorists Turn to the Web as Base of Operations," *The Washington Post,* August 7, 2005, A1.

7. Department of Defense, *National Defense Strategy of the United States of America* (Washington, DC: Chairman of the Joint Chiefs of Staff, March 2005), 13.

8. See <www.cert.org/stats/fullstats.html>.

9. Larry Greenemeier, "Estonian Attacks Raise Concern over Cyber 'Nuclear Winter,'" *Information Week,* May 24, 2007, available at <www.informationweek.com/news/showArticle.jhtml?articleID=199701774>.

10. See <www.icann.org/announcements/announcement-08mar07.htm>.

11. In 1999, two senior People's Liberation Army Air Force colonels recognized the PRC's weaker traditional military position vis-à-vis the United States and called for the use of "people's war" leveraging the Chinese advantage in numbers. Qiao Liang and Wang Xiangsui, *Unrestricted Warfare* (Beijing: PLA Literature and Arts Publishing House, February 1999), FBIS translation available at <http://cryptome.org/cuw.htm>.

12. As early as the 1980s, Toffler's work had already become standard reading for the PRC Politburo as detailed at <www.oycf.org/Perspectives/19_123102/eGovernment.htm>.

13. Kenneth Neil Cukier, "Who Will Control the Internet?" *Foreign Affairs* 84, no. 6 (November-December 2005).

Chapter 9

1. World Health Organization, "Assessment of Risk to Human Health Associated with Outbreaks of Highly Pathogenic H5N1 Avian Influenza in Poultry," May 14, 2004.

2. National Intelligence Estimate 99–17D, *The Global Infectious Disease Threat and Its Implications for the U.S.*, January 2000, available at <www.fas.org/irp/threat/nie99-17d.htm>.

3. Edward A. Gargan, "As Avian Flu Spreads, China Is Seen as its Epicenter," *The New York Times,* December 21, 1997.

4. Laurie Garrett, "The Next Pandemic?" *Foreign Affairs* 84, no. 4 (July-August 2005).

5. Hamish McDonald, "China's Unsafe Farming Practices May Be Breeding More Than Pigs," *The Sydney Morning Herald,* April 7, 2003.

6. Y. Guan et al., "Emergence of Avian H1N1 Influenza Viruses in Pigs in China," *Journal of Virology* 70 (1996), 8041.

7. David Blumenthal and William Hsiano, "Privatization and Its Discontents—The Evolving Chinese Health Care System," *New England Journal of Medicine* (September 15, 2005), 353, 1165–1170.

8. The Federation of International Trade Associations (FITA), available at <www.fita.org/countries/china.html>.

9. World Trade Organization (WTO), available at <http://stat.wto.org/CountryProfile/WSDBCountryPFView.aspx?Language=E&Country=CN>.

10. Ori Brafman and Rod A. Beckstrom, *The Starfish and the Spider: The Unstoppable Power of Leaderless Organizations* (New York: Penguin, 2006).

11. In chapter 2, Michael Moodie discusses the related conundrum that he terms the BW proliferation "latency" between the timing of intent and capability.

12. John B. Alexander, *Future War: Non-Lethal Weapons in 21ˢᵗ-Century Warfare* (New York: St. Martin's Press, 1999).

13. The term *campaign terrorism* was introduced in Richard Danzig, *Catastrophic Bioterrorism: What Is to Be Done?* (Washington, DC: Center for Technology and National Security Policy, 2003).

14. William Sims Bainbridge and Mihal C. Roco, eds, *Managing Nano-Bio-Info-Cogno Innovations: Converging Technologies in Society,* National Science Foundation, 2006, available at <http://wtec.org/ConvergingTechnologies>.

15. Proponents of human-enhancing technologies are sometimes called Transhumanists, and the field of study itself, Transhumanism, generally attempts to go beyond what is traditionally considered to be human.

16. James S. Albus et al., "A Proposal for a Decade of the Mind Initiative," *Science* 317 (September 7, 2007), 1331.

17. *Beyond Therapy: Biotechnology and the Pursuit of Happiness*, The President's Council on Bioethics, Washington, DC (October 2003).
18. Francis Fukuyama, "The World's Most Dangerous Ideas: Transhumanism," *Foreign Policy* 83, no. 5 (September-October 2004).
19. Matt Pueschel, "Pilot FBI Unit Links Medicine and Intelligence in Combating Bioterrorism," *U.S. Medicine* (May 2004), 14.
20. Neil A. Lewis, "Two Marines Who Refused to Comply with Genetic-Testing Order Face Court-Martial," *The New York Times*, April 13, 1996, A7.
21. Amanda E. Brooks and Randolph V. Lewis, "Probing the Elastic Nature of Spider Silk in Pursuit of the Next Designer Fiber," *Biomedical Science Instrumentation* 40 (2004), 232–237.
22. *Discover* (October 2007), Special Issue: The State of Science in America.
23. The current discussion does not take into account the most recent shift of corn production into ethanol manufacture. When more advanced technologies are developed—those that convert other forms of biomass than grain into ethanol—the market will adjust to the more rational level of less than 10 percent for nonfood/nonfeed needs.
24. National Agricultural Biotechnology Council, *Vision for Agricultural Research and Development in the 21st Century* (December 14, 1998).
25. Section 9003, "Bio-refinery Development Grants of the Farm Security and Rural Investment Act of 2002," authorizes development grants to build biorefineries to "develop transportation and other fuels, chemicals, and energy from renewable sources."
26. "A New Reality for Bioplastics," *NatureWorks* press release, November 21, 2006.

Chapter 10

1. Author interview with former officer, November 9, 2007.
2. Richard D. Lambert et al., *Beyond Growth: The Next Stage in Language and Area Studies* (Washington, DC: Association of American Universities, 1984), 260–281. This study was conducted for the Department of Defense (DOD) to fulfill the requirements of the House and Senate Conference Reports to the DOD Authorization Act of 1983, and under a separate grant from the National Endowment of the Humanities. It was intended to offer a comprehensive assessment of the status of language and area studies in the United States from the "broader perspective of the national interest" as viewed from the perspective of "various federal agencies," the "great universities," and private foundations.
3. Richard D. Lambert, *Points of Leverage: An Agenda for a National Foundation for International Studies* (New York: Social Science Research Council, 1986).
4. Lisa Wedeen, "Conceptualizing Culture: Possibilities for Political Science," *American Political Science Review* 96, no. 4 (December 2002), 713–728.
5. Modernization theory held that a hallmark of "modern" people and societies was to find rational solutions to personal and societal problems and to empower people to participate in governance decisions and decisions over their life. The sense of rationality offered was an acultural one. Modernity was seen as an enlargement of human freedoms and an enhancement of the range of choices as people began to "take charge" of themselves. Religion in modern life was thought to retain its influence only by conforming to such norms as "rationality" and relativism, accepting secularization and making compromises with science, economic concerns, and the state.

6. Fariba Adelkhah, *Being Modern in Iran*, trans. Jonathan Derrick (London: Hurst and Company, 1999).
7. Daniel H. Levine and David Stoll, "Bridging the Gap between Empowerment and Power in Latin America," in *Transnational Religion and Fading States*, ed. Susanne Hoeber Rudolph and James Piscatori (Boulder, CO: Westview Press, 1997), 75.
8. Samuel Huntington, "The Clash of Civilizations?" *Foreign Affairs* 72, no. 3 (Summer 1993), 22–49.
9. Francis Fukuyama, *The End of History and the Last Man* (New York: Free Press, 1992).
10. For Muslim societies see Paul Wheatley, *The Places Where Men Pray Together: Cities in Islamic Lands, 7ᵗʰ–10ᵗʰ Centuries* (Chicago: University of Chicago Press, 2001).
11. Dale F. Eickelman, "Islam and the Languages of Modernity," *Daedalus* 129, no. 1 (Winter 2000), 119–135, and S.N. Eisenstadt, "Multiple Modernities," *Daedalus* 129, no. 1 (Winter 2000), 1–9.
12. Dale F. Eickelman and James Piscatori, *Muslim Politics* (Princeton: Princeton University Press, 2003).
13. Alessandro Monsutti, *War and Migration: Social Networks and Economic Strategies of the Hazaras of Afghanistan* (London: Routledge, 2005).
14. Lambert, *Points of Leverage*, 95–96.
15. IntelCenter, "Destruction of the Destroyer USS *Cole*: Preparations," al Qaeda videos, vol. 7 (Arlington, VA: IntelCenter, 2005 [2001]).

Chapter 13

1. Muslims currently make up some 10 percent of the population of France—roughly the same percentage as the Latino population in the United States. Germany is home to over 2 million Turkish immigrants, perhaps a third of whom are Kurds.
2. Winston Churchill offered a striking retrospective view in his wartime memoirs—with some disturbing contemporary echoes. Reflecting on the prelude to the 1929 collapse and the onset of economic depression, he quotes the president of the New York Stock Exchange as saying that "we are apparently finished and done with economic cycles as we have known them." Churchill goes on to describe how "the prosperity of millions of American homes had grown upon a gigantic structure of inflated credit. . . . Easy loans, a vast array of purchase by installment. . . . All now fell together." Winston S. Churchill, *The Second World War*, vol. I, *The Gathering Storm* (London: Cassell and Company, 1948), 27.

Chapter 15

1. This crisis was triggered by an attack on the Indian parliament in December 2001 and reached another fevered peak with attacks against the families of Indian servicemen in battle-ready formations in May 2002.

Chapter 17

1. Principal contributors to this chapter included: John Garstka, John Geis, Ted Hailes, Rich Hughes, Sandra Martinez, and Lin Wells. Dr. Dave Alberts of the DOD Command and Control Research Program; BG Tan Yih San, Future Systems Architect of the Singapore Armed Forces; Air Commodore Martin Doel, Royal Air Force; and Professor Daniel Kuehl, National Defense University, offered valuable comments.
2. See "Converging, Combining, Emerging," Executive Summary of Highlands Forum XXXII, May 29–31, 2007, available at <https://www.hlforum.com/conferences>.

3. Thomas P.M. Barnett, *The Pentagon's New Map: War and Peace in the Twenty-first Century* (New York: Putnam, 2004).

4. Highlands Forum Executive Summary, January 27–29, 2008. Although focused at first on cyberspace, the "Collaboration, Competition, Conflict" construct is proving applicable in social, political, and economic spheres as well.

5. For example, Arthur K. Cebrowski and John J. Garstka, "Network-Centric Warfare: Its Origins and Future," *Proceedings* (January 1998), and David S. Alberts, John J. Garstka, and Frederick P. Stein, *Network Centric Warfare* (Washington, DC: Command and Control Research Program, 1999).

6. Secretary of Defense, *Quadrennial Defense Review* (Washington, DC: Office of the Secretary of Defense, February 2006).

7. The Maritime Strategy was signed jointly by the Chief of Naval Operations and the Commandants of the Marine Corps and the Coast Guard in October 2007. U.S. Army Field Manual 3–0, *Operations* (Washington, DC: Department of the Army, 2008), Introduction.

8. Highlands Forum XXXII Executive Summary, op. cit.

9. Ibid. Dr. Michael Crow, president of Arizona State University, reminds us that it is important that policymakers ask the right questions. In particular, the key environmental issues of the future may relate less to greenhouse gases than to interactions between the wild, dynamic, complex, and only partly understood processes of the planet on the one hand, and an increasingly urbanized, growing population on the other. In this model, the one unforgivable policy sin is the hubris of thinking that we, as a species, know all the answers about the interactions of complex, adaptive systems, or even that we *can* know them.

10. Ibid. Research by the DOD Command and Control Research Program, available at <www.dodccrp.org>, and others, is providing qualitative evidence that flat organizations are often more effective than hierarchical ones.

11. For example, a million-person rally in Colombia in February 2008 against the Revolutionary Armed Forces of Colombia was largely organized by citizens using cell phones, Facebook, and other information-age social software tools. In May 2006, the PCC criminal gang mounted an effective series of attacks against the Sao Paulo, Brazil, police, transportation, and other services, even though many of the PCC leaders were in prison.

12. Ashby's law of "requisite variety" comes from the field of cybernetics and refers to the need for sufficient variety (diversity) within a system to respond to the variety introduced by perturbations to the system. See chapter 11 in W. Ross Ashby, *An Introduction to Cybernetics* (London: Chapman and Hall, 1956), available at <http://pespmc1.vub.ac.be/ASHBBOOK.html>.

13. James Gleick, *Chaos: Making a New Science* (New York: Viking, 1987), popularized theories about nonlinearity and self-organization and the underlying tenets of chaos theory that were already well advanced in the natural sciences. Also, in 1984, prominent physicists, including Murray Gell-Mann and David Pines, founded the Santa Fe Institute to generate and focus transdisciplinary inquiry into complex adaptive systems. Within the last two decades, complexity theory, as a perspective for understanding reality, has gained a foothold globally. Since the early part of the 21st century, DOD, as well as the larger community of U.S. national security practitioners, has increasingly recognized the value of this paradigm, its potential for deeper understanding, and its implications for practice.

14. James Moffat, *Complexity Theory and Network Centric Warfare* (Washington, DC: Command and Control Research Program, 2003).

15. Robert Kegan, *In over Our Heads: The Demands of Modern Life* (Cambridge: Harvard University Press, 1994). Also, David Rooke and William R. Torbert, "Organizational Transformation as a Function of the CEO's Developmental Stages," *Organizational Development Journal* 16, no. 1 (1998).

16. Chris Argyris and Donald Schon, *Theory in Practice: Increasing Professional Effectiveness* (San Francisco: Jossey-Bass, 1974); C. Otto Scharmer, *Theory U: Leading from the Future as It Emerges* (Cambridge, MA: Society for Organizational Learning Press, 2007).

17. Chris Argyris, *Knowledge for Action* (San Francisco: Jossey-Bass, 1993), and William R. Torbert, *Action Inquiry: The Secret of Timely and Transforming Leadership* (San Francisco: Barrett-Koehler Publishers, 2004).

18. Donde Ashmos Plowman and Dennis Duchon, "Emergent Leadership: Getting beyond Heroes and Scapegoats," 109–127, in *Complexity Systems Leadership Theory: New Perspectives from Complexity Science on Social and Organizational Effectiveness*, ed. James K. Hazy, Jeffrey Goldstein, and Benyamin B. Lichtenstein (Mansfield, MA: The Institute for the Study of Coherence and Emergence); Scharmer, op. cit.

19. Plowman and Duchon; C. Otto Scharmer et al., *Presence: Human Purpose and the Field of the Future* (Cambridge, MA: Society for Organizational Learning Press, 2004).

20. Karl E. Weick, *Sense-Making in Organizations* (Thousand Oaks, CA: Sage Publications, 1995), and others have explored the importance of sense-making processes to decisionmaking and timely action. The systems-thinking group at MIT has shown the importance of learning for organizational sustainability and explored the leader's role as designer, steward, and teacher. See, for example, Peter M. Senge, *The Fifth Discipline: The Art and Practice of the Learning Organization* (New York: Currency Doubleday, 1990). From a technology perspective, see Clayton M. Christensen, *The Innovator's Dilemma* (Harper Business Essentials, 2000). BG Tan Yih San of the Singapore Armed Forces notes that there are active discussions within the forces to insert "a sense-making, learning-driven, decision-making module into the officer's training roadmap." Email, March 11, 2008.

21. Robert Gates, Landon Lecture, Manhattan, KS, November 26, 2007, available at <www.defenselink.mil>.

22. David S. Alberts and Richard E. Hayes, *Power to the Edge* (Washington, DC: Command and Control Research Program, 2005 edition).

23. David S. Alberts, "Agility, Focus, and Convergence: The Future of Command and Control," *International Journal of Command and Control* 1, no. 1, available at <www.dodccrp.org/html4/journal_v1n1.html>.

24. Mark E. Nissen, in "Enterprise Command, Control, and Design: Bridging C^2 Practice and CT Research," *International C^2 Journal* 1, no. 1 (2007), points out that "a noticeable chasm exists between well-established research in the cognitive and social domain and current Command and Control (C^2) practice" in military enterprise management. There are four domains related to NCO: physical, information, cognitive, and social. Until now, most of the research has been on the physical and information domains. However, recent progress in social and cognitive research suggests that these areas deserve much more attention by decisionmakers. See also "Complex Systems Leadership Theory: An Introduction," 1–13, in Hazy, Goldstein, and Lichtenstein.

25. Certain schools, such as the Information Resources Management College at the National Defense University, have included innovative, cross-cutting material, and

important courses have been taught as electives at several schools. However, Dan Kuehl, a respected teacher in this area, notes that involvement with these issues has been idiosyncratic, the incorporation of such material into core curricula has been "spotty," and the students taking the classes largely have been self-selecting.

26. Chairman of the Joint Chiefs of Staff Instruction 1800.1C, December 22, 2005.

27. The Special Areas of Emphasis (SAEs) for 2008 are: Countering Ideological Support for Terrorism; Military Support to Stability, Security, Transition, and Reconstruction Operations; Irregular Warfare; Strategic Communication; Defense Support of Civil Authorities; and Net-Centric Information Sharing. Chairman of the Joint Chiefs of Staff Memo CM–0189–08 of March 10, 2008, reads, "Where appropriate, please incorporate these SAEs into Joint Professional Military Education (JPME) curricula."

28. Robert F. Mills, Richard A. Raines, and Paul D. Williams, *Developing Cyberspace Competencies for Air Force Professional Military Education* (Wright-Patterson Air Force Base, OH: Center for Cyberspace Research, Air Force Institute of Technology, September 2007).

29. Allison Astorino-Courtois and Mathew Borda, "Reevaluating Deterrence Theory and Concepts for Use in Cyberspace," in *Deterrence 2.0: Deterring Violent Non-State Actors in Cyberspace*, ed. Carl Hunt and Nancy Chesser (Offutt Air Force Base, NE: U.S. Strategic Command Global Innovation and Strategy Center, 2008).

30. T.X. Hammes, discussion of 4th and 5th generation warfare, November 2007.

31. John C.F. Tillson et al., *Learning to Adapt to Asymmetric Threats* (Alexandria, VA: Institute for Defense Analyses, August 2005).

32. Charles Krulak, "The Strategic Corporal: Leadership in the Three-Block War," *Marines*, January 1999. His point was that new approaches to training and development were needed to prepare even the youngest Marines to handle urgent and unexpected situations of strategic importance. Increasingly, the outcome of a potential international crisis may depend on decisions and actions taken at the lowest levels of the rank structure under conditions of extreme stress.

33. Richard L. Hughes and Katherine C. Beatty, *Becoming a Strategic Leader: Your Role in Your Organization's Enduring Success* (San Francisco: Jossey-Bass, 2005).

34. Early in 2008, the Vice Chairman of the Joint Chiefs of Staff requested the support of the Service chiefs and the President of the National Defense University "in expeditiously including 'net-centric tenets and strategies'" into military school curricula. This process is under way. General James E. Cartwright, USMC, undated memo, "Net-Centric Information Sharing in Military Schools."

Chapter 18

1. Ray Kurzweil, "The Law of Accelerating Returns," 2003, available at <www.kurzweilai.net/articles/art0134.html?printable=1>.

Index

About the Contributors

Editor

Neyla Arnas is a Senior Research Fellow at the Center for Technology and National Security Policy (CTNSP) at National Defense University (NDU) in Washington, DC. Previously, she was the Policy Program Director at the Near East South Asia Center for Strategic Studies, and she has served at the U.S. Department of State as a Speechwriter and Public Affairs Officer to the Director General of the Foreign Service (2000–2004) and Special Advisor in the Bureau of European Affairs (1998–2000). Ms. Arnas is the recipient of the Department of State Superior and Meritorious Honor Awards. She is a graduate of Louisiana State University and holds a master's degree in Political Science.

Contributing Authors

Robert E. "Bob" Armstrong was a Senior Research Fellow at CTNSP. Previously, he served as a Life Sciences Intelligence Officer with the Central Intelligence Agency and as a Senior Government Executive at the U.S. Department of Agriculture. Dr. Armstrong held a BA in psychology from Wabash College and an MA in experimental psychology from Oxford University. He also held an MS in biology and a PhD in plant breeding and genetics, both from Purdue University. A veteran of the Vietnam War, Dr. Armstrong continued his uniformed service as an Army Reservist and held several staff and command positions before retiring as a colonel.

Ambassador (Ret.) William M. Bellamy joined the Center for Strategic and International Studies (CSIS) in October 2007 as Senior Resident Fellow in the Africa and International Security programs. Previously, he was Senior Vice President at NDU until his retirement from the Foreign Service in September 2007. A career diplomat, Bellamy was U.S. Ambassador to Kenya from 2003 to

2006, where he directed U.S. counterterrorism programs in the Horn of Africa. He served as Principal Deputy Assistant Secretary of State for African Affairs (2001–2003) and as Deputy Assistant Secretary for African Affairs (2000–2001). Ambassador Bellamy holds a BA in history from Occidental College and an MA in international relations from the Fletcher School of Law and Diplomacy, Tufts University. He is the recipient of a Presidential Meritorious Service award, the Chairman of the Joint Chiefs of Staff's Joint Distinguished Civilian Service Award, and a Distinguished Honor award and two Superior Honor awards conferred by the Secretary of State.

Geoffrey D. Dabelko is Director of the Environmental Change and Security Program at the Woodrow Wilson International Center for Scholars in Washington, DC. He is also an Adjunct Professor at the Monterey Institute of International Studies. He previously held positions with the Council on Foreign Relations, *Foreign Policy*, and Georgetown University's School of Foreign Service. He is coeditor of *Green Planet Blues: Environmental Politics from Stockholm to Johannesburg and Environmental Peacemaking* (Westview Press, 2004). Dr. Dabelko received a PhD in government and politics from the University of Maryland and an AB in political science from Duke University.

Mark D. Drapeau is the American Association for the Advancement of Science Science and Technology Policy Fellow at CTNSP. Previously, he was a National Institutes of Health Ruth L. Kirschstein Postdoctoral Research Fellow studying neurobiology and genomics at New York University. Dr. Drapeau has a PhD in ecology and evolutionary biology from the University of California (Irvine) and a BS in biology from the University of Rochester.

Dale F. Eickelman is Ralph and Richard Lazarus Professor of Anthropology and Human Relations at Dartmouth College, where he joined the faculty in 1989. His books include *Muslim Politics*, coauthored with James Piscatori (Princeton University Press, 1996); *The Middle East and Central Asia*, 4th ed. (Prentice Hall, 2002); and *Knowledge and Power in Morocco* (Princeton University Press, 1985). His recent coedited books include *Public Islam and the Common Good* (Brill Academic Publishers, 2004); and *New Media in the Muslim World* (Indiana University Press, 2003). He is a former President of the Middle East Studies Association and currently coordinates the American University of Kuwait-Dartmouth College project, involved in the development of Kuwait's first private liberal arts university.

David F. Gates is a Consultant to the Markets and Countries group at PFC Energy, where his focus is economic, energy, and environmental policies and prospects, market prospects, and business opportunities, especially in Asia. Until his retirement from Exxon Mobil Corporation in 2000, he was a Senior Advisor in the Corporate Affairs Department of Exxon Company, International. He holds a PhD in Economics from Princeton University.

Carl Haub is a Senior Demographer and holder of the Conrad Taeuber Chair of Population Information at the Population Reference Bureau in Washington, DC. Mr. Haub has also worked in demography at the U.S. National Academy of Sciences, the World Bank, and the U.S. Census Bureau. His publications include *The Global Demographic Divide, Understanding Population Projections, India's Population, Reconciling Change and Reality,* and *Population Change in the Former Soviet Republics,* all Population Bulletins produced by the Population Reference Bureau. He holds an MA in demography from Georgetown University and is a member of the Population Association of America and the International Union for the Scientific Study of Population.

Neil Jacobstein is Chairman and Chief Executive Officer of Teknowledge Corporation in Palo Alto, CA. He became a Senior Research Fellow in the Digital Vision Program at Stanford University in 2006 and is currently a Distinguished Visiting Scholar in Stanford's Media X Program. Mr. Jacobstein has been Chairman of the 501c3 Institute for Molecular Manufacturing since 1992, and he has served on the Technology Advisory Board for the U.S. Army's Simulation, Training, and Instrumentation Command and on a variety of industry and nonprofit advisory boards. He received his BS in environmental sciences from the University of Wisconsin, and an MS in human ecology from the University of Texas.

Peter Katona is Associate Professor of Clinical Medicine at the David Geffen School of Medicine at UCLA in Infectious Diseases. He has worked at the Centers for Disease Control and Prevention as an Epidemic Intelligence Service Officer in viral diseases and for Apria Healthcare as Corporate Medical Director. He has appointments at Louisiana State University's National Center for Biomedical Research and Training and the Los Angeles County Emergency Management Services Agency. He has been a consultant to the Los Angeles County Department of Health Services. He is cofounder of Biological Threat Mitigation, a bioterrorism preparedness consulting firm, and founder and president of the nonprofit Center of Medical Multimedia Education and Technology.

Michael Krepon is the cofounder of the Henry L. Stimson Center and is a Diplomat Scholar at the University of Virginia, where he teaches in the Politics Department. His publications include *Better Safe than Sorry: The Ironies of Living with the Bomb* (Stanford University Press, 2009), *Cooperative Threat Reduction, Missile Defense, and the Nuclear Future* (Palgrave Macmillan, 2003), *Space Assurance or Space Dominance? The Case Against Weaponizing Space* (Henry L. Stimson Center, 2003), and two edited volumes: *Nuclear Risk Reduction in South Asia* (Palgrave Macmillan, 2004) and *Escalation Control and the Nuclear Option in South Asia* (Henry L. Stimson Center, 2004).

Ian O. Lesser is Senior Transatlantic Fellow at the German Marshall Fund of the United States in Washington, DC, where he specializes in international security and Mediterranean affairs. He is also President of Mediterranean Advisors, LLC. Previously, he led a major study on the future of U.S.-Turkish relations at the Woodrow Wilson International Center for Scholars. Dr. Lesser has been Vice President of the Pacific Council on International Policy in Los Angeles and spent over a decade as a senior political scientist and research manager at the RAND Corporation. From 1994 to 1995, he was a member of the State Department's Policy Planning Staff, where his portfolio included Southern Europe, North Africa, and the multilateral track of the Middle East peace process.

Michael Moodie is an independent consultant specializing in issues related to the evolving security environment, particularly issues related to future conflict, proliferation, and globalization. He is a member of the National Intelligence Council's Long-Range Analysis Unit and the Global Futures Forum. He is also a Senior Associate at the Center for Strategic and International Studies and an Associate Fellow at the Royal Institute of International Affairs (Chatham House). In addition, Mr. Moodie teaches at Georgetown University and George Mason University.

Steven Pifer is a visiting fellow at the Brookings Institution. During over 25 years as a Foreign Service Officer with the State Department, he focused on relations with Europe and the former Soviet Union, as well as arms control and security issues. His assignments included Deputy Assistant Secretary of State, where he was responsible for relations with Russia and Ukraine (2001–2004); U.S. Ambassador to Ukraine (1998–2000); and Special Assistant to the President and National Security Council Senior Director for Russia, Ukraine, and Eurasia (1996–1997). He also served at the U.S. Embassies in Warsaw, Moscow, and London, as well as in Geneva with the U.S. delegation to the negotiations on intermediate-range nuclear forces.

Gregory J. Rattray is a Principal with Delta Risk Consulting. Previously, he served 23 years as a U.S. Air Force officer, retiring in 2007. His assignments included Director for Cyber Security on the White House National Security Council (NSC) staff, where he led national policy development and NSC oversight for cyber security programs and Iraq telecommunications reconstruction. He also served as an Assistant Professor of Political Science and Deputy Director of the U.S. Air Force Institute of National Security Studies at the U.S. Air Force Academy. He is the author of numerous books and articles, including *Strategic Warfare in Cyberspace* (MIT Press, 2001). He received a PhD from Fletcher School of Law and Diplomacy, Tufts University, a Master's in public policy from the John F. Kennedy School of Government, Harvard University, and a BS from the U.S. Air Force Academy.

Robert S. Ross is Professor of Political Science at Boston College; Associate, John King Fairbank Center for East Asian Research, Harvard University; and Senior Advisor, Security Studies Program, Massachusetts Institute of Technology. His current research focuses on Chinese security policy and East Asian security, including Chinese use of force and the role of nationalism in Chinese defense policy. He is the coeditor of *Normalization of U.S.-China Relations: An International History* (Harvard University Press, 2006), *Re-Examining the Cold War: U.S.-China Diplomacy, 1954–1973* (Harvard University Press, 2002), and *New Directions in the Study of Chinese Foreign Policy* (Stanford University Press, 2006) and is the author of numerous articles on Chinese security policy and U.S.-China relations in *World Politics, The China Quarterly, International Security, Security Studies, Foreign Affairs, Foreign Policy,* and *The National Interest.*

Edward Schumacher-Matos is the Robert F. Kennedy Visiting Professor in Latin American Studies at Harvard University. He formerly was a Bureau Chief for *The New York Times* in Buenos Aires and Madrid, Managing Editor of *The Wall Street Journal Americas*, and founder of the *Rumbo* chain of Spanish-language newspapers in Texas. Mr. Schumacher was awarded a bachelor's degree from Vanderbilt University and a master's degree from the Fletcher School of Law and Diplomacy, Tufts University. He was a Fulbright Fellow in Japan and a Bi-National Commission Fellow in Spain.

Linton Wells II serves as the Transformation Chair and a Distinguished Research Professor at NDU. Previously, he spent 16 years in the Office of the Secretary of Defense, including service as the Acting Assistant Secretary of Defense for Networks and Information Integration and Department of Defense Chief Information Officer. Dr. Wells, a 1967 graduate of the United States Naval Academy, was a career naval officer. He received an MSE from The Johns Hopkins University as well as a PhD in international relations and was graduated from the Japanese National Institute for Defense Studies in Tokyo. Recent projects include STAR-TIDES, an information-sharing research project in support of populations in stressed environments.

The Transformation Chairs Network is comprised of the Transformation Chairs and Force Transformation Chairs at 13 U.S. professional military education institutions, plus representatives from Australia, Singapore, Sweden, and the United Kingdom. The Transformation Chairs serve as authoritative champions for transformation studies at Department of Defense educational institutions, while creating courses, spurring research, and influencing curricula; are members of a network of educators including U.S., allied, and coalition partners; work to diffuse emerging knowledge while advocating for transformation in core curricula, collaborating in the development of courses, and developing case studies; and create new knowledge through original research and by acting as their institution's focal point for the Transformation Research Program.